"*Scaling Up Excellence* offers a strong antidote to the common pap—the delusions, impatience, and incompetence—that too often frustrate reforms and keep many good ideas from achieving their goals. Through engaging accounts of both organizational successes and colossal failures, Sutton and Rao offer practical wisdom for scaling improvements in complex institutions. Anyone involved in the work of improvement should hold this book close at hand." —**Anthony S. Bryk, President, Carnegie Foundation for the Advancement of Teaching**

"Growth and reinvention are key to winning, especially in tech. In *Scaling Up Excellence,* Sutton and Rao outline a real-world view of the challenges leaders face, and provide wisdom and practical tips about how to master them. I loved the insights." —**Shantanu Narayen, CEO, Adobe Systems**

"Rather than a one-size-fits-all recipe for what to do in scaling up your company, Robert Sutton and Huggy Rao offer guidelines for action in easy-to-read terms, based on case studies and research conducted over the last seven years. If you are interested in excellence using the principle of Less Is More, this is the book to read." —**Riccardo Illy, President, Gruppo Illy**

"*Scaling Up Excellence* is the best book I've ever seen on making an organization's vision come true. Sutton and Rao have created a deeply practical guide that is also a great read, grounded equally in astonishing stories and rigorous research. No matter what you do for a living, read this book to figure out how to link your 'short-term realities to long-term dreams." —**Teresa M. Amabile, Professor, Harvard Business School, and coauthor,** *The Progress Principle*

"Taking a small, manageable organization and making it into a big, successful enterprise is a major challenge in health care or any other industry. Robert Sutton and Huggy Rao take the mystery out of 'going large' with memorable mantras and fascinating case studies. *Scaling Up Excellence* shows the high roads—and the pitfalls—on the way to bigger and better." —**Delos M. Cosgrove, MD, CEO and President, Cleveland Clinic**

"Inspiring stories, compelling research, and actionable ideas masterfully woven together and immediately usable by any entrepreneur or manager." —**Clara Shih, CEO and Founder, Hearsay Social, and member of Starbucks' Board of Directors**

"Sustaining exceptional performance in growing organizations is critical in today's world. Sutton and Rao bring a wealth of knowledge and experience to identifying best practices in a straightforward and accessible way. If you want to grow your business, you need this book." —**Keith Ferrazzi, author of** *Never Eat Alone*

"Rao and Sutton have hit on an important challenge for leaders in every organization—companies, social sector, and government: How do you scale what works, and do it faster? The challenge of finding pockets of excellence and changing mindsets and behavior so that success becomes the norm, not abnormal, is very real for those who want to make excellence stick. *Scaling Up Excellence* is a useful road map for today's change leaders." —**Lenny Mendonca, Director Emeritus, McKinsey and Company, and Founder, Half Moon Bay Brewing Company**

"Robert Sutton and Huggy Rao's book provides insights on the key principles of scaling for excellence. For entrepreneurs or business leaders at the forefront of organizational growth, *Scaling Up Excellence* is a treasure trove of case studies and industry showcases." —**N. R. Narayana Murthy, Executive Chairman, Infosys**

SCALING UP EXCELLENCE

SCALING UP EXCELLENCE

GETTING TO MORE WITHOUT SETTLING FOR LESS

ROBERT I. SUTTON AND HUGGY RAO

RANDOM HOUSE CANADA

PUBLISHED BY RANDOM HOUSE CANADA

www.randomhouse.ca

Random House Canada and colophon are registered trademarks.

Library and Archives Canada Cataloguing in Publication

Sutton, Robert I.

    Scaling up excellence : getting to more without settling for less / Robert I. Sutton and Hayagreeva Rao.

Issued also in electronic format.

ISBN 978-0-307-36342-8

    1. Organizational effectiveness. 2. Performance—Management. 3. Success in business. I. Rao, Hayagreeva, 1959– II. Title.

HD58.9.S87 2014   658.4'02   C2013-901538-8

Text design by Elizabeth Rendfleish
Illustrations by motodan
Jacket design by Justin Gammon with Jess Morphew
Jacket photography by Shutterstock

Printed and bound in the United States of America

10 9 8 7 6 5 4 3 2 1

To our mothers,
Annette Sutton and Kamala Rao,
for all their love
and for always encouraging us
to think for ourselves.

CONTENTS

III. Parting Points

THE PROBLEM OF MORE

Scaling Up Excellence tackles a challenge that confronts every leader and organization—spreading constructive beliefs and behavior from the few to the many. This book shows what it takes to build and uncover pockets of exemplary performance, spread those splendid deeds, and as an organization grows bigger and older—rather than slipping toward mediocrity or worse—recharge it with better ways of doing the work at hand.

This challenge has been our constant companion since 2006, when we launched a weeklong management education program at Stanford on "Customer-Focused Innovation." It kept clobbering us over the head. No matter what we asked the participants to do—discuss a Harley-Davidson case study, interview JetBlue customers at the airport, or design solutions to improve the "gas station experience"—the same concern nagged and gnawed at them. It pervaded their comments and questions. They described it as the biggest obstacle to building a customer-focused organization. And their feedback drove us to devote more time to this challenge each year.

We started calling it the Problem of More. Executives could always point to pockets in their organizations where people were doing a great job of uncovering and meeting customer needs. There was always some excellence—there just wasn't enough of it. What drove them crazy, kept them up at night, and devoured their workdays was the difficulty of spreading that excellence to *more* people and *more* places. They also emphasized that the Problem of More (which they often called "scaling" or "scaling up") wasn't limited to building customer-focused organizations; it was a barrier to spreading excellence of every stripe.

The fascination and frustration that spilled out of those executives was infectious and troubling for us. No matter what the two of us were supposed to be talking about, the Problem of More soon dominated most of our conversations and e-mail exchanges. We were taken with the Problem because it was so widespread and so crucial to the fate of every leader and organization. The Problem also vexed us because the executives' questions were so good, yet our answers were so lame. And once people learned we were snooping around the "scaling stuff," we were peppered with tough questions. Leaders at places ranging from Google to the Girl Scouts deserved better answers than we could muster. Thus began the seven-year project that generated this book.

We did many things during those years to identify key differences between scaling well and scaling badly (see the Appendix for details). Yet regardless of what we did during any given week, we wove together two goals: uncovering the most *rigorous* evidence and theory we could find and generating observations and advice that are *relevant* to people who are determined to scale up excellence. It didn't matter whether we were writing a case study about the spread of lean manufacturing practices at Wyeth Pharmaceuticals, puzzling over the implications of group effectiveness research for managing the U.S. Navy Seals and McKinsey consultants, presenting half-baked ideas to Norwegian health care executives bent on spreading patient-centered practices, or coaching a student group that persuaded Stanford soccer players to wear bike helmets (via tactics such as scattering smashed watermelons around the practice field). We bounced back and forth between the clean, careful, and orderly world of theory and research—that rigor we love so much as academics—and the messy problems, crazy constraints, and daily twists and turns that are relevant to real people as they strive and struggle to spread excellence to those who need it.

This strategy fixed our focus on developing ideas that are grounded in great research, can help people spread and preserve excellence, and will grab and hold their attention. The chapters in *Scaling Up Excellence* spell out these lessons. Our efforts to boil down this challenge to its essence and develop practical recommendations were shaped by four big lessons that emerged during our journey. These lessons not only helped us write this book, they are useful mental provisioning for anyone contemplating—or in the throes of—the Problem of More.

Lessons from Our Journey

Our first big lesson is that, although the details and daily dramas vary wildly from place to place, the similarities among scaling challenges are more important than the differences. The key choices that leaders face and the principles that help organizations scale up without screwing up are strikingly consistent—whether the task is to grow a Silicon Valley start-up such as Pulse News from four to twenty people, double the number of lawyers at Google, spread best practices for selling beer from the most effective U.S. Budweiser distributors to the rest, open a new KIPP charter school in Washington, D.C., grow the Joie de Vivre hotel chain, open a See's Candies store in Texas, reduce drug treatment errors in San Francisco area hospitals, or open IKEA stores in China.

We dig into common and crucial decisions that shape how scaling unfolds. One of these universal decisions is whether and when to take a more "Catholic" or a more "Buddhist" path. Scaling well hinges on making the right trade-offs between mandating that new people and places become perfect clones of some original model (a "Catholic" approach) versus encouraging local variation, experimentation, and customization (a "Buddhist" approach). We show how the best leaders and organizations tackle this universal decision, along with other vexing trade-offs such as "more" versus "better" and scaling alone versus with others.

We drew on diverse case studies, our daily conversations and e-mail exchanges with scaling veterans, and hundreds of academic studies to develop five principles that guide successful scaling efforts. We began outlining one principle, for example, after a stretch when we led a workshop with executives who were trying to transform large prisons to focus on rehabilitation rather than punishment; talked with Yum! Brands CEO David Novak about how he developed leaders for the Taco Bell, Pizza Hut, and KFC chains; interviewed executives and engineers at Facebook about how they brought aboard over one thousand new engineers; and wrote a case on how executive Bonny Simi and her JetBlue team had implemented better practices for closing airports in bad weather. The same lesson popped up each time: just making a rational argument about why people ought to spread some form of excellence was rarely sufficient to provoke them into action. Skilled leaders found ways to stoke emotions that fueled tangible and desirable actions. This observation dovetails with research on the forces that explain both individual behavior and social movements. As a result, chapter 3 demonstrates how to propel scaling by linking "hot causes" to "cool solutions."

In *Scaling Up Excellence,* we show why this principle and others are effective and how to use each to spread new beliefs and behaviors. The upshot for people who spread some brand of excellence is that they often feel as if they are the first to travel down some bumpy road. But that probably isn't so. There are universal decisions and principles that can guide them along the way. And it's a lot easier (and less painful and expensive) to learn from the successes and failures of those who have already navigated a similar gauntlet.

Our second big lesson is that scaling entails more than the Problem of More. This four-word phrase is incomplete and takes people down the wrong path when they act as if they have something so wonderful that their only chore is to spread that perfection far and wide. Replication and repeatability will always be part of the scaling equation. Yet effective scaling isn't simply a matter of running up the numbers by replicating the same old magic again and again. It isn't enough to keep stamping out perfect clones of some original and idealized founding team, franchise, plant, quality effort, innovation process, charter school, or social services program.

Rather, the problem tackled here is one of both *more* and *better.* As Pixar's Academy Award–winning Director Brad Bird puts it, organizations that spread and sustain excellence are infused with a "relentless restlessness"—that often uncomfortable urge for constant innovation, driven by the nagging feeling that things are never quite good enough. Whether it happens in a young social media company like Twitter, the rapidly expanding KALAHI poverty program in the Philippines, a chain like Lulu's in California that opened only three restaurants in its first decade, a ninety-year-old hospital system with fifty thousand employees like the Cleveland Clinic, a massive multinational like Walmart, or a single KFC restaurant in Arkansas, scaling well requires never leaving well enough alone. It means constantly seeking and implementing better ways of thinking and acting across old and new corners of the system.

Our third big lesson is that people who are adept at scaling excellence talk and act as if they are knee-deep in a manageable mess. They believe that by considering the right decisions, following the right principles, and drawing on their skill and common sense, they will have some control over their collective fate and be able to crank up their odds of success. Yet at the same time they realize that scaling is so complex and fraught with uncertainty that there will always be stretches when they are pummeled with unpredictable and unpleasant events, when frustration and confusion reign, and when the stench of failure is in the air. The best leaders and scaling teams muddle through—and even revel in—these inevitable moments and months of messiness.

We learned the power of muddling forward from David Kelley, founding CEO and now chair of IDEO, one of the most renowned innovation consulting firms on the planet. We've followed and often worked with IDEO since 1995, as it grew from a product development firm with seventy-five people and three locations to a general innovation consultancy with some six hundred people and eight locations. They still develop products like the Faraday electric bicycle. But now IDEO's innovators do everything from inventing more humane experiences for people who donate blood, to designing dressing rooms for Prada's New York store, to shaping Samsung's innovation strategy. And through all this expansion, IDEO has somehow managed to sustain the playful spirit and thirst for excellence that we first admired nearly twenty years ago.

A big part of this success is that Kelley and other senior leaders have believed and behaved as if they had control over IDEO's fate as it grew and evolved. In doing so, they've applied many of the scaling principles spelled out in the coming chapters. Kelley is especially masterful, for example, at guiding people at IDEO to "stoke a hot cause" (see chapter 3) and to "cascade excellence" (see chapter 6) as they bring aboard new people and expand to new locations. But Kelley is probably at his best—and wisest—when everything seems to be going wrong, confusion abounds, tempers flare, and people are coming unglued. He reminds them that "life is messy sometimes. Sometimes the best you can do is to accept that it is messy, try to love it as much as you can, and move forward."

Our research revealed that IDEO isn't an aberration. Organizations that scale well are filled with people who talk and act as if they are in the middle of a manageable mess. This lesson also provides good guidance for applying the ideas in this book. The principles here can help you spread excellence from the few to the many without screwing up (or at least help you screw up less). But remember that you and your colleagues will always be subjected to messy, bewildering, and discouraging stretches during which nothing—including the advice here—seems to work. When that happens, it is best to embrace the mess and keep muddling forward until the path becomes more clear.

The fourth big lesson is that scaling starts and ends with individuals—success depends on the will and skill of people at every level of an organization. It isn't just something that senior executives need to worry about and understand. Sure, many scaling efforts start with those at the top. But it is impossible to spread excellence without the zeal, efforts, and imagination of people throughout an organization. For example, in 2007, Michael Kamarck, president of the manufacturing group at Wyeth Pharmaceuticals, made the initial decision, allocated the money, and staked his reputation on a program that changed the mindsets and actions of seventeen thousand employees. It would have been impossible, however, to cut costs by 25 percent while improving quality across Wyeth's thirty-seven manufacturing plants without the efforts of so many dedicated first-line supervisors and middle managers. They created the initial "minitransformations," the new pockets of excellence in each plant, which were then spread throughout each facility. At the biotechnology plant in Pearl River, New York, for example, Fysun "Fifi" Haknasar led the minitransformation on her team. The team systematically eliminated unnecessary steps and delays in changeovers between filling batches of syringes with vaccines. They slashed the average changeover time from fourteen to seven hours. Then, with Fifi as "changeover coach," these lessons were cascaded to other Pearl River teams.

Many organizations are born after some energetic individual discovers that something is broken and decides to fix it. That's what happened when anthropology PhD student Shannon May went to China to study economic development. As part of her job, she was required to teach English at a local elementary school. May was appalled by how poorly her fellow teachers understood what they were supposed to teach. She was also disgusted with their lack of attention to students, poor attendance, and penchant for getting drunk during lunch. She learned that horrible schools like that one fueled the cycle of poverty in developing nations throughout the world: an estimated 80 percent of the students they taught never became proficient at reading, writing, or simple arithmetic. May started talking with entrepreneurs Jay Kimmelman and Phil Frei; the trio "wondered why no one was thinking about schools in developing countries the way Starbucks thought about coffee." They soon raised money to start Bridge International Academies, a chain of high-quality, low-cost elementary schools designed to produce well-educated students. In 2009, they opened their first "Academy-in-a-Box" in the Mukuru slum in Nairobi, Kenya. They now operate over 210 schools in three African countries, where parents pay $4 to $10 a month for a highly standardized and exacting education (starting with children as young as three years old) that has chalked up impressive levels of student achievement, given hope to parents that their children can escape from grinding poverty, and created over two thousand good jobs.

Even in big companies, the impetus for creating and scaling excellence often doesn't start at the top. In smart organizations, people know that, although excellence might not be everywhere, it can start and spread from anywhere. Consider Doug Dietz, an engineer in General Electric's medical device business. Dietz had a revelation in 2005 when he visited a hospital to see a new magnetic resonance imaging (MRI) machine that he had helped to design. Dietz could hardly wait to see "his baby" in action. But all that pride evaporated when the first patient he saw was a terrified seven-year-old girl who was reduced to tears by that big white soulless machine and all the scary noises it made. Dietz's realization that "what we were designing sucked for kids" drove him to spend his next five years developing and spreading the "Adventure Series" in children's hospitals. These colorful rooms are designed around fantasy themes including "Pirate Island," "Jungle Adventure," "Cozy Camp," and "Underwater Adventure." They have pathways painted with pictures of animals and fish, machines painted to resemble submarines or pirate ships, theme music such as jungle noises or pirate songs, and "designer" smells including lavender water scent and piña colada. Dietz worked with hospital staff, fellow GE designers, parents, and his "Kid Advisory Team" to design a fun experience for each "adventure," such as having the child climb into a hollowed-out log or a sleeping bag for the journey. Approximately eighty such "Adventure Rooms"—for procedures including X-rays, nuclear medicine, and MRIs—are now used in some twenty hospitals. The result? Not only are kids less frightened by the experience (sedation rates are down 80 percent), satisfaction rates have also risen 90 percent, and many kids love the experience so much that they beg their parents to let them do it one more time.

Where to Start

When we teach the decisions and principles here to students, managers, and executives, or we coach people who are in the thick of a scaling effort, we often work with former Procter & Gamble executive Claudia Kotchka—who plays a starring role in our next chapter. People often ask Kotchka where to start. To us, her answer sums up this fourth big lesson pretty well. She says, "Start with yourself, where you are right now, and with what you have and can get right now." That advice doesn't just apply to kicking off the scaling process; it holds every day and every step of the way.

We now turn to the nuances of the Problem of More. Our first chapter begins with the most essential insight that we uncovered about scaling during our seven-year adventure. We then introduce seven scaling mantras, each a vital theme that runs throughout this book and a key ingredient in the successful scaling efforts that we studied.

I

SETTING THE STAGE

CHAPTER 1

IT'S A GROUND WAR, NOT JUST AN AIR WAR

Going Slower to Scale Faster (and Better) Later

Listen. This is the most important thing that we learned, the one to keep in mind every day if you are bent on spreading excellence to more people and places: those who master what venture capitalist Ben Horowitz calls "the black art of scaling a human organization" act as if they are fighting a ground war, not just an air war.

In the air wars of World War II, commanders typically ordered pilots to drop bombs or strafe some general area in hopes of damaging the enemy. Unfortunately, such attacks were woefully inaccurate. Political scientist Robert Pape estimated that, during World War II, "only about 18 percent of U.S. bombs fell within 1,000 feet of their targets, and only 20 percent of British bombs dropped at night fell within 5 miles." Even when air strikes were more accurate, Allied leaders learned that without ground operations—where soldiers were close to targets, gaining or losing territory a few yards at a time—victory was impossible. Even today, when guidance systems ensure that 70 percent of bombs fall within thirty feet of targets, an air war alone is rarely enough to defeat an enemy. After reviewing NATO's seventy-eight-day air war in Serbia that was meant to force Yugoslavian president Slobodan Milošević to ban ethnic cleansing, retired U.S. Air Force General Merrill McPeak concluded, "In a major blunder, the use of ground troops was ruled out from the beginning."

Similarly, savvy leaders know that just bombarding employees with a quick PowerPoint presentation, a few days of training, or an inspirational speech won't cut it if they want to spread some goodness from the few to the many. Certainly, there are junctures in every scaling effort when it is wise to choose the easier path or secure a quick victory. Yet as we dug into case after case, and study after study, we saw that every allegedly easy and speedy scaling success turned out to be one we just hadn't understood very well. Scaling requires grinding it out, and pressing each person, team, group, division, or organization to make one small change after another in what they believe, feel, or do.

That is what Claudia Kotchka learned during her seven-year effort to spread innovation practices at Procter & Gamble. As vice president of design innovation and strategy, Kotchka started with a tiny team and one project and ended with over three hundred innovation experts embedded in dozens of businesses. We asked her the most important lesson that she had gleaned about scaling. Kotchka responded that she was naturally impatient, someone who wanted things done "right now" and as quickly and easily as possible. This action orientation served her team well, driving them to make progress each day, find savvy shortcuts, and achieve quick wins. But Kotchka explained that her team would have failed to scale if this penchant for action hadn't been blended with patience and persistence. "My CEO, A. G. Lafley, reminded me how important it was again and again." Kotchka's advice is reminiscent of something a McKinsey consultant—a veteran of the scaling wars—told us: When big organizations scale well, they focus on "moving a thousand people forward a foot at a time, rather than moving one person forward by a thousand feet."

This kind of discipline is equally important in small and young organizations. It has been a way of life for Shannon May and her team since they launched Bridge International Academies, the chain of low-cost and standardized elementary schools that we described in the Preface. Consider the grueling gauntlet that Bridge created for screening and training new teachers. In early 2012, they hired eight hundred teachers for fifty-one new schools and eighty-three existing schools. These are tough jobs: students attend school from 7:00 a.m. to 5:30 p.m. each weekday and for half a day on Saturday, and teachers are required to maximize the time that students spend "on task and actively engaged." A thirty-person team from Bridge interviewed ten thousand candidates and gave each a battery of tests: reading, writing, and math exams. The team also had candidates give short speeches and hold one-on-one conversations with them to assess their ability to deliver material and interact with students. They invited 1,400 finalists (in two batches of 700) to a five-week training camp, where all were paid to learn Bridge's mindset, skills, and procedures. The team then selected the best 800 to teach Bridge's students.

The Bridge team doesn't just view scaling as the Problem of More. As they expand, their goal isn't just to maintain the status quo. The team works day after day to make their system *better*. They never leave well enough alone. For example, they keep improving the technologies and content delivered via the phones and "hacked" Nook tablets used to collect money from parents, pay staff, deliver teaching materials, and monitor student and teacher performance. May also described a new effort to deliver questions and assignments to teachers that are customized for students in the same class at different ability levels.

This kind of determination and discipline also defines people who spread excellence from the bottom or middle of organizations.

In 1991, Andy Papa graduated from Stanford, where he had played as a defensive lineman on the football team for four years. Through luck and persistence, Papa landed a job on a NASCAR racing team based in North Carolina, which included being on the pit crew that changed tires, poured in fuel, made adjustments, and did quick repairs during races. Papa asked when the crew practiced pit stops. The answer was they didn't practice; most worked as mechanics during the week and didn't have time. A lightbulb went off in Papa's head: by transferring "the athletic mindset" he had learned in football to pit stops, they could get faster and more consistent—a big advantage, as the gap between winners and losers is so small in NASCAR races, with less than one second often separating the first- and second-place cars. Papa talked his crew into practicing a couple times a week for just twenty or thirty minutes, he started analyzing film of pit stops, and he tested different techniques (such as coiling the air hose in a figure-eight shape instead of a circle to reduce tangles). The crew's average time dropped from about twenty-two to twenty seconds and, more important, the frequency of awful pit stops plummeted.

Papa eventually took this zeal for the "athletic mindset" to Hendrick Motorsports. He spent years as their "athletic director," overseeing the pit crews that serve elite drivers including Mark Martin, Jeff Gordon, Jimmie Johnson, and Dale Earnhardt Jr. Members of each crew are selected, trained, and coached by Papa and his colleagues, who enforce an exacting regimen of physical training, practice, and learning aimed at making stops faster (about fourteen seconds is the current goal) and more consistent during the thirty-six grueling races they compete in per year (each with six to twelve pit stops). This discipline has helped Hendrick win more championships than any NASCAR ownership group in history—including an unprecedented run of five Sprint Cup championships by Jimmie Johnson between 2006 and 2010.

Claudia Kotchka, Shannon May, and Andy Papa have traveled

different paths. But they all have something in common, an essential quality for grinding out the ground war and overcoming the inevitable setbacks and nasty surprises. These scaling stars have grit. Researcher Angela Duckworth and her colleagues found that grit "entails working strenuously toward challenges, maintaining effort and interest despite failure, adversity, and plateaus in progress. The gritty individual approaches achievement as a marathon, his or her advantage is stamina." Grit drives people to succeed, especially when they face daunting and prolonged challenges—a hallmark of every scaling effort.

Scaling Mantras

This book zeros in on how and where to focus such perseverance as your organization struggles and strives to scale up excellence. We've identified reliable signs that scaling is going well or badly, and we've distilled these signals into seven mantras. If you are embarking on a scaling effort, memorize them, teach them to others, and invent ways to keep them firmly in focus—especially when the going gets rough.

1. Spread a Mindset, Not Just a Footprint

There is a big difference between distributing your banner, logo, or motto as far and wide as possible versus having a deep and enduring influence on how employees and customers think, act, feel, and filter information. Scaling unfolds with less friction and more consistency when the people propelling it agree on what is right and wrong—and on what to pay attention to and what to ignore. Effective scaling depends on believing and living a shared mindset throughout your group, division, or organization. Scaling is analogous to a ground war rather than an air war because developing,

SCALING MANTRAS

1. Spread a mindset, not just a footprint.

Running up the numbers and putting your logo on as
many people and places as possible isn't enough.

2. Engage all the senses.

Bolster the mindset you want to spread with
supportive sights, sounds, smells, and other subtle
cues that people may barely notice, if at all.

3. Link short-term realities to long-term dreams.

Hound yourself and others with questions about what it takes to link
the never-ending now to the sweet dreams you hope to realize later.

4. Accelerate accountability.

Build in the feeling that "I own the place and the place owns me."

5. Fear the clusterfug.

The terrible trio of *illusion, impatience,* and *incompetence* are
ever-present risks. Healthy doses of worry and self-doubt are
antidotes to these three hallmarks of scaling clusterfugs.

6. Scaling requires both addition and subtraction.

The problem of more is also a problem of less.

7. Slow down to scale faster—and better—down the road.

Learn when and how to shift gears from automatic, mindless,
and fast modes of thinking ("System 1") to slow, taxing, logical,
deliberative, and conscious modes ("System 2"); sometimes
the best advice is, "Don't just do something, stand there."

spreading, and updating a mindset requires relentless vigilance. It requires stating the beliefs and living the behavior, and then doing so again and again. These shared convictions reduce confusion, disagreements, and unnecessary dead ends—and diminish the chances that excellence will fade as your footprint expands.

Facebook demonstrates what it takes to instill and sustain a mindset even when an organization's footprint is spreading like wildfire. The company's crazy climb began that legendary night in February 2004 when nineteen-year-old Harvard undergraduate Mark Zuckerberg pounded down beers and programmed the crude but captivating first iteration of the site. Facebook amassed over a million users by the end of 2004 and a billion by the end of 2012. Facebook's future is impossible to know. Despite stumbles including a botched public offering, some pundits predict it will become more dominant than Apple and Google; others predict that it will flail and fade away like America Online.

Whatever Facebook's fate, the twists and turns of how the company grew that colossal footprint in the eight short years before its 2012 public offering are instructive. By slowing down and shunning shortcuts when it came to developing the people who powered their expansion, leaders infused the company with the will, skill, and resilience to move quickly when and where it mattered. We've witnessed their ability to sustain this focus no matter how wild and out of control the ride became since 2006, when our conversations, interviews, and projects with people at Facebook began. They've done so despite brutal time pressures and distractions: adding as many as 3 million users per week and enduring intense media scrutiny (most start-ups aren't besieged with questions about toppling the Egyptian and Libyan governments), a Hollywood blockbuster that portrayed Zuckerberg in an unflattering light, nasty lawsuits, and withering user revolts—750,000 users objected to the News Feed feature in 2006 and millions complained about "Timeline" in 2012.

This devotion to growing and grooming Facebook's people happened informally at first. In the early years, Zuckerberg was jammed together with his employees in cramped offices. He talked constantly about his convictions and why they powered Facebook's strategy—and employees watched and worked with him as he lived those beliefs. Once the company got too big for Zuckerberg to personally influence every employee, it took to more systematic methods, notably "Bootcamp." Facebook engineers and other product developers are hired after rounds of grueling interviews to assess their technical skills and cultural fit. But they are not placed in a specific job until six weeks after coming aboard. Management has a hunch about which role each new hire will play. Yet the final decision is not made until the end of "Bootcamp," which is designed and led almost entirely by engineers—not the HR staff.

During Bootcamp, every new hire does small chores for a dozen or so diverse groups. Chris Cox, Facebook's thirty-one-year-old vice president of product, emphasizes that Bootcamp isn't just for figuring out which role is best for each newcomer. A more crucial aim is to infect each with the Facebook mindset. Bootcamp requires recruits to live Facebook's most sacred belief: "Move fast and break things." As Cox puts it, it is one thing to tell new engineers that they can change the code on the Facebook site. It is another thing for them to actually "touch the metal." He added, "We tell them, put your hand on it. Grab it. Now bend it." Cox told us about the newcomer whose dad called to say, "There's a problem with this drop-down menu." He called back the next day: "I fixed it, Dad. Did you see that?" That is the Facebook mindset—if you want people to move fast and fix things, they'd better feel safe to break some stuff along the way. When it comes to developing the site, going slow and trying to do things perfectly is taboo at Facebook. As engineer Sanjeev Singh explained, if you keep waiting for people to tell you what to do, don't ask for help when you get stuck, and won't show others your work until it is perfect, "you won't last long at Facebook."

Bootcamp instills other beliefs about what is sacred and taboo at Facebook. Engineers are expected to understand the code base, not just the part they tend to each day. Working on many different parts helps newcomers grasp the big picture. Rotating through many groups also sets the expectation that any role they play at Facebook won't last long. Chris Cox worked as a programmer, a product designer, a project manager, the head of human resources, and the vice president of product during his first six years at the company. After Bootcamp, these beliefs continue to be reinforced. Engineer Jason Sobel explained that Facebook doesn't just tell new engineers that they likely won't be in any job for long; they live this philosophy via a "nearly mandatory" program called "hack-a-month" where—each year—they are "loaned" to another group for a month.

Each newcomer is assigned a mentor—usually an engineer who isn't a manager—to help him or her navigate through Bootcamp. A new "class" of twenty to thirty hires was started roughly every two weeks in 2011—which meant that seventy or eighty engineers at a time were pulled away from their jobs to be mentors. This sometimes slowed crucial projects. Facebook's leaders, including Chris Cox and Chief Technology Officer Mike Schroepfer, are convinced that it is worth the cost—that their enduring success hinges on filling the company with people who live and breathe the right beliefs. Bootcamp also helps Facebook scale up talent because it enables mentors to "stick a toe in the management water." It helps engineers discover if they enjoy mentoring and leading others. And Facebook executives get useful hints about whether employees are management material.

No single mindset is right for every organization—or even different parts of the same organization. What is sacred in one organization can (and should) be taboo elsewhere. An executive from software firm VMware laughed when Sutton asked if they used the "Move fast and break things" approach. He said it was better for them to embrace the opposite belief, especially in their business unit that develops software for nuclear submarines! Or consider secrecy. At Apple, secrecy is revered. When Steve Jobs returned to run the company in 1997, several employees leaked an e-mail he wrote to the press. He fired them immediately and told everyone why he had done so. *Fortune* writer Adam Lashinsky reports that the one lesson "no Apple employee forgets" during employee orientation is "Scared Silent." Newcomers are told that if they reveal Apple secrets—intentionally or not—swift termination will follow. In contrast, at Mozilla secrecy is largely shunned. This open-source software firm is best known for its Firefox browser, which is used by over 300 million people and is translated into more than sixty-five languages. We followed Mozilla as it grew from twelve employees to more than five hundred. We were often taken aback by how open senior executives were about design flaws, competitive threats, mistakes, and internal disagreements. Former CEO John Lilly once told our Stanford class that he was going to abolish performance evaluations at Mozilla even though his human resources chief disagreed!

There is another sense in which one size does not fit all. The best mindsets provide useful guidance, but applying them to every case is a recipe for trouble. Sometimes it is wise to ignore or reverse even your most sacred beliefs. Secrecy at Mozilla is a good example. John Lilly told us that during "the first ten years of Mozilla's history all projects, no matter what stage, were essentially open to everyone at the moment of creation. But we learned (the hard way, often), that when ideas are nascent, they're fragile flowers—there are many, many, many reasons why they're crazy, they won't work, they're dumb to try." To protect these fragile ideas from getting killed off too early by the thousands of active helpers (and critics) embedded in Mozilla's open-source community, management started Mozilla Labs, "which had the explicit direction that they didn't have to open things up right away. This helped a lot, because it meant projects could get a little more definition, a little more momentum, and crazy ideas made it through a little more often, which was what we needed."

Finally, sustaining and constantly improving an organization's mindset is like being in a high-maintenance personal relationship. Constant vigilance is required. Even if you've got the best intentions, it is easy to ruin everything. When people get smug, operate on autopilot, take shortcuts, and choose the path of least resistance too often, they lose sight of the essence of their excellence. In their lust to run up the numbers and plaster their logo on as many people, places, and things as possible, the temptation to accept mediocrity—or worse—often proves irresistible.

Starbucks provides a cautionary tale. In 2007, Sutton saw firsthand how mediocrity had beset Starbucks during a three-day management seminar that he taught with fellow Stanford faculty Michael Dearing and Perry Klebahn to fifty executives in Abu Dhabi. The seminar was catered by a pair of Starbucks employees, who sat in the back of the room. The coffee was weak, cold, and tasteless. The juice smelled foul and tasted rotten. The sweet rolls were rock hard. And the two employees spent half their time slumped over, sound asleep. Starbucks has a huge footprint. But their once renowned devotion to hiring excellent people and providing first-class products had evaporated as they expanded too far and too fast. This isn't just our opinion. CEO Howard Schultz lamented Starbucks' drift toward mediocrity in an internal memo circulated in February 2007—which he admitted was genuine after it was leaked to the press. Schultz pointed to a string of decisions that had led to "the watering down of the Starbucks experience" as the company grew from one thousand to thirteen thousand stores. In his 2011 book, *Onward,* Schultz digs into how the "commoditization of the Starbucks experience" led them to lose that "warm neighborhood feeling," why such "dilution" happened, and what the company is doing to "get their groove back."

The key lesson? An organization rarely loses a healthy mindset and the resulting excellence all at once. It usually happens via a series of small and seemingly innocent moves that chip away at sacred convictions, eventually transforming those beliefs into hollow and hypocritical words.

2. Engage All the Senses

Howard Schultz's memo added that, because Starbucks no longer grinds coffee in stores, they "no longer have the soul of the past" that was once evoked by the sounds of grinders and smells of freshly ground coffee. So he reintroduced it. This lament dovetails with our second mantra. Mindsets are spread and sustained by subtle cues that activate all the senses. Many studies show how stimuli that people don't notice, barely notice, or strike them as trivial can nonetheless have potent effects on how they think and act. Our beliefs and behaviors are bolstered—and undermined—by the colors and kinds of images we see, the sounds we hear, the smells we encounter, the things we taste, and the objects we touch. We are also influenced by the voice tone and facial expressions that accompany the words people say, whether they look us in the eye, their posture, and many more seemingly inconsequential and irrelevant cues in the world around us.

Consider what happened when researchers examined the impact of playing French versus German music on wine purchases in a British supermarket. When French accordion music played, customers bought five times more French than German wine. When German oompah music played, customers bought two times more German wine. Customers were affected by the music, even though they didn't realize it. Smells have similar impacts. Dutch psychologists conducted a weird experiment in which, during eighteen two-hour train trips, they infused passenger cars with a citrus-scented cleaning product. They gathered and weighed the trash left by passengers in the scented cars and compared it to the amount of trash in those same cars during weeks that the cars weren't scented. Passengers left about three times more trash in unscented cars than in scented cars, perhaps because of "the non-conscious priming of cleaning-related motives and behaviors." These findings are similar to another study where people who smelled a "citrus cleaning product" tended to list "more cleaning-related activities in their plans for the day and to spill fewer crumbs when munching on a cookie."

The objects around us also pack a wallop. Psychologist Kathleen Vohs and her colleagues used various "primes" to turn attention to money—placing piles of fake money in front of people and showing them pictures of money. The researchers then presented people with challenges such as whether they asked for help while struggling to solve unsolvable puzzles or gave help to an (apparently) blind person who accidently dropped a bunch of pencils. The results are kind of scary. The money "primes" caused people to be less likely to ask for help, less likely to give others help, more likely to work and play alone, and more likely to put physical distance between themselves and new acquaintances. In the study with the "blind" person, subjects played Monopoly for seven minutes. Regardless of how the game had gone, they were left with a pile of $4,000 in Monopoly money, $200, or no money at all. Then an (apparently) blind person walked in and "accidentally" spilled some pencils. Subjects with big piles of money picked up far fewer pencils off the ground than those with a small pile or no pile. The money, noticed but not consciously registered, triggered associations about business, wealth, and capitalism, provoking people to become less helpful, more self-absorbed, and more self-sufficient.

Temperature and touch also influence our beliefs and actions. For example, a bit of barely noticed warmth or cold can have striking effects. Psychologist Lawrence Williams described his sneaky study where participants were randomly chosen to hold cups of hot versus iced coffee:

> We had a confederate meet participants on the first floor of the psychology building, and on their way up to the lab, she was holding some textbooks and a clipboard, and also a coffee cup that was either hot or iced. And, she just sort of incidentally briefly innocuously asked participants if they wouldn't mind holding her coffee cup as she jotted down some information—the time, their participation, their name—and then took the coffee cup back while they were on the elevator and then brought them into the lab. So, participants had no idea that holding that cup was the critical aspect of the experiment.

Participants who held the hot coffee rated the person who handed them the cup as warm, sociable, and generous. Those who got iced coffee rated that same person as colder, less generous, and more antisocial. Those who held hot coffee were more prone to buy a gift for a friend than for themselves; those who were handed the cold cup preferred to buy a gift for themselves!

The upshot is that you can bolster a mindset by weaving together subtle, even nearly invisible, cues that engage multiple senses. Take a page from the designers of Disney theme parks. Karin Kricorian, who leads Disney's efforts to study guest experiences, told us about dozens of small cues that Disney uses to spread happiness: smells, colors, uniforms, language, and simple guidelines that employees (called "cast members") apply when they aren't quite sure what to do. For example, when cast members talk to a child, they are taught to kneel down to get closer and come across as less threatening. Kricorian emphasized that, when it comes to small cues, it is especially crucial to spot and remove "dissonant details" that clash with the desired mindset. At Disneyland, for example, guests should never witness Mickey Mouse talking on a cell phone or Snow White chewing gum. Kricorian's advice reminded Sutton of a big energy company that he had studied in the 1990s. Senior managers repeatedly expressed frustration about how difficult it was to get their people to cooperate, share information, and take a long-term perspective (rather than focus on short-term profits). Every executive who registered this complaint had the same desktop screen saver: the company's current stock price. This "dissonant detail" clashed with the mindset those executives claimed they wanted to spread.

3. Link Short-Term Realities to Long-Term Dreams

A couple years back, we went to a talk by Bill Campbell at the Stanford Directors' College, a program for guiding people who serve on the boards of publicly traded firms. Campbell is the most revered director and mentor in Silicon Valley. He serves on the Apple and Intuit boards and is renowned for his role in developing dozens of influential executives, including leaders at Google, Apple, and Twitter. Everyone calls Campbell "the Coach" because he was head coach of the Columbia University football team until he was thirty-nine—before he left New York to work in Silicon Valley. During the final decade of Steve Jobs's life, Campbell and the legendary Apple CEO took a walk—and had a talk—together almost every Sunday. When someone at the Directors' College asked Campbell about the most crucial skill for a senior executive, he said it was the rare ability (which Jobs had in spades) to make sure that the short-term stuff gets done and done well, while simultaneously never losing sight of the big picture.

This is a tricky balance for us human beings. Research by New York University's Yaacov Trope and his colleagues shows that thinking about distant events is good because we focus on long-term goals—and it is bad because we manufacture unrealistic fantasies. We don't think enough about the steps required to achieve those ends, and when we do we underestimate how much time and effort they will take. But thinking only about looming deadlines and short-term goals is a mixed bag as well. We focus on what is feasible, on the steps to take right now, but we forget or downplay long-term goals. So we direct our efforts toward achievable milestones even when they undermine our ability to reach our ultimate destination.

Scaling requires the wherewithal to hound yourself and others with questions about what it takes to link the never-ending now—the perpetual present tense that every person is trapped in—to the sweet dreams you hope to realize later. When we interviewed Shannon May, the cofounder of Bridge International Academies, she emphasized that they started "building for scaling" in their very first school in Nairobi. Although her founding team was on site and could easily communicate face to face with staff, students, and parents, they insisted on doing so mostly via cell phones because, as Shannon put it, "with everything we did, we asked ourselves if it would work with one hundred schools."

Google took a similar approach. Shona Brown served as executive vice president of operations there from 2003 to 2011. She was the fourth-highest ranking executive in the firm, after founders Sergey Brin and Larry Page and CEO Eric Schmidt. Brown played a central role in scaling Google from one thousand employees in Mountain View, California, to thirty thousand employees across dozens of locations around the globe. Brown told us that, in every decision they made, Google's leaders tried to resist doing what was easiest now. They asked, "How will this work when we are ten times or a hundred times bigger?" They thought, "Let's not decide based on what is best now, let's decide based on what will be best in two or three years."

Brown said that this mindset created challenges in hiring. There was always a temptation to "bring aboard some warm body that could do the job right now." They usually forced themselves to resist because Google needed not only people who could do the current job. They waited to find people who were broad enough and curious enough to grow into new roles and take on more responsibility—and who would live and transmit the company's "lifeblood" to others, its culture of innovation. Google has always been notoriously slow to hire, involving large numbers of Google managers, executives, engineers, and other employees in interviewing and selecting every employee. Every new hire is still approved at the organization's highest levels. Brown emphasized that at times this picky process slowed growth, stalled product releases, and created heavier workloads for Googlers who needed help *right now.* But Brown believes this disciplined hiring process is a key reason that the company she left in 2012 had a culture so similar to the company she had joined in 2003. It is still a decentralized place filled with smart people who don't need much hand-holding to generate new insights, make good decisions, and implement ideas.

This focus on short-term actions that make scaling easier down the road doesn't apply just to growing an organization. It can help people and teams spread better practices across a mature organization. When we talked to Claudia Kotchka about spreading innovation practices at Procter & Gamble, she emphasized that her team needed some early wins. Yet, much like a game of chess, they needed the kinds of early wins that set the stage for future victories rather than defeats. The best quick wins help people start and persist on the scaling journey. These victories fuel optimism and excitement, make memorable stories, and convey that you are scaling something feasible. They also instill confidence and provide a protective coating of legitimacy to help your team weather future storms. With these goals in mind, Kotchka's team began by working with P&G's most troubled brands, where quick successes seemed possible and executives were hungry for solutions.

Their early successes with Mr. Clean, a stalled and stale brand, were crucial. Kotchka's team tapped into customer frustrations with annoying cleaning chores, along with feelings and memories associated with the Mr. Clean brand. These lessons led to the launch of Mr. Clean Magic Reach in 2005, which made it easier to scrub bathrooms. Magic Reach wasn't a blockbuster, but it sold well. The work with Mr. Clean enticed other P&G businesses to test the new innovation practices, and the shot of confidence helped sustain Kotchka's team during the journey ahead. That early win also set the stage for a big payoff. It taught Mr. Clean's leaders to think about their brand differently, which "led them to try new ideas beyond liquids, including the mega-hit Mr. Clean Magic Eraser."

4. Accelerate Accountability

This mantra pops up under numerous guises in the coming chapters, especially when we discuss the most crucial talents for propelling scaling. Accountability means that an organization is packed with people who embody and protect excellence (even when they are tired, overburdened, and distracted), who work vigorously to spread it to others, and who spot, help, critique, and (when necessary) push aside colleagues who fail to live and spread it. The trick—and it is a difficult trick—is to design a system where this tug of responsibility is constant, strong, and embraced by everyone, and where slackers, energy suckers, and selfish soloists have no place to hide.

There are many ways to create this brand of urgent, all-hands-on-deck accountability, but the goal is always the same—to bake-in that constant pressure to do the right thing. Michael Bloomberg strove to create such accountability during his long reign as mayor of New York City by jamming himself and his fifty-one most crucial staff members into a "bullpen" that was the center of his administration—a small and often noisy room where the mayor sat in the center. Each resident sat in a small cubicle with a low partition. Everyone could see, and often hear, what everyone else was doing, and the burden to do the right thing—especially to support the sacred tenet of open communication—weighed heavily upon everyone in the room. A former bullpen resident told *New York* magazine: "As a work space, it is something that you do not think that you can ever get used to. . . . But when you see the mayor hosting high-level meetings in clear sight of everyone else, you start to understand that this open-communication model is not bullshit. And that it works."

Jamming people close together is just one way to build an organization filled with people who can't escape relentless pressures to do the right thing, to live a mindset and hold others to it as well. Bloomberg's method can't be used when people are dispersed across different cities or countries. But there are ways to design such organizations so that members feel that constant tug of accountability. Stanford faculty Chuck Eesley and Amin Saberi organized and taught a free Stanford entrepreneurship class called "Technology Entrepreneurship" that attracted thirty-seven thousand students from more than seventy-five countries—one of the first big "MOOCs" (massively open online courses) at Stanford. For decades, versions of this course had been taught to classes of fifty to sixty tuition-paying Stanford students at a time, who gathered in a traditional classroom twice a week. The key to scaling the class to a wider audience was the technology platform called Venture Lab that Eesley, Saberi, and doctoral student Farnaz Ronaghi developed. The platform was used to deliver proven content to the thirty-seven thousand students who signed up for the class. The course included lectures on marketing, technology, and finance; interviews with interesting guests, including one with Stanford president and Google board member John Hennessy; and readings and tips for starting a company. The teaching team used the platform to scale up a temporary organization during those twelve weeks. It wasn't just a website that blasted out content; the team built in numerous clever and easy-to-use social features to create a peer-powered network that would link, organize, evaluate, and mentor students.

Their technology allowed for an initial "dry run" to establish students' willingness to work hard and collaboratively. Students were initially assigned to groups on the basis of geography—those from the same cities and countries were grouped together. Then students with varied skills, technical backgrounds, and industry experience were mixed together. Each newly formed team was asked to come up with their five best and five worst start-up ideas and to submit a video within a week. This simple task quickly separated the doers from the slackers. Students in each group were asked to evaluate their peers, and these ratings were displayed to everyone in the class. After that, classmates were free to form new groups, leave for other groups, or recruit new members—armed with data about free riders and hard workers.

The platform also enabled peer-reviewed homework: rather than placing the burden of grading thirty-seven thousand students on the teaching team, students (after completing an online tutorial) graded each other. To their delight, Eesley and Saberi discovered that this system resulted in tougher grading standards. The teaching team graded assignments for a random subset of students to develop guidelines and verify the quality of peer reviews: peers graded each other far more harshly than the Stanford faculty. The faculty and student teams also recruited approximately two hundred veteran entrepreneurs to serve as mentors, who used the platform to find teams that matched their skills and interests.

We visited the site on July 23, 2012, at 10:00 a.m. It showed that 563 class members had been active that day and that one or more interactions had occurred on 190 teams. Naveen Bagrecha, an undergraduate in civil engineering from India, had submitted an assignment that day—a video he made for pitching a start-up. One team was working on their final presentation entitled "Core Complexity Reduction," an idea for a company that developed tools for "more efficient structuring of organizations based on the analysis of interactions of its members." This nine-person team was formed by Roger Sen, a computer engineer from Spain. The remaining members were four students from Germany and one each from France, Italy, the United States, and South Africa. Their mentor was Benson Yeung, a founder and senior partner at Triware Networld Systems, based in the San Francisco area.

Social pressure and monitoring helped to ensure accountability in this online class. Each of the initial thirty-seven thousand students could see how all the others performed—if they handed in their homework, how they were graded, how their contributions were rated by teammates, when they had last logged on, and how many contributions they made to the discussion forum. These pressures to do the work and to be an active class member drove down the class size from thirty-seven thousand at the start to ten thousand at the end. This attrition among free riders and weak performers was accelerated in week 6 of the class, when the faculty urged teams to communicate with and confront members who weren't pulling their weight. This message convinced some two thousand students to drop the class before the deadline and led teams to expel another two hundred or so deadbeats. Many of these students would never meet their teammates face to face, but the teaching team used their powerful platform, extreme transparency, social pressures, and tough policies to scale up a sizable teaching organization that was thick with accountability. By fall of 2013, at least fifty-five courses at Stanford and other universities were using the platform, and, with Saberi as CEO, a company called NovoEd was formed to develop, sell, and spread it.

5. Fear the Clusterfug

In 2011, we had a rollicking dinner with Marc Hershon. The alleged purpose was to discuss the title of this book, and, more broadly, the best words and phrases for describing scaling. Hershon is supremely well suited for this challenge, as he makes a living naming things—including Dasani water, the Swiffer, and most famously, the BlackBerry. Hershon is an all-around "creative," writing jokes for comedians such as Jay Carney and Jay Leno, numerous TV scripts, and a couple of books. He is also a syndicated cartoonist and teaches improvisation and stand-up comedy. After batting around book titles, we turned to a related question: What word best captures horrible scaling, the opposite of spreading excellence? Someone soon suggested *clusterfug*. We laughed and agreed it was among the most colorful and compelling words in the English language but decided that "No More Clusterfugs" would be a misleading and overly shocking title. (As you've probably guessed, we actually used a slightly different word during that conversation. We are censoring ourselves here—borrowing Norman Mailer's euphemism *fug* from *The Naked and the Dead*—because some readers found that profanity offensive.)

We never forgot that dinner. As our research unfolded, we realized that the definitions of that cussword in the *Urban Dictionary* captured many elements of the most mangled and misguided scaling efforts. The origin appears to be a "military term for a situation caused by too many inept officers, *cluster* referring to the insignia worn by majors and Lt. Colonels, oak leaf clusters." Definitions like this one came even closer: "the state of affairs resulting from too many staffers and not enough *trained* staffers on a project." As we read such definitions, and studied cases where scaling had turned ugly, three elements kept popping up:

Illusion: Decision makers believe that what they are scaling up is far better and easier to spread than the facts warrant.

Impatience: Decision makers believe that what they are scaling is so good and easy to spread that they rush to roll it out before it is ready, they are ready, and the organization is ready.

Incompetence: Decision makers lack the requisite knowledge and skill about what they are spreading and how to spread it, which in turn transforms otherwise competent people into incompetent ones.

When these three elements collide, you've got a classic clusterfug. This trifecta causes scaling efforts to fail big and late rather than early and cheaply. A related hallmark is that decision makers don't recognize when they are on the verge of subjecting victims (and themselves) to overwhelming mental load, distress, and turmoil. So, at least at first, they don't hold themselves accountable when things turn ugly and can't resist heaping excessive blame on the casualties of their incompetence.

Stanford University's effort to upgrade its IT systems in 2003 illustrates this terrible trio all too well. A team of internal IT people and outside consultants decided to abandon the homegrown legacy system that supported accounts payable, procurement, and HR and to replace it with something called Oracle Financials. Decision makers were antsy because their original plan to roll out the system in phases during 2002 had slipped a year. Even though the new system was unfinished and unproven, they somehow deluded themselves into deciding that a "big bang" implementation was the way to go. They pulled the plug on the legacy system and forced over four thousand inadequately trained and poorly supported users to start using the new system on September 1, 2003.

Just before the big bang, leaders began admitting to Stanford staffers that hiccups were on the horizon: data might be missing, transactions might be delayed, and the system had a steep learning curve. They even gave users a little punching bag to pummel when they couldn't contain their frustration. The leaders were trying to make light of the situation, but staff members weren't amused. Instead they (accurately, as it turned out) viewed the gift as another omen that their superiors were starting them on a forced march that would soon degenerate into a colossal clusterfug. Sutton first spotted one of those punching bags in the office of an unusually loyal and hardworking Stanford staffer. She was on the verge of tears, worried that she would never master the system. From what she could tell, no one at Stanford was really accountable for helping her navigate the tough months ahead.

University leaders were somewhat aware that they were about to unleash confusion and chaos on four thousand people, but they did not fear the clusterfug sufficiently. They were plagued by collective *illusions* about when the system would be completed, how far it was from being ready for the big bang, how easy it would be to teach and learn, and how quickly they could fix snags and snafus. Despite their knowledge of major risks and problems (in concert with their ignorance and denial of many others), they were so *impatient* that they elected to impose the system on four thousand unprepared victims anyway. The punching bag freebies implied an attitude of "Although we are not ready, you are not ready, and this will make your life miserable—we are doing it anyway. Suck it up and deal with it." The decision makers' *incompetence*—including their inability to foresee the hell that the big bang would inflict on their own lives—had the ripple effect of turning four thousand otherwise competent people into incompetent ones, rendering these employees anxious and embarrassed because they were no longer able to do their work.

The first year of the Oracle Financials rollout was a nightmare. By December of 2003, there were over five hundred unresolved requests from staff members for help from IT. The IT team was overwhelmed as they struggled to assist hundreds of upset and often inadequately trained staffers, while simultaneously trying to repair bugs and flaws that made the system difficult or impossible to use for even the most skilled staff. During public forums, both Stanford's IT team and staff members portrayed themselves as "in crisis." Chief Information Officer Chris Handley was hauled in front of the Stanford faculty senate in February of 2004, six months into the botched implementation. He admitted that most administrative processes still took two or three times longer than under the old system. Missing and flawed data made managing money "difficult, if not impossible, right now." Handley confessed further, "Morale is low. . . . The toll on individual administrators in schools and departments is very high right now. These are all people who pride themselves on doing their work, people who pride themselves on having the information for you. And at the moment, they feel completely disarmed, embarrassed, and ashamed because they can't actually get the information for you." Handley met with the faculty senate for the last time in October of 2004, reporting persistent "slow progress in smoothing out the many problems." He resigned a couple weeks later, citing a need to "focus on his family."

6. Scaling Requires Both Addition and Subtraction

As we say in the Preface, scaling is the Problem of More. So it is no surprise that the language of More pervades talk on this topic. Ask any group of executives or nonprofit leaders about scaling; search the Internet for the keywords *scaling* or *scaling up;* read articles, cases, and academic research on the subject. You will find that the dominant words and phrases are all about addition and multiplication: *grow, expand, propagate, replicate, amplify, amass, clone, copy, enlarge, magnify, incubate, accelerate, multiply, roll it out to the masses,* and so on. Ben Horowitz echoes this spirit by kicking off a 2010 blog post on scaling with lyrics from rap singer

Dorrough's song "Get Big," in which the words "Get Big" are repeated over and over.

We use the language of More throughout this book as well. Yet the addition and multiplication that define successful scaling depend on equally relentless subtraction (and division too, as chapter 4 shows). As organizations grow larger and older, as the footprint of a program expands, and as the consequences of past actions accumulate, once useful but now unnecessary roles, rules, rituals, red tape, products, and services build up like barnacles on a ship; to make way for excellence to spread, these sources of unnecessary friction must be removed.

In particular, a hallmark of successful scaling is that leaders remain vigilant about what "got us here but won't get us there," as author Marshall Goldsmith would put it. These are beliefs, behaviors, and rituals that once bolstered excellence but now undermine it. All-hands meetings in growing organizations are a prime example. When an organization is small enough that each member can have a personal relationship with every other, or at least recognize all their faces and names, gathering everyone for regular meetings makes sense. But there comes a point when the place gets so big that having an intimate gathering with, say, five hundred of your best friends isn't feasible. Sutton saw this happen at the renowned innovation firm IDEO. In the 1990s, when IDEO had sixty or seventy people working at their Palo Alto headquarters, founder and then CEO David Kelley did a masterful job of orchestrating the all-hands meeting every Monday morning. Kelley is such a skilled facilitator that nearly every person in the room added at least one comment or joke during each of these hourlong gatherings. Once the company grew to hundreds of Palo Alto employees, however, even Kelley couldn't sustain the intimacy. So, the Monday all-hands meeting became a vestige of the past and was replaced with smaller gatherings organized around studios and design practices.

All-hands meetings in Palo Alto were dialed back to once a month and then, as IDEO continued to expand, to a few times a year.

Strategic subtraction clears the way for people to focus on doing the right things. As you will see, chapter 4 shows how important it is to keep whittling away at the cognitive and emotional burdens generated by scaling. And chapter 7 shows how crucial it is to clear out bad behaviors and beliefs to make way for good things to spread. Veteran retailer Barry Feld used such a strategy when he took charge of the struggling retail chain Cost Plus World Market in 2005. Cost Plus has over two hundred stores in the western and midwestern United States that sell specialty foods and home furnishings. In 2005, the company was on the verge of bankruptcy. The stock was teetering at under $1, sales had plummeted, and the brand reputation was in tatters—few consumers had even heard of Cost Plus, and most who did recognize it had negative perceptions of the brand. Stores were messy and disorganized, skilled managers were quitting in droves, and employees were dispirited. Feld visited almost every store to provide coaching and encouragement, determine what needed to be changed, and help decide which stores to shutter.

We invited the charming and down-to-earth Mr. Feld to speak to our scaling class. When we asked him which employee behaviors were most destructive, Feld responded that bad things happen when employees treat customers as if they are invisible. When he noticed that employees failed to greet customers, he pressed them (and their managers) to develop a ritual of stopping for a moment when stocking shelves, serving other customers, or chatting with coworkers to look customers in the eye and say "Hello" or "Let me know if I can help." These small acts are crucial, according to Feld, because when employees offer greetings, customers are less likely to steal and more likely to buy something. This was only one of the hundreds of changes that Feld's team made to turn around the troubled chain.

Sales, profits, and the stock price kept climbing until the chain was sold for a healthy $22 per share to Bed Bath & Beyond in 2012.

The upshot is that scaling isn't just a problem of *more*. Scaling is a problem of *less* too, and subtraction is often an essential tool for doing it better.

7. Slow Down to Scale Faster—and Better—Down the Road

Nobel Prize winner Daniel Kahneman demonstrates that human beings are blessed and cursed with the ease and speed with which we can make judgments and take instant and largely mindless actions—"the automatic System 1" as he calls it. Human organizations, with their ingrained histories, rules, practices, standard operating procedures, and, of course, mindsets, are similar. When people who work together share the right skills and the right motivation, coordinated (and often complex) action can unfold rapidly and with few errors. When it comes to scaling, this happens when an organization is packed with people who embrace and act on a shared mindset.

But there is danger in relying on ingrained behaviors too early and too often, even though people and organizations are prone to do so. A study by Clifford Holderness and Jeffrey Pontiff examined the fate of 122,765 American prisoners of war captured during World War II—93,666 by Germany and 29,099 by Japan. They examined whether the senior officers among the POWs replicated the military's rigid hierarchy or moved to a flatter and more flexible organizational structure in the camps. The results were striking: prisoners in the most hierarchical camps suffered a death rate about 20 percent higher than their counterparts in the least hierarchical camps. Traditional hierarchies are effective given the need for quick and coordinated action on the battlefield. But they are too rigid given the flexibility and individual judgment required in prison camps. Captured senior officers who automatically replicated and clung to the traditional military mindset created inferior organizational structures compared to those officers who realized that a different model was required (and then acted on such beliefs).

The broader lesson is that mastering "the black art of scaling a human organization" requires learning when and how to shift gears from fast to slow ways of thinking. As Kahneman suggests, slowing down and thinking about what you are doing and why—shifting to that laborious, reasoned, deliberative, and conscious "System 2" thinking, as Kahneman calls it—is the best defense when "you are in a cognitive minefield"—when you don't know enough, risks are high, or you are stuck. Shifting to "System 2" often requires forcing yourself to pause rather than plow ahead. This shift is demonstrated by some advice that Jerome Groopman got when, as a young doctor, he was unsure of a patient's diagnosis. "Master craftswoman" Dr. Linda Lewis instructed Groopman: "Don't just do something, stand there." When it comes to scaling, "System 2" thinking requires constant vigilance so that those easy and automatic responses that are hallmarks of "System 1" thinking don't impair your efforts to spread, sustain, and keep improving excellence.

Nissan CEO Carlos Ghosn put it well: "You have to be like a race car driver—you need to know when to accelerate, when to brake, and when to change gears." Recall the approach used by Chuck Eesley and Amin Saberi to teach entrepreneurship to some ten thousand online students. They used a compelling blend of "System 1" and "System 2" thinking. The teaching team often slowed down to think about, build, and test solutions that later reduced the burden on themselves by making it easy for students to post and grade work, to judge one another's effort and skill, to form and work in teams, and for mentors to select and guide teams. In Ghosn's lingo, Eesley and Saberi figured out when to take their foot off the gas, downshift, and hit the brakes so that later on they (and their students) could put the pedal to the metal and fly down the road.

The Ground War Mindset

We've emphasized that scaling excellence requires the kind of grit required to run a marathon rather than a sprint. If anything, this analogy understates the challenge. Scaling is akin to running a long race where you don't know the right path, often what seems like the right path turns out to be the wrong one, and you don't know how long the race will last, where or how it will end, or where the finish line is located. Yet it is one of the fundamental challenges that every organization faces, whether it's small or large, new or old, or somewhere in between. And the good news is that plenty of people and teams find ways to master this mess, take satisfaction in their daily accomplishments, and take pride in spreading constructive beliefs and behaviors far and wide. Those who succeed think and act as if they are fighting a ground war, not just an air war. This "ground war mindset" (along with the seven mantras) reverberates throughout the coming chapters on key decisions and scaling principles.

CHAPTER 2

BUDDHISM VERSUS CATHOLICISM

Choosing a Path

Stanford's Hasso Plattner Institute of Design, or, as everyone calls it, "the d.school," was founded in 2005 to teach and spread design thinking—a hands-on approach to creativity that focuses on identifying and filling human needs. In the d.school's early days, a group of us were sitting around debating our scaling philosophies. The conversation heated up after Michael Dearing, a faculty member and venture capitalist, asked a brilliant question. It went something like: "What is our goal? Is it more like Catholicism, where the aim is to replicate preordained design beliefs and practices? Or is it more like Buddhism, where an underlying mindset guides *why* people do certain things—but the specifics of *what* they do can vary wildly from person to person and place to place?"

Dearing's question sparked a conversation about "flexing" design thinking to fit particular people and places—as well as the dangers of changing or watering it down so much that it doesn't work or, even if it does, it ought to be called something else. His question still haunts the d.school. Certain elements do pop up in every flavor of design thinking that we apply, including empathy (understanding human emotions, goals, and needs that a design ought to address) and rapid prototyping (developing quick and cheap solutions and updating them rapidly in response to users' actions and suggestions). Yet d.school professors have become more "Buddhist" over the years. We've learned, for example, that bankers are less confident in their creativity than Girl Scouts and thus require more coaching, cajoling, precise instructions, and emotional support—and so we teach them differently. We've also learned to "flex" our methods for other cultures because most were developed in the United States.

In the fall of 2010, Sutton, along with the d.school's Perry Klebahn, led a teaching team that helped twenty-four middle managers from Singapore's Ministry of Manpower to learn and spread design thinking. The managers traveled to Palo Alto, where they spent the day observing and doing interviews at the Stanford Blood Bank. They then used the insights gleaned there to generate ideas and prototypes for improving the "blood donation experience." The first day ended with the d.school's usual debriefing practice: "I like, I wish." Klebahn asked the group to talk about what worked ("I liked when Perry jumped in to help us interview that nervous donor") and what was lacking or ought to be changed ("I wish Bob had spent more time helping our team"). But the debriefing was a flop. The usually rambunctious Singaporeans squirmed and stared at the floor as everyone suffered through one painful silence after another. Eventually, the teaching team declared defeat and headed for the solace of a nearby bar.

It was teammate Yusuke Miyashita who saved the day. A gifted designer, Miyashita had been born and raised in Japan. He explained that, unlike the Westerners that "I like, I wish" had been developed with, Asians were less comfortable with openly expressing strong individual opinions in a freewheeling fashion. They worried about embarrassing themselves and criticizing Stanford faculty, whom they saw as authority figures. Miyashita suggested a small change: ask each manager to first jot down "I like" and "I wish" statements on Post-its, and then ask each one to read them aloud. Klebahn tried it the next day. The managers laughed and teased each other as they each read thoughtful, and often blunt, comments. This small change resulted in, as Miyashita put it, a reversal of social pressure, so that silence became more embarrassing than speaking out, and *not* criticizing the teaching team felt like defying authority. These twenty-four managers (who call themselves "the Alphas") have since taught design thinking to many of their colleagues in Singapore. "Yusuke's flex" is part of their bag of tricks—whether they realize it or not. Sutton watched them use it effectively, for example, during a workshop that they ran for sixty employees of Singapore's main library.

"Yusuke's flex" is reminiscent of so many other scaling stories because Dearing's "Catholicism-Buddhism" continuum plays a starring role. Every time we describe this continuum to people who are knee-deep in their own scaling efforts, they smile, nod, and tell us that it captures one of the most important challenges they are up against. We've heard this from Budweiser distributors, team leaders at Twitter, hospital administrators in Cincinnati, middle managers at JetBlue, senior executives from General Electric, California high school principals, the chief justice of the Wyoming Supreme Court, and on and on. In every case, managing the tension between replicating tried-and-true practices and modifying them (or inventing new ones) to fit local conditions weighs on decision makers, shapes key events, and leads to success or failure.

Navigating the Continuum

Numerous cases and studies support both ends of this "replication-adaptation" continuum. At the "Catholic" end, where common practices are replicated with little deviation, it is hard to quarrel with the success of In-N-Out Burger and See's Candies. These beloved U.S. chains shun local customization. The product mix, employee uniforms, training, and procedures (and just about everything else) in each In-N-Out or See's store are faithful replications. Or consider Intel's Copy Exactly! philosophy, first implemented by the semiconductor giant in the 1970s: "Stated in its simplest form, everything which might affect the process, or how it is run, is to be copied down to the finest detail, unless it is either physically impossible to do so, or there is an overwhelming competitive benefit to introducing a change." After Copy Exactly! became routine at Intel, yield rates and quality improved dramatically in both existing and new plants. This philosophy works because the manufacturing system is so exact and consistent. It enabled Intel to quickly spot and learn from any unexpected sources of variance. A salesperson for an Intel vendor once told us about a chip-making machine that produced unexpectedly higher yield rates at one plant. Upon closer investigation, Intel discovered that the vendor had accidentally installed the machine a tad off-center (by ¼ inch) at this particular plant. Intel copied the exact position of this machine in its other twenty or so plants—and yield rates improved across the board.

The power of cloning is reinforced by evidence from a company with 2,444 franchise stores that were tracked by Wharton's Sidney Winter and his colleagues between 1991 and 2001. The researchers did not reveal the brand, but they sound like Mail Boxes Etc. or UPS stores, as they provide mailing and copying services and sell office supplies. When the franchisees that operated these stores added "nonstandard" services such as passport pictures or money wiring, bad things happened. These nonconformist Buddhist moves were linked to lower store revenue and a greater risk of being shuttered. The researchers concluded that the best practice was "copying elements of the original template as precisely as possible."

Yet despite the success of Copy Exactly! and Winter's research, requiring every employee, team, business, or location to reproduce the exact same practices or business model isn't always a recipe for success. Educational research on everything from the CATCH program for improving heart health among elementary school kids to Artemis, a tool for helping middle-school kids do more effective research on the Internet, provoked Martha Stone Wiske and David Perkins to rail against the "replica trap," the misguided belief that "we can accomplish the same result widely by simply doing the same thing all over the place."

The replica trap can plague companies too. Just ask Home Depot's leaders. "You can do it, we can help" was the slogan for the twelve Chinese Home Depot stores opened in 2006. This "do it yourself" (DIY) approach works in America, but it clashes with the "do it for me" (DIFM) mindset in China. Most people in China do not have the space or tools to do home improvements and aren't raised with the DIY mindset. Labor is also a lot cheaper in China, so customers who can afford to shop at Home Depot can usually afford to pay someone to do their projects. Home Depot's DIY approach flopped: the last Beijing store closed in 2011, and the remaining seven stores were closed by late 2012. China experts—and even a Home Depot spokesperson—chalked up the failure to the company's rigidity and ignorance of the market. The University of Florida's Steven Kirn explained that being in tune with the local culture is essential: "You can't just parachute in." In contrast, Yum!, a conglomerate that owns fast-food chains including KFC, Pizza Hut, and Taco Bell, has taken a far more Buddhist approach. Yum! is thriving in China, with over four thousand KFCs and Pizza Huts, because it is "the ultimate example of a company that does adapt its strategy to China." For example, KFC sells "egg tarts, soy milk, and other items that aren't offered on menus outside of China."

Buddhist approaches also create alternatives for customers who face a sea of seemingly identical and soulless replicants. Founding CEO Chip Conley relied on a Buddhist strategy to grow his Joie de Vivre hotel chain—thirty-five varied hotels that Conley ultimately sold to Geolo Capital for $300 million in 2010. Conley used a clever technique to guide the look and vibe of each of his hotels: pick a magazine that best defines aspirations of target customers, choose five words that describe the hotel's essence, and devise ways for customers and employees to experience them via their five senses.

Conley invented this technique in 1987 after raising a million bucks to buy his first property. At that time, the Phoenix Hotel was a dilapidated mess in San Francisco's seedy Tenderloin district, renting rooms by the hour to prostitutes. Conley's first management team meeting degenerated into an unfocused argument about how to transform the place. Then he had an inspiration: Why don't we each pick a magazine that best personifies our target customer? All but one person came back with *Rolling Stone*. The team then generated five adjectives to capture the essence of the Phoenix: *funky, irreverent, adventurous, cool,* and *young at heart*—and aimed at rock 'n' roll musicians. Those adjectives shaped everything from the art (e.g., a statue of a frog playing a guitar), to services (parking for musicians' tour buses, opportunities to donate money to musicians suffering from hearing loss), to the staff (funky, irreverent, and often tattooed music lovers). The now legendary rock 'n' roll hotel has attracted guests such as Nirvana, Linda Ronstadt, and Johnny Depp. By 2010, this "magazine method" had helped Joie de Vivre grow into California's largest boutique hotel chain. For example, in 2002, Conley's team selected the *New Yorker* to personify the Hotel Rex on San Francisco's Union Square. The five defining words picked by the team were a far cry from the funky Phoenix: *clever, literate, artistic, worldly,* and *sophisticated.*

The best leaders and teams often strike the right balance between replication and customization, between Catholicism and Buddhism, by acting much as if they are working with Lego "bricks." There are some elements—not just individual bricks, but "subassemblies" of multiple bricks—that they replicate over and over for every person and place, even if other factors vary widely. For example, Apple teaches and enforces secrecy among all employees, from "geniuses" in Apple stores to senior vice presidents. Similarly, McDonald's french fries are cooked the same way with the same ingredients all over the world, even though the menus, store designs, employment policies, and prices vary widely from country to country.

Even leaders who boast about their Buddhism standardize many things. Executives at the Four Seasons take pride in making their luxury hotel chain a cultural chameleon that is "Italian in Italy, French in France," because "If you are going to go global, you cannot be one way." As vice president David Crowl tells it, "We are not a cookie-cutter company. . . . When you wake up in our Istanbul hotel, you know that you are in Turkey. People know that they will get 24-hour room service, a custom-made mattress, and a marble bathroom, but they also know that they are going to be part of the local community." In addition to the marble bathroom and other common amenities at every location, Four Seasons specifies 270 "service culture standards" (down from 800 in the 1990s) that capture lessons from hotels across the globe, provide guidance for managers and frontline employees, and ensure predictability for guests. Yet, given Four Seasons' Buddhist bent, these standards are flexed to fit each location: "All uniforms are required to be immaculately pressed and clean, and well-fitting," but staff wear shorts in Bali and long pants in Chicago.

The challenge, then, isn't whether it is generally better to lean toward a Catholic or a Buddhist approach. Rather, it is deciding when to move toward one end or the other for a given organization, person, location, or decision point. Although there is no magic formula or instant cure that will make the vexing tensions and trade-offs vanish, the best leaders and teams stay on the lookout for signs of overkill. They search for signs of excessive "localization" or "standardization"—signs that it is time to move a little, or a lot, toward the other end of the continuum. We've identified three diagnostic questions that can help you detect when a move is wise, which direction to head, and how to make it happen.

1. Do You Suffer from Delusions of Uniqueness?

There are times when the need for local customization is crystal clear. Researchers, led by Stanford's Pamela Hinds, have been tracking a software firm with outposts in the United States and India for several years. The first location opened in Silicon Valley. Much like the offices at Facebook, Twitter, IDEO, and other California companies that are renowned for creativity, the software firm's Silicon Valley office had concrete floors and other rough unfinished surfaces. The Indian location was opened with concrete floors as well. But locals objected to how crude and low class it looked by local standards. The floors also became dirty quickly because there was more dust outside than at the Silicon Valley location. This created problems in India because female employees wore saris, which became dirty as they dragged across the dusty floor. So the company wisely set aside its Catholic approach and installed carpeting.

We described how Home Depot flopped in China because its American "do it yourself" approach didn't transfer to a "do it for me" culture. IKEA faced similar challenges when they opened their huge stores in China: IKEA furniture is infamously difficult to assemble, and its big and bulky items are difficult to cart home. In addition to the DIFM culture, many people living in China don't own cars, and, if they do, most are small. To use the Lego analogy, IKEA kept most of their tried-and-true subassemblies but tweaked some older ones and built key new ones to better mesh with the culture. They customized the product line a bit (smaller beds, for example, sell better in China), added Chinese foods to their cafeteria to join the famous meatballs, and increased staffing levels and trained employees to deal with the armies of visitors—including the sixty thousand people who visit the Beijing store each weekend—who treat IKEA as a tourist attraction (with free coffee and beds to sleep in). The *China Business Review* adds: "IKEA has built its PRC stores near public transportation lines, offers local home delivery and long-distance delivery to major cities in China for a fee, maintains taxi lanes, and offers fee-based assembly services." In particular, "In China, where labor is cheap, the DIY notion has not taken hold, so Chinese customers use IKEA's assembly services more than customers in other countries."

IKEA treats this adaptation as a two-way street, nudging Chinese consumers to change their buying patterns as well. Advertising, brochures, and employees chip away at the Chinese "all or nothing" approach to home improvement, conveying "that change can be easy, and that it is okay to make small changes, step-by-step." One advertisement pictures an old man in his shorts and T-shirt, on "a typical cement-and-tile balcony in China with plants, drying laundry, and a newspaper," sitting in a new red IKEA chair. This two-pronged strategy is working so far. The eleven IKEA stores operating in mainland China racked up 950 million in sales in 2012—up 21 percent from 2011.

The contrast between Home Depot's failure and IKEA's success demonstrates that shrewd adaptations to local constraints are essential for expanding a footprint. But beware of leadership teams that balk at replication because they—or the settings they are in—are so "special" or "different." They may be suffering from delusions of uniqueness that foster misguided Buddhism. Too often, we humans convince ourselves that proven rules or technologies don't apply to us or the apparently unique place or situation we are in, when, in fact, we are fooling ourselves.

Such delusions explain why many of the franchisees that Sidney Winter studied couldn't resist straying from the company's standard product line, even though it hurt profits and drove some franchisees out of business. Similarly, Atul Gawande shows how delusions of uniqueness can amplify health care costs and undermine quality. Gawande argues that hospitals and doctors could learn a lot from the standardized approaches used by restaurant chains such as the Cheesecake Factory. Each of the Cheesecake Factory's 160 restaurants has the same menu, but employees cook each dish to order with fresh ingredients. He points out that health care economics are forcing many doctors in a similar direction. Gawande, a surgeon himself, blanches at the administrators and insurance companies that now look over his shoulder and insist on replication and consistency—much as the Cheesecake Factory does with its cooks. Nonetheless, he points out the virtues of taking a similarly standardized approach to surgery.

Despite Gawande's expertise, he had trouble selecting a surgeon for his mother's knee replacement. In his home city of Boston, no statistics were available about which surgeons from the three major hospitals performed best (and worst). Comparisons were further muddled because local surgeons used wildly varied kinds of artificial joints, anesthesia methods, and physical therapies. Ultimately, Gawande selected New Zealander John Wright from his own hospital, Brigham and Women's. Wright wasn't the most famous knee surgeon in town, but his approach reminded Gawande of the Cheesecake Factory. Wright had devoted a decade to standardizing joint replacement surgery at the hospital.

His mindset was that, from surgery through physical therapy, "Customization should be 5 percent, not 95 percent of what we do." Wright fought a prolonged battle with the other eight joint replacement surgeons at Brigham and Women's over which types and brands of implants they ought to use. Wright's colleagues initially dismissed his arguments because "knee surgeons are as particular about their implants as professional tennis players are about their rackets." Wright kept fighting because the data were so clear. The average price for knee hardware is $8,000, but some brands cost twice as much—even though no evidence shows that they are superior. Many of his fellow surgeons also enjoyed the challenge of trying new makes and models on patients. But Wright pressed them to stick with old models because new ones cost more and fail more often.

Wright has largely won his battle against excessive Buddhism. Brigham and Women's now uses the same manufacturer for 75 percent of operations. The increased bargaining power with that single supplier has helped cut the cost of operations in half. This, along with many other standardized steps (including increasing physical therapy from once to twice a day), means that knee-replacement patients stand earlier, walk farther the day after surgery, require less pain medicine, and return home about a day earlier than before Wright went on the warpath. For Gawande's mother, this meant that, although before surgery she had insisted on taking five days to recover at the hospital, she was comfortable going home after only three: she could get out of bed on her own, walk without pain, and climb stairs—all without narcotic pain-killers.

Despite all this good news, half of Wright's colleagues "at best" tolerate these changes, and "one or two" remain downright hostile. Apparently, they see themselves as special people who face many special circumstances and thus should be free to exercise un-fettered judgment—even when it is clear such delusions do more harm than good. They don't like it much, but Wright's insistence on standardization has dragged them down the path to excellence.

This story also illustrates a broader lesson about accountability. Scaling depends on people like Dr. Wright, those often unsung heroes who strive to influence the people they encounter every day to embrace better moves and mindsets. Gawande put it well: "The biggest complaint that people have about health care is that no one ever takes responsibility for the total experience of care, for the costs, for the results. My mother experienced what happens in medicine when someone takes charge."

2. Do You Have a Successful Template to Use as a Prototype?

Finding the right blend of "standard" and "custom" when you are scaling up an organization often requires a messy, time-consuming, and costly process of trial and error. But some strategies speed such learning. If you aren't sure, a good general rule is to start with a complete model or template that works elsewhere and watch for signs that certain aspects of the model aren't working and need to be rebuilt, replaced, or removed. We recommend resisting the temptation to roll out an unproven mishmash of best practices if you can avoid it.

Wharton's Gabriel Szulanski provides a cautionary tale. In the 1990s, Xerox's European operation (then called Rank Xerox) had a big initial success when specific and complete "recipes" that worked in one country were transferred to others. For example, an integrated approach to selling color copiers that worked in Switzerland was transferred to numerous other countries. It cost about $1 million to scale up these programs—but saved about $200 million. Executives were so thrilled that they rolled out a bigger "best practices sales process," where "they cherry-picked bits and pieces of best practices from different companies." This untested collage was never successfully implemented in even a single place because Xerox's leaders and teams—try as they might—had no "working examples that demonstrated feasibility" and thus had a poor "sense of what was expected and how to proceed." Szulanski explains, "Rank Xerox violated one of the basic rules of replication: It is essential to identify a template that can be 'seen' and 'touched' in a single, specific location."

That is exactly what the Girl Scouts of Northern California did as they worked with the Thrive Foundation for Youth between 2010 and 2013. The Girl Scouts were one of several nonprofits selected by Thrive to translate social science research into programs to help young people between ages eleven and eighteen to reach their full potential. Thrive's materials draw on Carol Dweck's groundbreaking book *Mindset,* Chip and Dan Heath's bestselling book *Switch,* and other rigorous research. These materials were first tested and refined during a twenty-four-day pilot program in Redwood City, California, for incoming ninth graders who were at risk of dropping out of high school. The program incorporated lessons about identifying "sparks" in young people ("the things that light you up and engage you more than anything else in your life"), developing a "growth mindset" (viewing your abilities as changeable rather than fixed in stone), and setting and pursuing goals.

During their first three years, the Girl Scouts staff and Thrive's team learned much about tailoring this program without undermining or diluting Thrive's learning goals. The Girl Scouts of Northern California serves some fifty thousand girls each year, most of whom participate through volunteer-led troops and camps. Many adult volunteers begin working with troops when their daughters are kindergartners, so as their girls move into adolescence they need new teaching tools, which Thrive provides. When Heather Vilhauer, the Girl Scouts' Thrive program director, first presented the program to forty adult volunteers in 2010, they loved the concepts but found the materials too "school-like." Vilhauer explained that "school-like" meant "a lot of sitting down and writing and reflecting, a lot of worksheets. It wasn't a lot of hands-on, get up, move around, talking." Another challenge was that the materials had been developed largely by researchers who insisted on precise repetition of the steps and language used in controlled studies and pilot programs. The first couple of times that Vilhauer presented the program, Thrive staffers on hand advised, "You're using the wrong words to present that" or "It needs to be stated like this." They insisted that she parrot the materials perfectly—even as the volunteers tuned out those dull words. Vilhauer believed that Thrive's concepts—if translated well—could help the thousands of girls they served. But she was concerned: "I grew up in Girl Scouts, was a Girl Scout leader, and then a volunteer before I became staff. I knew that probably wasn't feasible— that our leaders weren't going to take a script and read it word for word, that they were going to give the gist of it."

Vilhauer and her Girl Scouts colleagues worked with the Thrive team to make the program "less school-like," which entailed "less talking at the girls" and allowing the girls to "lead more of the activities themselves." The drastic contrast between the classrooms where the materials had been piloted and the setting at Girl Scout camps and events was another reason that lockstep replication wasn't wise. A lecture on brain science might seem interesting when your other classes are remedial reading and math. But it will seem dull when your other activities include singing, hiking, climbing an adventure tower, and building a Lego robot. The Girl Scouts staff shortened teaching modules and spiced them up with games that got the girls moving around and giggling, but in ways that brought home the concepts. For example, to demonstrate the science of neurons and synapses "they toss around a ball to show that if you do it in the same pattern you can get quicker each time you go around."

Developing and spreading the Girl Scouts' Thrive program has been messy and difficult at times. The journey has been punctuated by healthy exchanges among adult volunteers, girls, Girl Scouts staff, Thrive staff, and leaders in the field of youth development—especially about which elements are essential to the Thrive concepts and which can be omitted, simplified, or spiced up. In an early training program, adult volunteers resisted rating girls' skills at managing goals on a scale where "1" indicated "lacks skill" and "5" indicated "mastery." For example, they were asked to rate girls on how badly or well they shifted gears when things got tough. Volunteers objected because "Girl Scouting is always so positive and this felt very judgmental." Shari Teresi, Girl Scouts' senior director of volunteer resources, calmed the waters by asking the volunteers if changing the rankings to stages of a butterfly's development might "feel different." They liked that idea.

The Thrive program remains a work in progress, but the key players agree that it keeps getting better and more engaging for girls and adults and is helping girls identify their sparks, develop growth mindsets, and set and manage goals. In 2012, some six hundred adults and five thousand Girl Scouts participated in the program. To use the Lego analogy, some of the original "subassemblies" have been discarded and many have been rebuilt. But some subassemblies have been changed little, if it all. Vilhauer tells us that, from the beginning, tips about offering praise based on the "growth mindset" have been received enthusiastically by volunteers and girls. For example, instructions to comment on how hard a girl worked to get an "A" on a test or to complete the ropes course (rather than on her natural ability) are easy to remember and implement and—as Carol Dweck's studies show—can bolster a girl's courage and confidence.

The Girl Scouts' approach to Thrive reminds us of how Howard Schultz developed what eventually became the Starbucks coffee empire. In 1986, he started a small chain of coffeehouses in the Seattle area called Il Giornale. At first, each store was a faithful replication of an Italian espresso bar, but Schultz kept making changes to fit American tastes. So when customers complained about the stand-up coffee bar and blaring opera music that he had imported from Italy, Schultz added chairs and changed the music to jazz and other tunes better suited to American tastes. Both the Girl Scouts and Schultz took much care to replicate a complete template that worked elsewhere. Then, when evidence emerged that some elements didn't travel well, they had the humility and flexibility to remove, revise, and replace them with better solutions.

3. Will Bolstering Buddhism Generate Crucial Understanding, Commitment, and Innovation?

Relying on prebuilt, replicable, and proven "subassemblies" usually produces cheaper, faster, and more reliable solutions. As we saw with those Boston knee surgeons, there are times when—no matter how mightily people object—replication is a superior strategy. Delusions that each of us is a special person in a special place can gum up the works. Yet injecting a bit of Buddhism has advantages (beyond just enabling customization) that should be factored into scaling decisions.

For starters, laboring to create a local translation of a mindset magnifies the feeling that "I own it and it owns me." Researcher Cynthia Coburn concludes that most scaling studies in schools focus on the "expansion of numbers" and maintaining "fidelity" (i.e., precise replication of the original model). The role of local "reform ownership" is usually ignored. Yet giving people the power to tailor the template they implement can bolster understanding throughout a team or organization. If, say, a team from a U.S. shoe store chain is opening the first store in Moscow, they will understand their customer service practices more deeply if they are asked to think about and experiment with adjustments to fit locals' tastes and expectations—rather than implementing prepackaged and standardized practices exactly as they are used in all U.S. stores. As renowned psychologist Kurt Lewin said, "If you want truly to understand something, try to change it." Local ownership also creates commitment because the adjustments that locals decide to make will help determine success or failure; such responsibility—and the justified credit and blame that often go with it—fuel the feeling that a scaling effort is "mine" or "ours."

This blend of understanding and commitment helps explain the findings from a three-year study that tracked some one thousand elementary school students in the CATCH program, which taught kids about heart health. Teachers who tinkered with the language, exercises, and timing of prepared materials had a more positive impact on their students' "dietary self-efficacy and knowledge" than teachers who delivered the materials exactly as instructed. The researchers suggest that teachers who modified the materials were "more motivated and creative." Local ownership also helps explain the success of the Girl Scouts' Thrive program. Although Heather Vilhauer and her colleagues admired the Thrive concepts, the more they worked to customize the materials, the more they felt as if the Thrive program was partly "their" creation, not just words handed down by experts that they were required to parrot.

Tilting toward Buddhism is especially useful when you have the right mindset in your organization or project but don't yet have a complete template that has worked elsewhere. If there isn't a proven model to start with, you need to experiment with different solutions to figure out what works. The approach taken by University of California at San Francisco (UCSF) researchers to reduce drug treatment errors in hospitals is a good example. There is compelling evidence that distractions and interruptions cause nurses to administer the wrong medicines and the wrong doses at the wrong times. It is much less clear how to combat such interruptions. So the UCSF researchers worked with teams of nurses at nine San Francisco area hospitals to develop tailored solutions. Nurses at several hospitals wore bright yellow vests or sashes to alert others that they were counting or administering drugs. Nurses at St. Rose Hospital in Hayward sorted drugs and planned treatment in an "isolation room." At San Francisco General, nurses covered windows after realizing that "they were constantly being interrupted in the medication room because their colleagues could see them." The result? Drug treatment errors dropped in these hospitals by 88 percent between 2006 and 2009.

Even just a dash of Buddhism can spur motivation and innovation. McDonald's is an instructive case study. Although the company is known for standardization, local franchisees still have leeway to introduce variation and to experiment with new practices and menu items—which has proven essential for expanding its gigantic footprint. There are especially big differences across countries: McDonald's serves alcohol in France and serves lamb rather than beef in India. There is also a history of local experimentation. In the United States, some of the most successful innovations come from local franchisees—not just corporate labs. The Big Mac was first made and sold by Pittsburgh franchisee Jim Delligatti in 1967. He based it on a burger sold by the Big Boy fast-food chain. Delligatti developed it because he got tired of losing customers to Big Boy. At first, corporate executives opposed the Big Mac because, at 45 cents, it was twice the price of a regular McDonald's burger and they feared the high cost would drive away customers. They also worried that assembling this complex burger "would throw a monkey wrench into the finely-tuned store operations system." Eventually, McDonald's vice president and operations guru Fred Turner grudgingly allowed Delligatti to try selling these double-deckers in his stores. Sales shot up 12 percent. By 1968, Big Macs were rolled out to all U.S. McDonald's, and in 1969 they accounted for 19 percent of national sales.

The lesson from the Big Mac story is that innovations that ought to be scaled won't happen *everywhere* but can happen *anywhere*. Sure, there may be conflict and uncertainty. There always is, even in the best organizations. But McDonald's was Buddhist enough to tolerate bottom-up innovation. And when executives discovered that the Big Mac worked, the company took a sharp turn toward Catholicism to ensure that every Big Mac would look and taste the same.

Alone Versus Together

The Buddhism-Catholicism dimension plays a big part in every scaling story. Success only makes matters more difficult because such choices get tougher—and put more people and places at risk—as a footprint expands. Of course, there are numerous other key scaling choices, including national culture versus organizational mindset (How strongly should you weight each when you expand to a new country?); careful advanced planning versus learning by doing (How and when do you make the trade-off?); centralization versus decentralization (How much power should rest with a few people at the top versus many people throughout the organization?); and the "make," "buy," or "rent" decision (Is it better to create your own pocket of excellence, buy an existing team or smaller organization that has what you need, or rent consultants to develop and spread excellence to your people?). At one point, we had compiled a list of more than fifty different scaling decisions.

We devoted many hours to studying such choices, mulling them over with people who were in the throes of scaling efforts, and cataloguing studies about them. We originally planned to cull them to a short list and generate advice about tackling each one. After plowing away at this for a few years, we realized, as the American baseball player and folk philosopher Yogi Berra would put it, that it was "déjà vu all over again"—and again and again. While each decision unfolded differently, our analysis always seemed to end up in the same place: the trade-offs and tensions between encouraging versus forbidding departures from some template, practice, or behavior took center stage. In other words, we eventually circled back to the Buddhism-Catholicism continuum no matter where our journey had begun.

Take the choice between going it alone versus working with partners. A partner can provide you with resources, expertise, and the ability to reach more people and establish more locations, which allows you to create a bigger footprint (and do it faster). But maintaining the purity of some original model is more difficult when your partner has a different history or different ideas, tastes, skills, and information than you have—as they always do. Partnerships generate Buddhist pressures. In-N-Out Burger is among the most successful and admired fast-food chains in the United States—with the proudest employees we've ever encountered at any such chain. Unlike major competitors, including McDonald's, Burger King, and Wendy's, the company owns and operates all its stores, which helps it maintain strict control over food quality, physical design, and customer experience. In-N-Out was founded in 1948, but by 1978 it had only about twenty restaurants, all of them in California. In contrast, after Ray Kroc began selling McDonald's franchises in the 1950s, the influx of cash and local knowledge allowed the company to open its five thousandth restaurant in 1978 (in Kanagawa, Japan). By 2013, In-N-Out had a far better reputation among U.S. customers than did McDonald's. But their decision to go it alone meant that they had opened only about three hundred restaurants, all in five western U.S. states—each a nearly identical clone of the others. Meanwhile, by 2013, there were some thirty-four thousand McDonald's restaurants in over one hundred nations—which, despite considerable standardization, varied far more than In-N-Out restaurants, especially across different countries.

In-N-Out has shunned partners, in part, because they believe that loss of control will mean a loss of excellence—rather than useful adaptations to local tastes or an influx of great ideas. Pixar, the renowned creator of animated films including the three *Toy Story* films, *A Bug's Life*, *Ratatouille*, *Up*, *Brave*, and *The Incredibles*, has shunned filmmaking partners for similar reasons. They partnered with Disney from the very beginning to distribute and advertise their films. But they are zealots about creating and controlling everything in the films themselves. When we interviewed Pixar executive Tom Porter in 2011, he emphasized that every part of every Pixar movie made thus far (and of all films in the pipeline) was created by full-time permanent Pixar employees at their Emeryville, California, headquarters. This moat around Emeryville has endured even though Pixar was acquired by Disney in 2006. Pixar executives Steve Jobs, John Lasseter, and Ed Catmull were careful to structure the deal so that Pixar remained in control of its destiny—which was possible, in part, because Jobs became Disney's largest shareholder as a result of the sale.

The variance or new ideas that come with partnering can also fuel rather than stifle innovation, as we've seen from McDonald's success in countries such as India and China. The opportunity to blend your ideas with others is part of the reason to partner with others. In 2000, Procter & Gamble CEO A. G. Lafley decided that this giant firm needed to become more creative—to sell more innovative products and spread creative thinking throughout the company. As part of this effort, P&G formed numerous "Connect & Develop" relationships with other companies, even working with competitor Clorox to develop a food wrap called Glad Press 'n Seal (which quickly became the market leader).

More Versus Better

Purists and perfectionists despise this trade-off. Yet there are times when even bad Buddhism is worth living with, at least for a while. To spread your footprint faster and further, it is sometimes worth sacrificing a bit—or a lot—of short-term excellence. Dips in excellence are temporary and predictable effects of the learning curve. As a doctor at the Stanford Hospital explained to Rao, when the hospital spreads practices from an exemplary unit to others (such as methods for reducing infection rates), some "voltage loss" is inevitable at first. Studies of learning curves in automobile plants, semiconductor factories, hospitals, pizza parlors, and shipyards find that new locations almost always perform worse than existing ones—and it can take months or years before they perform as well. During World War II, sixteen U.S. shipyards built over 2,600 Liberty Ships. These seven-thousand-pound cargo ships were desperately needed to transport the supplies and troops required to fight the Germans and Japanese. Carnegie Mellon's Linda Argote shows that, when Liberty Ships were first built in January of 1941, it took about six months to complete each one. By late 1943, it took about thirty days; but whenever a new shipyard started building Liberty Ships, it still took a year or so before the new shipyard become that efficient.

Unfortunately, learning doesn't always happen so quickly or well. The burdens of expansion can be enduring, and disastrous, especially when bad assumptions are made about new locations, employees, or customers. The demands of shouldering the additional load or learning new skills can push people to the breaking point and beyond. Getting such decisions wrong can wreak havoc in organizations of any size. John Bentley's, a fancy restaurant near Stanford University, struggled to operate a second restaurant. The overloaded chef and owner—Mr. Bentley himself—eventually sold one of the restaurants to employees because "I can't be in two places at once." On a larger and more tragic scale, a firestorm of anger and blame erupted in England after officials revealed that 43 of the 181 babies that had received open-heart surgery at Bristol Hospital had died—a mortality rate that was 50 to 100 percent higher than in similar hospitals. Bristol administrators attributed those 43 deaths between 1991 and 1995, in large part, to "the learning curve."

Or consider the fiasco that unfolded after Walmart began opening stores in Germany in 1997. Walmart ran up enormous losses year after year and left in disgrace in 2006 after selling eighty-five stores for a bargain-basement price to a German chain. A pair of German researchers concluded that Walmart had faltered because management was arrogant about the ease of entering the market, was ignorant of local conditions, and failed to deliver on its legendary value proposition "We sell for less—always" in concert with "excellent service." In their lust for expansion, in 1998, Walmart paid almost a billion dollars for seventy-six Spar "hypermarkets" in Germany, even though most of these stores were in poor condition, wildly varied in size and format, and were located in "less well-off inner-city residential areas." The financial performance of these stores ranked among the worst of all large German retail stores both before and after the acquisition. When Walmart fled from Germany in 2006, they still had failed to "upgrade most of these stores and to implement a uniform design to build brand recognition."

Despite such cautionary tales, there are still times when a bad imitation of a good solution is far better than nothing or what the organization had before. These are times when, to quote Rod Park (Sutton's late father-in-law), "snowballs are better than no balls." Sutton first heard this expression in the 1980s on a windy day on San Francisco Bay, while racing Park's sailboat, *Jazz*. Part of the steering mechanism (the tiller extension) broke. Park grabbed the tangled mess, did a quick repair with duct tape, and handed it back to his son, Malcolm, who was struggling to steer the boat. Park said, "Try this. Sometimes snowballs are better than no balls." It was an ugly and clumsy imitation of the original, but it worked far better than steering the boat without it.

The same logic goes for spreading solutions that are inferior imitations of some splendid model or solution that exists elsewhere but is too expensive or impractical to reproduce in all its glory—at least for now. Xiao Wang, a former New York City schools administrator, explained to us that the cash and commitment devoted to the top charter schools are often impossible to replicate in new charter schools that draw on similar mindsets and methods, especially when they have less money than the original schools. "Voltage loss" is hard to stop, and fewer resources may mean that new locations lag behind. Then Wang raised a great question: "But wouldn't we want to spread inferior imitations if, say, the new schools were only *half* as good as the great charter schools, but *twice* as good as what they have now?" In other words, there are times when tilting—or lurching—away from Catholicism doesn't produce excellence but is still the best path forward because, as Rod Park would have said, "snowballs are better than no balls."

Striking a Balance: Using Guardrails at Kaiser Permanente

Health care giant Kaiser Permanente (KP) undertook a prolonged scaling journey that shows how the choices—and many specific lessons—in this chapter fit together. This journey especially reinforces how central the Buddhism-Catholicism continuum is for shaping decisions about what excellence means and how to spread it. In the decade before 2002, KP suffered a string of failed attempts to develop and implement electronic health record systems. The turning point came when its leaders realized that to scale up a records system that made life better for patients and employees (and contained costs too) the organization needed to break from its history of extreme Buddhism and regional silos that operated as largely separate, autonomous businesses.

Kaiser Permanente is the largest integrated health care system in the United States, with over 9 million members and 170,000 employees (including 17,000 medical doctors and 49,000 nurses) in thirty-seven hospitals and six hundred medical offices; its eight regions serve nine U.S. states, as well as the District of Columbia. Between 2004 and 2010, KP scaled up a massive electronic health record system called KP HealthConnect. It was first implemented in one of the smallest regions, Hawaii, between 2004 and 2006. The rollout across the largest region, Southern California, was completed in 2008, and it was "live" in every region by 2010. In 2012, some 4.3 million patients used MyHealthManager (the personal health record part of the system) over 100 million times— scheduling some 3 million appointments and filling 12 million prescriptions.

We first heard about KP's journey from Dr. Louise Liang during a scaling conference at the Cincinnati Children's Hospital in early 2013. As a senior vice president, Liang led KP HealthConnect between 2002 and 2009. We then learned more about this effort after talking to Liang and other KP leaders, as well as from Liang's book, *Connected for Health,* which documents this change program (with chapters contributed by many key players). The grit and persistence of the "Tiger Team" that spearheaded this prolonged rollout reinforce our message from chapter 1: effective scaling requires conducting a ground war, not just an air war. Before CEO George Halvorson recruited Liang in 2002, KP had endured a decade of failed regional efforts to implement electronic health records. It took the Tiger Team—working with thousands of KP employees and millions of patients—nearly another decade and over $4 billion to develop and roll out KP HealthConnect.

Liang's Tiger Team started "with the end in mind." The mind-set they developed in early 2003 to guide KP HealthConnect was a marked change in how patients and providers construed and engaged with KP's health care system. The centerpiece of this new mindset was "Home as Hub," the view that "the home and other nontraditional settings" would become the main places where patients received health care and that the "care delivery team would expand beyond the physician." Liang explained that KP moved earlier than most U.S. providers to embrace what she called "the 180 degree shift in how health care is seen throughout the world." She continued, "It was once seen as an encounter that happened in a few limited places at a few specific times. We've had to realize that it is not all about us (the health care providers) or our buildings. It is about serving patients where they are and when they want."

Among the biggest obstacles to spreading this mindset and rolling out KP HealthConnect was—in Liang's words—that KP operated under a "paradigm of eight siloed regions with a loose relationship to national functions." To succeed, KP HealthConnect required far more collaboration among regions and a more "Catholic" approach to scaling than ever before. Yet KP's history and culture of local autonomy meant the Tiger Team couldn't insist that the exact same system be implemented in the exact same way in each region. They had to strike a balance between the commitment, creativity, and customization that permeated KP's Buddhist operating principles, while still nudging regional leaders toward Catholicism.

KP HealthConnect required local leaders to learn from and imitate other regions; Hawaii's early success created challenges because, in the past, large regions such as Southern California had set the tone for systemwide changes. But as Liang put it, "Little Hawaii took the lead and taught everyone else" and began "going live" in 2004. By the end of 2006, Hawaii's rollout was complete, initial fears and resistance had vanished, and local doctors, nurses, and patients reported that it was making their lives easier. As we saw with Thrive, Starbucks, and Xerox, risk goes down and efficiency goes up when—early on—leaders and teams have a complete template in a single specific location that they can see and touch (even if some elements are later changed to fit local needs and sensibilities). Another reason that Hawaii succeeded was that—in contrast to many past KP failures—they didn't implement it alone. The Tiger Team, along with dozens of KP HealthConnect leaders from other regions, traveled to Hawaii to observe and help out—providing lessons and hands-on experience that guided and sped rollouts down the road.

The Tiger Team struck a balance between Buddhism and Catholicism by specifying a few crucial constraints for every region as it implemented the system—dubbed "guardrails." Local leaders still had much leeway in what they did and how they did it. But a short list of "non-negotiables" helped ensure that each rollout was efficient, regions could learn from each other, the integrated system worked properly, and patients and KP staff could learn and use one version rather than eight. The first "non-negotiable" was the name. In contrast to past KP change efforts (including many failed electronic records projects), the Tiger Team insisted that every region call the system "KP HealthConnect." A name may seem like a small thing. But Liang pointed out that this constraint clashed with a culture where—for decades—"operational issues were left to regional discretion" and "variation was the norm, not the exception."

The second guardrail was "interoperability": no modifications could be made to KP HealthConnect that hampered KP's ability to maintain a single, integrated system. Any software developed by a region—or a hospital or function—had to work well with the rest of the system.

The third non-negotiable guardrail was a "common data model":

every local software system had to use uniform data elements and common definitions. This mandate enabled each region to generate consistent and comparable data so performance differences could be identified, problems spotted, improvements made, and comprehensible reports generated for KP's leaders and regulators.

The fourth guardrail was "configuration, not customization." Liang's team saw that "needless delays, cost, and complexity" emerged when existing software was customized for KP or entirely new software was written. And these were usually regional, not national, solutions. When Liang took charge, more than three hundred contractors were working on such customization. To use a restaurant analogy, rather than ordering a meal from "the menu" of available "dishes" from software providers, regions were drastically modifying existing dishes or cooking up entirely new ones from scratch just for themselves. The Tiger Team stopped this practice. They allowed regions to select their own "configuration" of existing "off-the-shelf" software but not to sink time and money into programs that were built or heavily customized just for them.

The final guardrail mandated that the look, feel, and function of any "customer-facing" part of KP HealthConnect had to be consistent across regions. As the project unfolded, the Tiger Team added related constraints to ensure more consistent patient experiences—such as expectations that providers would return patient e-mails within twenty-four to forty-eight hours. A few regions resisted this standard, including one region that at first told patients it would take a week to answer their e-mails, but later caved-in to pressures from other regions and patients.

This "guardrail" strategy eliminated many costly, time-consuming, and destructive aspects of local customization, while still harnessing the ownership and motivation generated by KP's traditional Buddhism. There was still local customization. Yet there was far more consistency in KP HealthConnect across regions than most KP leaders had ever expected. This happened partly because the guardrails constrained choices and partly because of the Tiger Team's relentless efforts to break down regional boundaries. For example, when a new region "went live," dozens of staffers from regions that had already completed implementations were "on loan," as were people from regions that had yet to do so. They were on hand to pitch in, not just to teach and learn. During the first days after a system went live, the goal was to help any KP employee who had trouble using it within minutes.

As KP regional leaders discovered, it was easier, faster, and cheaper to imitate solutions that work elsewhere than to invent something from scratch every time. Liang's team also enticed these leaders with incentives. Their policy was that, if a region elected to use software that was not common across KP, they would have to make and pay for it themselves, as well as required yearly updates. But if they adopted software that was standard throughout KP, then updates would be made and paid for by the national organization.

Steering rather than forcing people toward change also meant that KP's people felt more free to form their own opinions. After looking at the facts, talking to peers, and learning about successful IT implementations, many local leaders decided that a less Buddhist path was best. Richard Fitzpatrick, a project consultant, described a "tipping point" at a retreat in Sonoma, California, for forty physicians who were KP HealthConnect leaders from the eight regions. "Then it happened. A physician stood up and said, 'You know, up till now the rule was that everything varies unless you could make a compelling case that something ought to be standardized, and that was fine. Until now. From here on the rule is everything is standardized, unless you can make the case it ought to vary.'"

KP HealthConnect also reflected a decision by KP's senior executives, and its board of directors, to take enough time, spend enough money, and mobilize enough people to avoid making long-term trade-offs between scaling to more places and scaling more effectively. Yet KP certainly made plenty of short-term trade-offs, opting for "better" over "more" (and "faster"). After the first rollout in Hawaii was completed in 2004, it took six years before patients and staff in the final KP region had access to the full system. As Liang explains in *Connected for Health,* saving money was encouraged, but skimping on staff, training, equipment, and other expenses that would undermine the quality or schedule was unacceptable.

As a result, KP HealthConnect is now the largest nongovernmental electronic health record system in the United States (and arguably one of the best). It includes about 80 percent of the tasks performed by KP employees. In 2003, 95 percent of the care that KP provided patients was through face-to-face encounters, 5 percent by telephone, and virtually none via e-mail. By 2011, 28 percent of interactions with patients were via e-mail and 17 percent were by phone—and the number of patient contacts with providers increased by over 10 percent. A host of metrics show that the easier communication and more accurate information (for patients and providers) have increased the quality of care—including a 50 percent decrease in hospital stays for diabetics. Because KP employees have instant access to patient records, including information about past tests and treatments, there has also been a big drop in unnecessary tests. Liang reports that since the implementation physicians work somewhat longer hours, but that they are more satisfied with their work and spend more of their time helping patients rather than doing administrative chores. Most telling is that virtually no KP physician would be willing to revert to the old system.

KP HealthConnect, in concert with other cultural and operational changes, has produced marked improvements in employee and patient satisfaction, as well as the quality of care at KP. In 2013, the National Center for Quality Assurance ranked the eight

KP regions among the top 25 private health plans in the United States (out of 484 plans) and ranked Kaiser Permanente first in the nation on 13 measures of effectiveness of care, including breast cancer screening, cervical cancer screening, and controlling high blood pressure.

The key to using the guardrail strategy is specifying as few constraints as you possibly can—picking those precious few that matter most and pack the biggest wallop, and then leaving people to steer between and around them as they see fit. Keeping the list of constraints short also reduces the burden on leaders and teams that are charged with scaling, and on frontline employees who are asked to live the new behaviors and beliefs. As chapter 4 shows, reducing unnecessary complexity and cognitive load propels effective scaling. Finally, the guardrail strategy offers a promising middle ground for scaling efforts that are plagued with excessive standardization and replication. In contrast to what KP's Tiger Team faced, in such cases, the guardrail strategy becomes an exercise in subtraction rather than addition. The challenge is to strip away as many unnecessary constraints as possible—to select a few crucial guardrails, tell and (especially) show everyone that crashing through such barriers produces unpleasant consequences—but otherwise allow people to take the paths that they believe are best.

II

SCALING PRINCIPLES

CHAPTER 3

HOT CAUSES, COOL SOLUTIONS

Stoking the Scaling Engine

We teach a Stanford graduate course called "Scaling Up Excellence." The students study some of the cases here and learn our scaling principles. We also ask them to tackle a tough scaling challenge, because there is no substitute for learning by doing. In 2012, the students worked to increase bike helmet use among Stanford students. Bikes are students' main means of traversing the large campus. Distracted bikers—often talking on phones or texting—create constant near misses and minor accidents. At least one student is injured badly enough most weeks to warrant a trip to the emergency room. A helmet cuts the odds of a serious head injury during an accident by 85 percent, yet fewer than 10 percent of our undergraduates wear them (percentages are higher for graduate students and staff). Many undergraduates actually wore helmets before coming to Stanford. They stop because few peers wear them, the serene campus seems so safe to pedal around, and, as Ariadne Delon Scott, coordinator of Stanford's bike programs (and a member of our teaching team) explained, helmets are inconvenient, mess up your hair, and "don't look cool."

Many students in our class didn't wear helmets either. So we asked a survivor of a bad bike accident, Kali Lindsay, to tell the class her story. Kali wore a helmet during her first weeks at Stanford but stopped after classmates called her "helmet girl" and a "dork." Later that year, she was pedaling to the library (sans helmet, of course). The next thing she remembered "was my parents getting to the hospital about 2:00 a.m. . . . more than twelve hours later." Kali crashed and suffered bleeding between the skull and the brain. The resulting dizziness, memory loss, and fatigue forced her to take a term off. Kali thought she could bounce right back: "I am a Stanford student, and thought I could do anything." But she couldn't read quickly and suffered panic attacks. It took her a year and a half to return to her old self. Our class was moved by Kali's story. Several students cried. She emphasized that their feelings were useless unless something changed—it was up to them to help spread the helmet habit. Kali's story was a "hot cause." It triggered attention, emotional energy, and commitment among our students. Many bought and started wearing helmets.

From Hot Causes to Cool Solutions

We divided students into groups and assigned each to increase helmet use among students in a particular dorm, fraternity or sorority, or sports team. For example, Carolin Christiansson, Sarah Chou, Ivan Chua, Aaron Ng, and Jim Tomczyk were charged with convincing the fourteen bike riders on Stanford's men's soccer team to don helmets. Only a single player wore a helmet before the intervention—so this was an effort to spread "pro-helmet" beliefs and behavior from the one to the many. This group learned that athletes are especially resistant to this and other safety measures.

They see themselves as too tough and coordinated to need helmets; soccer players don't even wear helmets when playing their sometimes dangerous sport. Our students faced the challenge of changing the team's mindset and of creating the felt accountability required to sustain it—that urge to do the right thing even when nobody is looking. They also hoped that once this safety mindset was instilled, players on the men's soccer team would help spread it to other Stanford athletes.

Much like other leaders who strive to change teams or organizations, this group had to decide whether they should concentrate first and foremost on changing the players' beliefs or on changing their behaviors—we call it "the B2B choice." The argument over which path is best for provoking action and change has raged for hundreds of years. The nineteenth-century American writer Ralph Waldo Emerson wrote, "The ancestor of every action is a thought," while his contemporary, British Prime Minister Benjamin Disraeli quipped, "Thought is the child of action."

The question of whether beliefs are largely the causes or consequences of behavior has key implications for scaling up change. Many studies show, as Emerson would have it, that first altering people's beliefs via persuasive and emotionally charged slogans, stories, and arguments induces behavior change. We saw this when Kali's story moved some students to start wearing helmets. Other studies, as Disraeli contended, find it is best to start by changing behavior no matter what people believe. In other words, what they *do* shapes their thoughts and emotions. These studies show that regardless of initial convictions, when people are enticed to behave in concert with some belief (for example, by arguing a point of view they don't believe or volunteering to eat a food they dislike), they often change beliefs to match their behavior to avoid seeing themselves—and being seen by others—as hypocrites.

Given this controversy, where is the best place to start a scaling effort? Our research suggests that the answer is *anyplace you can.*

While arguments will persist over whether it is most effective or logical to first change beliefs or behavior, the two strategies are mutually reinforcing. So, as a practical matter, you can stoke the scaling engine by targeting beliefs, behavior, or both at once. The key is creating and fueling a virtuous circle.

Communicating a hot cause entails creating and sharing stories, symbols, language, reasons—the beliefs and emotions that flow from a mindset. An effective hot cause unleashes strong feelings such as pride and righteous anger. Such feelings make people feel powerful and in control of the world around them, which in turn triggers assertive and confident action. The way that advocates communicate a hot cause is as important as its content; nonverbal behaviors are especially crucial. Although Kali's words certainly moved our class, her presentation would not have packed such a wallop without her compelling expressions of anger, sadness, and joy, as well as the rise and fall in tension in her voice. Kali's physical stance seemed a bit shriveled as she talked about the difficult months after her accident. But Kali turned upright and confident—shoulders back and chin up—as she listed her successes at bouncing back from the injury and at convincing fellow students to wear helmets. Emotions are contagious. Psychologist Elaine Hatfield shows that expressed feelings like those displayed by Kali (facial expressions, voice tone, and body positions) spread most readily during face-to-face interaction. When it comes to getting people to rally behind a hot cause, the key is creating experiences that generate "communities of feeling."

The Watermelon Offensive

The students who worked with the Stanford men's soccer team learned how—and how not—to galvanize people around a hot cause. They started by reciting safety statistics, which had no effect whatsoever. After brainstorming and prototyping possible ways to stir strong feelings among the players, the group discovered that smashed watermelons provided a vivid if cartoonish metaphor for a cracked skull—and directed attention and energy toward helmet use.

Thus began the "Watermelon Offensive." Before meeting with the players, the group scattered smashed watermelons around the field and put up posters depicting helmetless and apparently unconscious students lying on the ground with smashed melons by their heads. They printed smaller versions of these pictures, coated them in plastic, and attached one to each player's handlebars. Then they gathered the soccer team, shared a laugh about the melons, and smashed a few more. They called their crusade "Love Your Lobes," shorthand for "Love your life and serve your team by taking care of your brains," and concluded by relaying Kali's story and reciting those safety statistics. This brew aroused the soccer team's energy and commitment and triggered the strong and shared emotions—the communities of feeling—that are hallmarks of an effective hot cause.

Next, the group needed to link these feelings and intentions to action—they convinced players to sign a pledge to wear their helmets, post pictures of themselves and teammates wearing helmets on the Watermelon Offensive's Facebook page, and promise, "If I catch another member of the team not wearing a helmet, I will throw a watermelon at them, with photographic evidence if possible." The group provided the players with a supply of watermelons, which they threw at helmetless teammates and smashed and spread around the field to reinforce the "Love Your Lobes" mindset.

The players who made and lived the pledge became more committed to the cause because they did so in the presence of teammates and our student group. It is harder to break a commitment when you have proclaimed it publicly (rather than just announcing it to one or two people). The pledge, the Facebook postings, and the silliness of throwing watermelons amplified accountability because each athlete was part of a small community that had committed to live the helmet mindset and that exerted enough peer pressure on members so that they kept their promises.

Every member of the soccer team wore a helmet during the intervention, even one who at first insisted, "Nothing will ever make me wear a helmet." The players came to understand the "Watermelon Offensive" tactics as well as the students in the scaling group and had the will and skill to help with the next stage: spreading it to other teams. Soon, all ten bike riders on the women's field hockey team and seven of the nine riders on the women's soccer team were wearing helmets.

The Valentine's Day Massacre and JetBlue: Focusing on Cool Solutions First

The Watermelon Offensive is a simple example of how one group triggered a hot cause, linked it to a cool solution, and kept that virtuous cycle spinning—so that the players' behaviors and beliefs were mutually reinforcing. We studied a more complex initiative at JetBlue Airways that demonstrates how to trigger the virtuous circle by focusing on cool solutions first. It all started when mid-level JetBlue executive Bonny Simi took it upon herself to influence her colleagues to change their behavior in ways that, in turn, helped create belief in a better mindset.

On February 14, 2007, an ice storm hit Kennedy Airport in New York City, shutting down the airport for six hours. JetBlue, which has a big operation at Kennedy, was caught off-guard, and its systems and infrastructure weren't up to the challenge. The airline left hundreds of passengers stranded on nine planes for over ten hours on the airport tarmac that day and canceled over one thousand flights in six days. The airline was ridiculed in the press and lampooned on talk shows for making a mockery of their mission to "bring humanity back to travel." This nightmare eventually contributed to the ouster of founding CEO David Neeleman— even though he was graceful and forthright in taking responsibility for the fiasco and announced efforts to repair the system.

The operational and cultural challenges that gave rise to "the Valentine's Day Massacre" were tough to fix. Former American Airlines executive Russell Chew led a top-down repair effort at JetBlue in 2007 and 2008 that seemed promising at first. But an onslaught of thunderstorms in July and August of 2008 led to 814 JetBlue flight cancellations. JetBlue's inconsistent responses to these storms revealed that systemic coordination and communication problems still plagued the company. As a scrappy start-up founded in 1999, JetBlue had grown from a few planes to over one hundred partly because when unexpected problems reared their ugly heads, heroic individuals went beyond the call of duty to keep flights on schedule and delight customers. Unfortunately, the heroic mindset that had once fueled their success was no longer enough by 2007. JetBlue faced a textbook example of the "what got us here won't get us there" problem raised in chapter 1: something that had once propelled scaling, but that now needed to be changed or discarded given the organization's greater size and complexity.

To understand how this "heroic" mindset worked—and its flaws—consider what happened when JetBlue captain and director of customer experience Bonny Simi was a passenger on a flight departing from Kennedy Airport on August 10, 2008. Coincidentally, JetBlue Chairman Joel Peterson was onboard the flight to San Jose as well. Nasty weather hit New York and shut down Kennedy for a couple hours. Simi talked to the plane's flight crew and then called members of the JetBlue "Crew Services" group that she knew. She learned that many delayed Kennedy flights would be canceled because pilots were close to "timing out," exceeding FAA regulations about how long they could work. Unfortunately, the JetBlue System Operations group (which coordinated flights) did not have this information yet because the systems used by crew schedulers, dispatchers, and flight controllers were not connected.

After spending a couple more hours waiting in a long line of aircraft after Kennedy opened, Simi realized her flight's crew was about to time out, so she contacted the JetBlue controller (whom she also knew) and asked if he could work with Kennedy Air Traffic Control to negotiate an earlier departure time. A few minutes later, Air Traffic Control instructed the captain of her plane to taxi to the head of the line. They took off for San Jose just in the nick of time. While their flight did get airborne, Simi explained to Peterson that such flight-by-flight interventions were not scalable now that JetBlue operated over eight hundred flights a day. JetBlue would continue to struggle without better standardized processes, upgraded and integrated systems, and a new way of thinking about managing irregular operations ("IROP") during bad weather. Simi was convinced that the best way to solve IROP problems was to stop relying on individual heroics or a top-down approach and instead to recruit frontline crew members to root out and repair trouble spots and build in better communication within JetBlue and between JetBlue and passengers.

Chairman Peterson, CEO David Barger, and COO Rob Maruster agreed to support Simi's "wisdom of the crowds" approach. In the fall of 2008, Simi gathered 120 or so managers and frontline employees to tackle this challenge—a diverse group including reservation agents, pilots, dispatchers, and crew schedulers. Simi proposed that JetBlue needed to weave together isolated functions and actions and tone down their beloved "heroic" mindset. She asked them to join together to fix the IROP problem and instill a "systems" and "continuous improvement" mindset throughout JetBlue. The IROP Integrity team's mantra was to improve how

JetBlue "canceled, recovered, and communicated." She proposed an ambitious goal: when bad weather hit Kennedy or another airport and it had to be closed, JetBlue would contain major disruptions to the day of the event. The system would fully recover within a day after the bad weather had passed.

COO Maruster asked members of that first group how many believed such changes were possible. Only a few raised hands; most were skeptical and several were downright cynical. Their doubts were justified. After all, a major improvement effort had just failed. And this new effort required getting people throughout the company to map the steps required to open and close an airport (dealing with crews, passengers, airports, regulations, thousands of little things) and to identify and repair every flawed practice. Simi did not dwell on the skepticism or looming obstacles. Instead, she took a "do, then speak" approach: she asked the group to humor her and spend just one day mapping out—with Post-it notes—the steps required to shut down and then reopen JetBlue's Kennedy operations when bad weather hit. She also asked them to put a pink Post-it at every juncture where the system needed to be changed. In a few hours, the group created a huge map composed of several thousand Post-its—including over one thousand pink ones, indicating over one thousand pain points.

This "process mapping" exercise revealed numerous flaws in the system, and many employees in that first group remained skeptical. Yet all agreed to try Simi's approach a bit longer and to recruit other JetBlue employees to join the effort. Simi, with support from senior executives, persisted with this "do, then speak approach" as the IROP project expanded to twelve teams. Each team worked on improving different parts of the system (in good weather and bad). These teams identified and implemented solutions that stemmed from their deeper understanding of the people, activities, and connections that made JetBlue tick. They completed over one hundred improvement projects, creating changes such as more accurate and up-to-date information for passengers and crew members about bad weather, flight cancellations, and delays; clear and jargon-free language on the website for customers; and better communication "handoffs" between employees who played different roles and worked different shifts. Operations began to improve, and crew members started embracing a new mindset—one that emphasized understanding, building, and repairing the links among parts of the system and relied less on individual heroics.

The first big test came when an ice storm hit Kennedy Airport on February 10, 2010, one considerably more severe than the Valentine's Day storm in 2007. Yet, just as Simi had proposed to all those skeptics in 2008, disruptions were largely limited to the day the storm hit, and the system had fully recovered a day later. In comparison, it had taken six days after the weaker 2007 storm before operations returned to normal, and it had cost JetBlue about $41 million. The 2010 storm cost the company about $500,000. More impressively, the cost for all weather delays in 2010 totaled only about $10 million.

A far tougher test came during Hurricane Sandy in 2012, when—along with all other airlines—JetBlue canceled nearly all flights (over one thousand) over three days as the largest Atlantic hurricane on record slammed into the Eastern seaboard. JetBlue leaders and team members from multiple departments planned together during the days before the hurricane hit to develop best- and worst-case scenarios. The IROP Integrity project had taught them to better understand how their individual roles and responsibilities fit together. The IROP mantra "canceled, recovered, and communicated" was evident in thousands of intertwined large and small actions by JetBlue's people, from a massive social media campaign to spread the word about closed airports and canceled flights to heroic efforts by JetBlue employees across the country to help passengers and coworkers deal with the disruptions, distress, and property damage inflicted by the storm. JetBlue resumed flights within an hour after the Federal Aviation Administration granted permission to reopen each airport that had been closed by Sandy's onslaught. Crew members were especially proud that, when Kennedy reopened, a JetBlue flight was the first to take off.

And these successes all started with a group that didn't believe the "systems mindset"—or anything else—could improve JetBlue's response to irregular operations. But those skeptical pioneers were willing to listen, put their toes in the water, and take a little action. Brian Towle, general manager of the San Diego Airport and an early IROP team member, put it this way: "When I first looked at it [IROP Integrity], I thought, 'How the heck can you break this down?' When I was watching Bonny, I thought, 'What kind of mind takes something so huge and just breaks it down to a pink sticky?' It's just amazing how impactful a little sticky can be. It's taught me that nothing is impossible."

Talking About a Mindset Is Not Enough

Organizational life is rarely so cleanly organized that scaling can be launched via a pure "belief" or "behavior" strategy. No matter where you start, if people continue to talk and talk about some hot cause or mindset but fail to enact cool solutions, commitment will wane, and accountability—that pressure to live the mindset and to insist that others do too—will be weak. When the emphasis is on triggering beliefs alone, compelling talk may spread, but the constructive actions that are hallmarks for successful scaling usually will not. Remember the ancient proverb: "What I hear I forget, what I see I remember, and what I do I understand."

Alas, over the years, we've been involved with too many

organizations where internal champions have taught hundreds, even thousands, of employees to talk a good game about "lean" or "quality" techniques, design thinking, or patient-centered care. Yet when we ask where and how such excellence is lived in their organizations, they offer vague plans or fantasies about efforts that haven't started (and probably never will) or success stories that are irrelevant to the brand of excellence in question. These are symptoms of what Sutton and Jeffrey Pfeffer call "the smart-talk trap," where people treat planning, conferences, corporate retreats, brainstorming, storytelling, and other kinds of talk as substitutes (rather than motivation) for action. For example, at the height of the Total Quality Management (TQM) movement in the early 1990s, Sutton and then PhD student Mark Zbaracki met with a Silicon Valley executive about his company's efforts to use statistical process control, flow charts, Pareto diagrams, design of experiments, and other bread-and-butter quality tools. When they asked questions about his company's efforts, the executive kept changing the subject and talking about conferences he attended, gurus he knew, great stuff happening at other companies, and the excitement his quality team was creating in the company. His bluster quickly evaporated when Zbaracki wrote down a list of TQM methods and asked where they were used in the company. The executive sheepishly admitted that the team was focused on spreading enthusiasm about TQM, not the use of any actual TQM practices.

Don't be that guy. Take a page from the Watermelon Offensive and JetBlue: stoke the scaling engine by connecting beliefs and behaviors. Remember, Facebook's sacred belief: "Move fast and break things." As Chris Cox explained, veterans talk with newcomers about it, but their commitment to and understanding of this mindset is cemented only after they start living it—after a new engineer has made a change to the site during their first week on the job, and then another ten or so more, and shows colleagues, friends, and family, "Look, I did that."

Stoking the Virtuous Circle

To scale up excellence, leaders and teams need to keep finding ways to bolster belief in a hot cause (and the underlying mindset), persuade others to live that mindset (whether they believe in it or not), or, better yet, work both belief and behavior angles at the same time. Here are some strategies for starting, sustaining, and accelerating this virtuous scaling circle.

1. Name the Problem

In late 2004, a small nonprofit called the Institute for Health Improvement (IHI) launched an eighteen-month effort to reduce preventable deaths in U.S. hospitals. IHI identified six simple packages of evidence-based practices that hospitals (especially nurses) could employ to chip away at mortality rates. These practices included washing hands and performing related hygiene measures to reduce the spread of infections, forming rapid-response teams to treat patients showing signs of rapid decline, and using a checklist to reduce the risk of pneumonia for patients on respirators. Every hospital that joined this "100,000 Lives Campaign"—eventually 3,200, over 75 percent of U.S. beds—agreed to implement at least one package. IHI estimated that U.S. hospitals had saved 122,300 lives by June of 2006, in large part because of the campaign.

Before the campaign, CEO Donald Berwick and his staff learned a valuable lesson from feminist author and activist Gloria Steinem. She explained that, to generate collective emotion and attention around a cause, it is wise to "name the problem." Steinem described "date rape" as something that had always occurred but that was not recognized as a problem in America until it was given a name, one that made it seem more troubling, real, and specific. The right name provides a compact summary that helps people understand a challenge, explain it to others, and guides them to cool solutions. A compelling name such as "date rape" can also fuel a moral imperative and convey that inaction is ethically suspect, thus cranking up accountability pressures.

Inspired by Steinem, IHI decided to name the problem "Preventable errors are killing too many people." The problem of "needless deaths" compelled hospital leaders and other powerful industry players to act because, if they didn't, they risked be seen as uncaring, immoral, or incompetent. This set the stage for a speech by a nun and CEO of a big hospital system at the 2004 conference that kicked off the "100,000 Lives Campaign." Sister Mary Jean Ryan—CEO of a large U.S. Catholic hospital system— told the four thousand people in the audience that "'no needless deaths' is fundamental to any health care organization, so I think that CEOs should really worry more about not declaring commitment to this goal than to declaring it," implying that it was a moral imperative. Her subtext, it seems, was that providers who didn't join the campaign risked eternal damnation! Sister Ryan's plea stirred the crowd, as did a horrifying tale by Sorrel King about how her eighteen-month-old daughter Jodie had died from preventable errors made by Johns Hopkins Hospital. King not only brought many audience members to tears but also pressed them to turn their feelings into action by signing up for the campaign, because Jodie would still be alive if Johns Hopkins had used the practices that IHI aimed to spread.

IHI channeled this heat, especially the initial attention, energy, and commitment it aroused, to convince leaders from hundreds of hospitals to sign up for the Campaign on the spot. The next step was to steer those beliefs, those feelings and good intentions, toward evidence-based practices—cool solutions that flowed from the hot cause of "preventing needless deaths." And thus began a virtuous circle that saved thousands of lives in over 3,200 hospitals across all fifty U.S. states.

Naming the problem is a hallmark of effective scaling in many companies and industries. CEO Alan Mulally used this strategy in the early days of Ford's celebrated turnaround. Poor communication plagued the manufacturer. Ford's executives had been pitted against each other for decades. There was little incentive for sharing information across the business or using your expertise to help others succeed. There was often nastier cutthroat competition inside Ford than against the other car companies that Ford was supposed to be besting in the marketplace—especially between different Ford brands and regions. Mulally named this problem when, after coming on board in 2006, he decided to "create one Ford." When asked if Ford was pursuing a merger, he answered, "Yeah. We're going to merge with ourselves."

Mulally started down this road with weekly review meetings where he asked each senior executive to present his or her group's performance data and insisted that treating the gathering as a blood sport was forbidden. He made these Thursday meetings a safe place to share information (including about failures and setbacks) and to ask executives from other departments for help. Mulally made numerous other symbolic and structural changes that enabled Ford to "merge with ourselves," such as placing operations in Europe, Asia, and several other subsidiaries and divisions under one name. After managers grew confident that cooperation was not a career-limiting move, fact-based decisions and transparency began to spread and take hold. Even today, those Thursday meetings are attended by an outsider who ensures that executives treat each other as friends rather than enemies, are open to discussing setbacks and potential problems, and act as if they are part of "One Ford."

2. Name the Enemy

This is a more hard-core variation of naming the problem, one that adds a healthy dose of team spirit and righteous anger. The hot cause is amped up by pointing to some vile outside enemy that people must join together to defeat. Research on sports teams, combat teams, corporations, political movements, and warring countries shows that, when people feel threatened by an external threat, solidarity and cooperation usually shoot up. As celebrated social activist Saul Alinsky advised, "Pick a target, freeze it, personalize it, and polarize it."

The late Steve Jobs was the master of this ploy. He routinely rallied and focused the attention of his employees and customers by provoking images of Apple's evil, uncool, and idiotic corporate enemies. In Apple's early days, Jobs likened IBM to an evil dictatorship bent on taking over the world with its soulless wares. He demonized and belittled Microsoft and Bill Gates, famously saying, "The only problem with Microsoft is they just have no taste. . . . I don't mean that in a small way, I mean that in a big way. In the sense that they don't think of original ideas, and they don't bring much culture into their products." He later lambasted Disney and especially CEO Michael Eisner (until Jobs sold Pixar to Disney and became Disney's largest shareholder), and during the final months of his life, he turned to blasting Google and its CEO Larry Page for their lack of creativity and their imitation of Apple's ideas.

Jobs's ability to demonize and ridicule enemies and use them to provoke emotion and commitment among his followers is seen in a report from John Lilly, the venture capitalist and former Mozilla CEO we met in chapter 1. Lilly worked at Apple in 1997, right after Jobs returned as interim CEO. He went to a gathering where Jobs was "all fired up" and talking about "how Apple was going to completely turn things around and become great":

> It was a tough time at Apple—we were trading below book value on the market—our enterprise value was actually less than our cash on hand. Someone in the audience asked him about Michael

Dell's suggestion in the press a few days previous that Apple should just shut down and return the cash to shareholders, and as I recall, Steve's response was: "Fuck Michael Dell."

Good god, what a message from a CEO! He followed it up by admitting that the stock price was terrible (it was under $10, I think—pretty sure it was under $2 split-adjusted), and that what they were going to do was reissue everyone's options on the low price, but with a new 3-year vest. He said, explicitly: "If you want to make Apple great again, let's get going. If not, get the hell out." I think it's not an overstatement to say that just about everyone in the room loved him at that point, would have followed him off a cliff if that's where he led.

This is a classic example of "naming the enemy" to crank up emotion, inspiration, and commitment—energy that Jobs funneled to provoke Apple employees to embrace a new mindset—one where pride and persistence took center stage. Jobs reinforced his emphasis on grit and taking the long view with the new stock vesting, giving Apple employees an incentive to think three years ahead. And he demanded accountability—insisting that if you weren't there to make Apple great again, you'd better "get the hell out."

The "name the enemy" strategy can be extremely effective. But it can also backfire. It loses its punch when you try it over and over and repeatedly fail to best your enemies. It can do more harm than good if your claims are seen as delusional or inauthentic. And it can be dangerous when people embrace it so strongly that they will do anything to destroy a rival. As Irving Janis's classic research on groupthink shows, when a tight-knit group is battling a real or imagined enemy, they can develop delusions that their cause is so just and their enemy is so inherently evil that they feel entitled to take unethical and unlawful actions. For example, in the 1990s, Virgin Atlantic Airways won a libel suit against rival

British Airways (BA) after BA admitted to a "dirty tricks" campaign. BA employees called Virgin customers to lie to them that their flights were canceled and hacked into Virgin's databases so "BA could use this information to crush them by swamping their routes with alternative flights and cut-price deals." BA employees also spread false rumors that Virgin CEO Richard Branson had the AIDS virus and that garbage collectors balked at collecting trash from Branson's nightclub because it was riddled with HIV-infected needles.

3. Do It Where All Can See

In 1930, Mahatma Gandhi led the Salt March, a twenty-three-day, 240-mile protest march against the British salt monopoly in colonial India. Gandhi wanted the marchers to adhere to the strictest principles of nonviolent civil disobedience, so he started the trek with devotees from his own ashram who were committed to living this mindset. As Gandhi traveled from village to village on his journey to the sea, tens of thousands of people cheered him on and gathered to hear him speak. Fifty thousand supporters greeted him when he reached the seaside village of Dandi. Here, he boiled some mud in seawater to produce a bit of salt—breaking British laws requiring all Indian residents to buy only salt sold (and taxed) by their government-controlled monopoly. Gandhi urged his followers to make their own salt too and, no matter what the British did to them, to engage in only nonviolent protest. This movement spread like wildfire even though some sixty thousand protesters were jailed for breaking the salt laws. Violence by British soldiers and police erupted repeatedly in subsequent protests, but the protesters' adherence to nonviolent principles persisted.

After Gandhi was jailed for planning a march on a salt factory and the protest continued without him, a Western journalist reported:

Not one of the marchers even raised an arm to fend off the blows. They went down like ten-pins. From where I stood I heard the sickening whacks of the clubs on unprotected skulls. The waiting crowd of watchers groaned and sucked in their breaths in sympathetic pain at every blow. Those struck down fell sprawling, unconscious or writhing in pain with fractured skulls or broken shoulders. In two or three minutes the ground was quilted with bodies. Great patches of blood widened on their white clothes. The survivors without breaking ranks silently and doggedly marched on until struck down.

The Salt March and related protests did not lead the British to make immediate changes in laws or eliminate the despised taxes, let alone grant India the independence that Gandhi and his followers sought. But it was still a brilliant strategy that enticed tens of thousands of people to take public actions that demonstrated their commitment to the principles and goals of the independence movement, which soon spread to tens of millions more. Each of them said and did things in the presence of families, friends, and coworkers to support the movement, which ultimately won India its independence.

Persuading people to take "public" actions that demonstrate a commitment to a mindset or a belief is a powerful means for stoking the behavior-belief cycle. As psychologist Robert Cialdini contends: "Whenever one takes a stand that is visible to others, there arises a drive to maintain that stand in order to *look* like a consistent person." Public commitments foster especially strong accountability pressures in long-term relationships. As others see you act in a certain way, you become surrounded by witnesses who impose pressure on you to remain true to your new behavior. These forces were present in spades in both "the Watermelon Offensive" and JetBlue's IROP project. The soccer players bought helmets, signed pledges, and pedaled away from practice wearing helmets in the presence of teammates. Similarly, during the first meeting that Bonny Simi led at JetBlue, and dozens of subsequent IROP meetings, employees gathered together to live the mindset: mapping the process, placing pink Post-its where problems lurked, and inventing ways to improve the system. The lesson gleaned from these and many other scaling cases is that mindsets spread further and are held more strongly when people have no place to hide.

4. Breach Assumptions

Sociologist Harold Garfinkel was obsessed with social norms, those often unspoken dos and don'ts that every group, organization, and society enforces. Norms can infect members' souls so thoroughly that they are barely noticed even as they animate a host of feelings, thoughts, and actions. Garfinkel devised a series of "breaching experiments" to reveal how such taken-for-granted assumptions guide behavior. In one ploy, his undergraduates acted as if they were boarders in their parents' homes—exuding extreme politeness and agreeing with everything that their parents said. This strange behavior provoked shock, confusion, and anger. Parents asked: "What's the matter?" "Are you sick?" "Are you out of your mind or are you just stupid?" Those miffed moms and dads calmed down only when their children revealed that Dr. Garfinkel had instructed them to mess with their minds. Another experiment sent students into grocery stores to negotiate with clerks over the prices of canned foods—and most got a few cents knocked off the advertised prices.

Breaching experiments reveal the contours of unwritten social rules. Garfinkel saw them as "aids to sluggish imagination" and added that "they produce reflections in which the strangeness of an obstinately familiar world can be detected." These "aids" reveal—and challenge—existing mindsets. Gandhi's Salt March was a breaching experiment that induced millions of Indians to question British rule and all the taken-for-granted assumptions about how they ought to act that came with it.

Breaching can also be a powerful tool for bolstering desirable mindsets and moves. Sutton encountered such a case when visiting IDEO's Palo Alto headquarters a few years ago. As he turned the corner to the main floor, Sutton saw CEO Tim Brown sitting just where he expected the receptionist to be stationed. He did a double-take. Brown, he remembered, had a nice private office. Yet there he was, working in what would be deemed a low-status place in most companies, with no privacy and no gatekeeper to stop colleagues and visitors like Sutton from interrupting him. Sutton asked why he wasn't sitting in his office. Brown answered that he had abandoned it and decided to become "the most public person on the floor." Brown had never had a private office at IDEO before becoming CEO some five years earlier and found the isolation "vaguely embarrassing and frustrating." So Brown and several other IDEO leaders converted their offices into conference rooms and moved into the open. Brown added that, although he meets in conference rooms for confidential matters, when he visits other IDEO offices—such as London, Chicago, New York, Boston, Shanghai, and San Francisco—he sits in the center of the action because "when I am there to visit and get to know the people and how they work, I can't learn much sitting in a private office."

We realized that Brown's breach made crucial, and often unspoken, elements of IDEO's mindset more vivid to both old-timers (who sometimes forget them) and newcomers (who are assumed to know them but often don't). At IDEO, Brown and other keepers of their culture believe that the best ideas emerge when many intertwined smart people fret over, tweak, and critique them. Status differences that are irrelevant to the problem at hand and physical barriers between people are thought to damage the creative process. Brown's move reminded everyone to keep living those norms—and to find new ways to dial these constructive social pressures up a notch.

5. Create Gateway Experiences and On-Ramps

The Paris Peace Accords of 1973 resulted in the so-called "peace with honor" that ended the Vietnam War and won Henry Kissinger and Le Duc Tho of North Vietnam the Nobel Peace Prize. Before discussions about the accords began, the parties spent months haggling over seemingly silly issues—most infamously, over the shape of the negotiating table. The South Vietnamese insisted on a square table, while the North Vietnamese insisted on a round one. Eventually, they agreed on a round table with square tables placed off to the side for staff. Why did this objectively trivial issue take up so much valuable time? Certainly, the issue was symbolic: adversaries facing each other head on at opposite sides of a square table versus sitting as equals around a circular table. Just as important, however, was that bargaining over the table was a "gateway experience."

Donald Winnicott, a pediatrician and developmental psychologist, described gateways as transitional objects or experiences to which children can transfer feelings of attachment as they break away from their mothers or other caregivers. Gateways may include a teddy bear brought to day care or Linus's ever-present "security blanket" in Charles Schulz's *Peanuts* cartoon strip. Winnicott proposed that teddy bears and blankets create "holding environments," which foster security and comfort and enable children to develop confidence to become more independent. For the negotiators of the Paris Peace Accords, the table was their teddy bear. They attached many of the same feelings to this transitional object that they would to the eventual negotiations about ending the Vietnam War. Discussions about the table also served as a stepping-stone that helped the negotiators develop relationships with each other and establish useful precedents about making decisions and compromises.

Gateway objects and experiences are equally valuable for paving the path to excellence—especially for guiding transitions to new behaviors and beliefs. Consider what Fiat CEO Serge Marchionne did when he took charge of Chrysler. In 2009, the U.S. government loaned Chrysler over $6 billion in hopes of rescuing the company. In the process, Fiat acquired over 50 percent of the company and Marchionne became Chrysler's CEO. Chrysler was the most beleaguered of the "big three" U.S. auto companies, and numerous experts declared it beyond repair. Yet Marchionne and his team somehow turned it around, and by the end of 2010, Chrysler's factories were humming and the loans were repaid. By 2011, the company had returned to profitability and was making far more desirable cars than just a few years earlier.

When he took over, Marchionne detected "the smell of fear" among Chrysler employees—an aroma he had encountered when leading Fiat's turnaround several years before: fear of the firm's death, loss of income and camaraderie, and loss of control over one's fate. Marchionne decided that restoring pride and confidence ought to be the first order of business. For example, the Jefferson North plant in Detroit was lousy with leaky roofs and decrepit bathrooms and was down to a single shift. Instead of closing the plant for renovation and laying off assembly workers in the interim, Chrysler paid the workers to clean up and repair the plant (for the first time since 1991). They painted the place, installed new locker rooms, and constructed an atrium break area. They repaired conveyance systems that moved parts and cars around the plant. Then, rather than having industrial engineers tell these hourly workers how to design and do their jobs, Marchionne brought in two dozen Fiat workers from Italy to teach them "World Class Manufacturing" methods—to "use analytical tools to help them understand each process in the 400 or so workstations on the floor—for example, What's the most efficient and most ergonomic way of tightening a seat bolt?"

The cleaning of Jefferson North was a transitional project for the workers, a gateway for developing and directing many of the same motivations they would need to revive Chrysler. Their pride was palpable and they did the work with little supervision, setting the stage for the increased accountability—and decreased supervision—that was required for the transition to Fiat's World Class Manufacturing program. The gratitude they felt toward Marchionne amplified the weight of obligation to do the right thing—as well as their confidence in his support and trust in the future. The cleaning of the Jefferson North plant demonstrates how the right transitional experience can serve as a stepping-stone to scale up a new mindset and turn hope into reality.

6. New Rituals, Better Rituals

Rituals can serve as on-ramps for creating or reinforcing a mindset—especially when they are performed in front of others, done by all, and repeated over and over. Such public displays of commitment are difficult to revoke or reverse, and as people perform them over and over they become ingrained habits. Rao spoke to CEO and founder Randall Lipps about the little things Lipps had done to spark and spread excellence at Omnicell, a leading provider of systems that help health care providers order, store, protect, and dispense pharmaceuticals. Lipps reported that during Omnicell's early years he wanted to remind his senior team to focus on facts rather than on feeding their egos. So he created a little ritual where they used the coatrack as a place both to hang their jackets and to symbolically check their egos at the door. The coatrack and the mundane act of using it quickly became a symbol of the mindset that the senior team sought to sustain and spread. Every time these executives hung up a coat, passed by the rack, or saw coats hanging from it, they were reminded of which beliefs and behaviors were sacred and taboo at Omnicell.

Similarly, when a new leader or team takes charge, they can help modify the reigning mindset by changing the interaction rituals. In one faculty group we are part of, a new leader wanted to change the existing norms so that all members' voices were heard—not just those of a few high-status and overbearing faculty. So he started a ritual where—when an important decision was to be made—each of the thirty or so members was limited to a short statement (under a minute). He called on the most junior people in the room first and worked his way up to the most senior (and didn't allow people to interrupt). This change required members to expend effort to live a new mindset: that status differences mattered less and that everyone ought to have a voice in major decisions. The ritual also required faculty to demonstrate public commitment to these new beliefs and behaviors, which amplified pressures to hold each other accountable to the new norms—and all but one or two embraced the new routine. A big pile of studies shows that putting forth effort to do something, doing it in front of others, and doing it voluntarily add up to a potent recipe for changing hearts and minds—and that is exactly what this new ritual accomplished.

7. Lean on People Who Can't Leave Well Enough Alone

When Serge Marchionne took over Fiat in 2004, it was bleeding red ink and veering toward an ugly and irreversible collapse. He needed people with the will and skill to change things and move the company forward faster. So he plucked young and talented executives who had been confined to backwaters of the company and gave them wide-ranging mandates. He anointed people who were running small brands or working in small markets such as Latin America to take on key leadership roles. He found that these executives "felt free to take initiative" because "the head office was far away and people from there wouldn't be over every week to ask some idiotic question." He ejected Fiat senior managers who had become insulated in a clubby environment where titles and glad-handing mattered more than competence. At Chrysler, he repeated the same approach, rewarding merit rather than seniority, excellence rather than mediocrity, and especially leaders who were drawn to big and bold objectives and didn't mind taking risks.

Picking people who will jump at the chance to live the new mindset—and sidelining or even firing those who resist such change—is often the first step to scaling up a new mindset. Cornell professor Shaul Oreg developed a "resistance to change" survey that reveals the kinds of people best—and worst—suited to embrace and live a new mindset. Four hallmarks of "change resisters" emerged from this research:

1. "Routine seekers" who agree with statements like "I would rather be bored than surprised."
2. People who have strong negative emotional reactions to change, those who become "tense," "stressed," and "uncomfortable" at the prospect of doing or dealing with new challenges and chores.
3. Short-term thinkers, those who agree with statements like "When someone presses me to change something, I tend to resist even if I think the change may ultimately benefit me."
4. People who are "prone to cognitive rigidity," who agree that "once I come to a conclusion, I am not likely to change my mind."

Oreg found that people who agreed with such statements weren't any more or less intelligent than others. But he did find that they were more resistant to change. Students who scored higher on his resistance measures were less likely to change their course schedules after the start of the semester. Cornell faculty who scored higher on his scale were less apt to adopt a new technology for moving course materials online compared to those with lower resistance scores. Those change-resistant professors remind us of a story recounted by one CEO about a distraught employee that she encountered in the parking lot. Her nonprofit organization had just gone through a major merger, responsibilities were shifting, some of their clients were up in arms, and cost cutting was under way. The employee asked, "Can you tell me one thing? When is the change going to end?" The CEO gave her a warm but wary smile and said, "I am sorry, but the changes are never going to end."

These are the kinds of people that you ought to exclude from your scaling effort, at least in the early days. They will slow the effort, and, worse still, their fear and foot-dragging can spread to others like a contagious disease. Instead, you want people who get bored with stable routines, don't stress out—or, better yet, take pleasure—from new challenges, have a penchant for long-term thinking, and are prone to change their minds when new information comes along. You want people who—even when they express skepticism or outright disbelief—still can't resist the temptation to try something new, to make things a bit better for themselves and others, and who don't freak out and freeze up when confronted with the confusion and dead ends that are inevitable as we learn new ways of thinking and acting.

This is just what Charlotte Beers did when she became CEO of the iconic advertising agency Ogilvy & Mather in the early 1990s. This agency was in such financial and emotional turmoil that Beers defined her main job as "removing 'beleaguered' from our name"—every press report about the agency seemed to use that word, and it captured how most of Ogilvy & Mather's seven thousand employees felt. The recent loss of anchor clients such as

American Express and Campbell's Soup had been especially devastating. The approach that Beers used to recreate and spread excellence throughout the agency was "painful, messy, and chaotic" at times. But a new mindset emerged: "The purpose of our business is to build our clients' brands," or, more briefly, "brand stewardship." Beers and her team pressed and persuaded employees in Ogilvy & Mather's 272 offices around the world to embrace and live this mindset. For example, Beers worked on rolling out "brand audits" throughout the company, "a series of questions designed to unveil the emotional as well as the logical significance of a product in users' lives." Answers to questions such as "What memories or associations does this brand bring to mind?" were used, in Beers's words, to "guide each brand team to the rock-bottom truth of the brand."

Clients embraced the idea of brand stewardship and new tools such as the brand audit so enthusiastically that the agency stopped losing old accounts, landed new ones such as Jaguar Motors, and reclaimed the lost American Express account. The word *beleaguered* no longer seemed to be part of its name; indeed, the press announced that "Ogilvy & Mather is back on track."

One of Beers's most crucial early moves was to select nine executives for "the thirsty for change group." Beers asked them, "Will you please join me . . . in re-inventing our beloved agency. I chose you because you seem to be truth-tellers, impatient with the state we are in and capable of leading this revised, refreshed agency." In other words, they were picked by Beers for their discomfort with the status quo, enthusiasm for new challenges, penchant for long-term thinking, and flexibility—and impatience to start rebuilding the company. The group that turned around Ogilvy & Mather would score mighty low on Professor Oreg's resistance-to-change survey.

Poetry, Plumbing, and Scaling Up Excellence

We've emphasized how managers, leaders, and teams can link hot causes to cool solutions. People are motivated to match what they say to what they do, in part, because glaring gaps between beliefs and behaviors make us feel like hypocrites. Yet there are times when striving for a perfect match between behavior and belief is neither practical nor wise.

Stanford emeritus professor James March—arguably the most prestigious living organizational theorist—suggests that one root of such necessary inconsistency is that every skilled executive, manager, and supervisor is both a "poet" and a "plumber." The poetry part is mostly about communicating hot causes: creating beliefs via words, stories, ceremonies, mission statements, goals, and strategic plans to inspire and guide others. The plumbing part is mostly about cool solutions—especially the nitty-gritty behavior required to ensure that planes or trains run on time, widgets or cars are built, grapes are grown and put in bottles of wine, or in our case, students are taught and those books and papers written. March asserts that leaders and their followers yearn for compelling poetry and related joys even when they have unclear and impractical implications for concrete beliefs or behaviors. Sometimes people need to hear comforting and inspiring words, hear beautiful songs and music, and eat, drink, dance, joke, and laugh together, even when such pleasures have no tangible link to achieving victory or success—it makes them feel glad to be alive, enjoy the company of those around them, and develop the bonds and trust required to keep moving forward together.

The art of scaling up excellence is very much about knowing when to create a tight connection between poetry and plumbing versus when to stretch, flex, or even set aside your most precious beliefs. We've seen the power of beautiful but seemingly unrealistic poetry, such as Gandhi's calls for nonviolent resistance and Donald Berwick's passion and impatience about saving one hundred thousand lives in U.S. hospitals. As March explained, such poetry reflects the sometimes useful "ability to refuse to accept the constraints of reality"; skilled and savvy poets can sometimes lead people "to accomplish wondrous things that would not be deemed possible in a 'rational' world."

But compelling poetry also has a dark side. Dogmatic, mindless, and inflexible application of any mindset can get you or your organization in big trouble. A mindset should be treated like a compass or the global positioning system in your car or on your phone. It is something that points you in the right direction most of the time. But you can't follow it blindly; otherwise, every now and then, you will plow into obstacles that you should have steered around or miss your destination. As we saw in chapter 1, wise leaders resist taking a "one-size-fits-all" approach. They keep a sharp lookout for situations that require ignoring or rewriting their favorite poetry.

Consider Apple's obsessive penchant for protecting its intellectual property. Apple is infamously secretive and aggressively attacks any competitor or person that puts the company's ownership claims at risk. In explaining why the company was pursuing a lawsuit against HTC, Steve Jobs offered typical Apple poetry, "We can sit by and watch competitors steal our patented inventions, or we can do something about it. We've decided to do something about it." This mindset has served the company well many times, such as during the billion-dollar lawsuit it won against Samsung in 2012 for encroaching on Apple's smart phone patents. There have been other times, however, when such mindless devotion has made Apple come across as a band of idiotic bullies, as when nine-year-old Shea O'Gorman sent Jobs a letter with some suggestions for improving her iPod. Apple's lawyers responded with a letter "stating that the company doesn't accept unsolicited ideas and telling her not to send in any more suggestions." This caused Shea to burst into tears and generated bad publicity for Apple—earning them a place on *Fortune*'s list of "101 Dumbest Moments in Business." Apple wanted to make sure that Shea couldn't sue them if they ever used her idea of having lyrics appear on the screen (to help her sing along with her favorite songs). Perhaps they should have "flexed" their policy before sending a threatening letter to a nine-year-old girl who loved her iPod. Indeed, the uproar caused Apple's lawyers to apologize to Shea and to tweak their legalistic language to avert such embarrassment in the future.

CHAPTER 4

CUT COGNITIVE LOAD

But Deal with Necessary Complexity

"Rules, tools, and fools." The University of Michigan's Robert Kahn once joked that these key ingredients make every organization tick. Kahn's definition is instructive to those charged with scaling. The process requires adding new rules, processes, and technologies; adding more people; and placing them in roles, teams, regions, divisions, plants, retail stores, companies, ships, and such. These additions are inevitable and necessary parts of spreading excellence. But the associated mechanics and mental gyrations can stretch people and systems to the breaking point. This chapter digs into why the "more more more" of scaling can wreak havoc throughout a team or organization. And it provides solutions for avoiding predictable pitfalls.

Whether the challenge is to spread better ways to gas up cars across four Hendrick Motorsports pit crews, bring aboard hundreds of newcomers at Facebook or Bridge International Academies, roll out new practices for "irregular operations" at JetBlue, or instill customer-centered design throughout Procter & Gamble, scaling entails subjecting people to an onslaught of unfamiliar, difficult, and upsetting changes and chores. The sheer volume and complexity often overwhelms the "working memory" of the individuals who do it, which produces blind spots and bad decisions and saps their willpower.

Researchers call this condition "cognitive overload," and its unfortunate effects are well documented. For example, marketing researcher Baba Shiv randomly split students into two groups: one group memorized two digits (e.g., "16") and the other seven (e.g., "2257324"). Before reporting the number to an experimenter, students walked down a hall where they were offered a choice of fruit salad and chocolate cake with a cherry on top. Students working to recall the seven digits were 50 percent more likely to choose the cake. Why? The mental effort required to remember those extra five digits induced them to take the easy way out and gobble down the less healthy cake.

It is no accident that Shiv used seven digits. Seven is the "magic number" for memory researchers. In 1956, psychologist George Miller showed that people could hold "seven, plus or minus two" numbers in short-term memory. Yet organizational designers rarely heed the implications of Miller's Law or thousands of subsequent studies on the hazards of overtaxing our brains. As organizations expand and mature, rather than rationing or subtracting load, leaders and teams often pile on so many metrics, procedures, and chores that people lose the capacity and willpower to do the right things.

Kevin Peters, president of Office Depot, provides a revealing example. When Peters took charge in 2010, he faced two clashing facts: evaluations by "mystery shoppers" (who secretly observe and record employee actions) were at all-time highs, but store sales were falling. After visiting seventy stores in fifteen states, Peters found that clerks and managers felt so pressured to do tasks like sweeping floors and stocking shelves that they routinely ignored customers' questions and needs: their bellies faced the shelves and their backs faced customers. Office Depot's mystery shopping metrics diverted attention from customers—even though every employee believed that serving and selling to customers ought to be their top priority.

As Office Depot discovered, the more tasks that people do, the worse they tend to perform each one. Research on multitasking reveals a similar lesson. The rise of information technologies, especially smart phones, has transformed us into creatures who do many things at once. We text, e-mail, or surf the Web, while simultaneously trying to listen and talk with colleagues, teachers, or loved ones, and—for good measure—perhaps do housework, write a report, or drive a car to boot. Despite claims that younger people who grew up with these gizmos are more adept at such juggling acts than their parents or grandparents, numerous studies show that multitasking undermines everyone's competence. The late Cliff Nass and his Stanford colleagues also found that multitasking skills aren't honed with practice. "Heavy multitaskers" performed worse than "light multitaskers" on every task examined—they were even worse at multitasking! Nass concluded, "They're suckers for irrelevancy. . . . Everything distracts them."

A study of twenty-three neonatal intensive care units (NICUs) underscores the dangers of burdening people with extra chores. These NICUs asked frontline staff including nurses, doctors, and respiratory therapists to get more involved in sharing information and making decisions. When staff collaborated to improve care—learning and teaching ways to control infections, for example—infant mortality rates were lower. But getting staff involved in management ("shared governance") was linked to higher mortality rates. When they participated in hiring, performance appraisals, and budgeting, more babies died! We discussed these findings—which were first observed for 2002—with Harvard's Anita Tucker, one of the researchers. She conducted additional analyses for 2003 and 2004 for this book and found that higher death rates in NICUs with "shared governance" persisted over all three years. Tucker wrote us that "physicians we talked with about shared governance on clinical outcomes felt this was a very accurate finding because it pulled nurses away from the bedside and diverted their attention from clinical care."

Bigger and Dumber?

In short, cognitive load is another reason that scaling is the Problem of More. It can tax human minds and organizations beyond what they can bear. When that happens, people ignore their best intentions, work on the wrong tasks, shift focus too often, and perform less well at everything they attempt. Scaling provides a potential antidote: adding people to share the load. Most scaling adventures—whether starting a restaurant chain or spreading better practices in hospitals—begin with one or two people, or perhaps a small team. And if there is a whiff of success, they add or attract more help.

Unfortunately, although extra hands and minds can lighten the burden, these additions carry nasty side effects. As teams get bigger, individual performance suffers. Bradley Staats and his colleagues documented this decline in an experiment that compared two- and four-person teams. Each was asked to assemble a fifty-piece human figure with Legos. The bigger teams did assemble the figure faster: an average of 28 minutes versus 36 minutes for smaller teams. Yet the "labor efficiency" of two-person teams was higher: 72 "person-minutes" of labor versus 112 for four-person teams. Bigger teams lost those 40 minutes because each member had to coordinate and make decisions with three people rather than one. A similar story emerges from Jennifer Mueller's study of twenty-six innovation project teams (with three to nineteen members), which she tracked for two to eight months. Ratings by leaders and peers revealed that the bigger the team, the worse each member performed. Employees in bigger teams gave each other less support and help because it was harder to maintain so many social relationships and to coordinate with more people.

After devoting nearly fifty years to studying group effectiveness, the late J. Richard Hackman concluded that, for most tasks, the best size is four to six: "My rule of thumb is that no work team should have membership in the double digits. . . . The number of performance problems a team encounters increases exponentially as team size increases." Miller's magic number (seven, plus or minus two) pops up again: once a team has more than nine members, the trouble really starts. As Miller and Hackman would have it, retired marine captain and former U.S. senator James H. Webb Jr. explained why the "fire team"—the basic combat fighting unit— shrank from twelve to four during World War II. Webb wrote in the *Marine Corps Gazette* that this "12 man mob" was "immensely difficult" for marine squad leaders to control under the stress and confusion of battle. Coordination problems were rampant, and close relationships—where soldiers fight for their buddies—were tougher to maintain in twelve-man teams.

As Intuit CEO Brad Smith says, "When it comes to building a culture of innovation, less is often best." Much as teams do at online retailing giant Amazon, Intuit lives this philosophy with the Two-Pizza Rule: "Our development teams can be no larger than the number of people who can be fed by two pizzas," which helps members "stay nimble and make decisions quickly." This lesson applies to tiny organizations too. Pulse News, a "news aggregator" app for phones and tablets, was started in mid-2010. Communication breakdowns and misunderstandings flared up after it grew slightly from three to eight people. Founders Akshay Kothari and Ankit Gupta told us that, after they divided those eight people among three teams, people produced better software, did it faster, and argued less. When Pulse expanded to about twelve people (working in four teams, all in the same room), each team maintained a bulletin board that captured their current work to help everyone at Pulse follow what they were doing. Every afternoon at about 3:30 p.m., each team also gave a short talk to the company about what they were working on and where they needed help. Pulse relied on small teams as it grew to twenty-five employees and 30 million users; it is now part of LinkedIn, which bought Pulse for $90 million in April 2013.

The finding that bigger groups weigh more heavily on the mind is echoed in research by Oxford anthropologist Robin Dunbar, which was popularized by Malcolm Gladwell. Dunbar proposed that the size of a primate group is limited by the cognitive capacity of members to maintain social bonds. Gladwell explains:

> If you belong to a group of five people, Dunbar points out, you have to keep track of 10 separate relationships: your relationships with the four others in your circle and the six other two-way relationships between the others. . . . If you belong to a group of twenty people, however, there are now 190 two-way relationships to keep track of: 19 involving yourself and 171 involving the rest of the group. That's a fivefold increase in the size of the group, but a twentyfold increase in the amount of information processing needed to "know" the other members of the group.

Like Hackman, Dunbar finds that communication and coordination challenges multiply exponentially: when more than four or five people gather, face-to-face communication starts getting cumbersome. Dunbar believes these limits explain studies that found the average restaurant reservation was for 3.8 patrons and that most committees in big U.S. corporations had between five and eight members. Dunbar calculated that when enough people and small groups compose an organization so it has more than about 150 people (between 100 and 230), the demands outstrip what the human mind can handle.

Dunbar focuses on the burdens of "grooming activities." Baboons and other nonhumans devote many hours sitting with members of their group, scratching and petting them, and picking out twigs and bugs from their coats. Grooming promotes hygiene, but its main value is sustaining social bonds. Dunbar argues that gossip and small talk play a similar role for humans. He calculates that, in an organization of 150, people devote about 42 percent of their time to "grooming." At 200, it jumps to 56 percent. This is why, he says, organizations should and often do divide into smaller units at about 150 people. At about 200 or 250, conflict, coordination, and performance problems will be rampant. These limits seem to explain why, going back to at least the Romans in 104 BC, armies have relied on a company size of about 150 members (never exceeding 230)—and still do so, despite vastly improved communication technologies. Modern studies of online behavior bolster Dunbar's number. A 2012 analysis of 1.7 million Twitter users in the *Bulletin of the American Physical Society* found they could maintain only one hundred to two hundred active online relationships at a time.

Related research shows that as organizations grow and age, "maintenance," "coordination," and "grooming" costs accelerate as decision makers add layers, form teams and departments, and pile on rules and processes. Administrators are often added at a faster rate than those who perform the organization's main work. Universities seem to be especially cursed with this penchant for administrative bloat. The *Economist* reported: "Between 1993 and 2007 spending on university bureaucrats at America's 198 leading universities rose much faster than spending on teaching faculty. For example, Harvard increased its administrative spending per student by 300%. . . . In some universities, such as Arizona State University, almost half the full-time employees are administrators."

The U.S. Department of Education reports that, in 1976, U.S.

universities had about fifty "non-faculty professionals" per hundred faculty members. By 2009, this ratio reached ninety-eight per hundred, much like Arizona State. Naval historian and management satirist Northcote Parkinson observed a similar pattern decades earlier. In 1914, the British Navy had sixty-two large ships, 146,000 officers and sailors, and 2,000 "Admiralty officials" (civil servants to support their work). By 1928, the post–World War I navy was down to twenty large ships and 100,000 officers and sailors, but Admiralty officials had nearly doubled to 3,569. Between 1935 and 1954, the percentage of Admiralty officials rose year after year (at 5 to 7 percent), regardless of whether the rest of the navy was expanding or contracting.

As organizations and programs expand and age, they often propagate ever more convoluted procedures and processes. Ballooning brigades of administrators must justify their existence. So they busy themselves by writing more rules and requiring colleagues to jump through more hoops—stealing bandwidth, effort, and willpower from more essential work. In the worst cases, the result is "BDC" or "Big Dumb Company" disease, as venture capitalist John Greathouse calls it. Rao saw this malady at a chain of West Coast gas stations he worked with several years ago. When Rao asked frontline workers how they solved customer service problems, they said it wasn't worth the trouble. They were required to get nine approvals for even small acts of goodwill, such as refunds or replacing damaged goods. The company didn't trust workers, and managers didn't trust each other—even minor customer complaints took months to resolve on the rare occasions that employees had the will to battle all that red tape.

Geoffrey West, a physicist at the Santa Fe Institute, asserts that this penchant for organizations to devote more and more resources to the care and feeding of the bureaucracy and less and less to the work itself spells their ultimate doom. West and his colleagues studied twenty-three thousand corporations and found that, as companies grew, profits-per-employee shrank. He contends that small companies focus on delivering great products and services. As they grow, "Management starts worrying about the bottom line, and so all these people are hired to keep track of the paper clips." West argues that bloated bureaucracies overwhelm the advantages of greater scale; ballooning overhead and shrinking profits mean that even minor marketplace disturbances can cause catastrophic losses. He concludes, "Companies are killed by their need to keep on getting bigger."

Despite such hazards, bigger can be better—or at least pretty good—under the right conditions. For starters, most organizations are too small to suffer from Big Dumb Company disease. In 2008, of the 6 million U.S. firms with employees, more than half had four or fewer employees and only 981 had more than ten thousand. Similarly, in 2012, 1.6 million nonprofit organizations were registered with the IRS; just 25 percent had revenues over $100,000 and 4 percent exceeded $10 million. There are several hundred nonprofits with revenues over $50 million, including about two hundred founded since 1975, such as Habitat for Humanity and Teach for America—so a lot of good is being done by fast-growing newcomers. Massive multinationals such as Apple, General Electric, Walmart, Yum!, and McDonald's may eventually collapse under their own weight, but these giants have endured and grown for decades. These firms are tiny infants compared to the Catholic Church, which is over two thousand years old, has over a billion members, and has been led by 266 popes. The church faces many problems, including sex scandals and accusations of rigidity. Yet despite massive scale, the church has repeatedly risen to the challenges of spreading excellence and reversing bad behavior during its long history.

Debates over the limits and hazards of size have raged since the 2008 financial meltdown. Executives, politicians, and academics wrestle over "megabanks"—whether giants like Bank of America and Citibank with trillions of assets are "too big to fail" and should be broken up. Some giants may indeed be too large for protecting financial markets and their own long-term viability—as even Sandy Weill, Citibank's former CEO, now asserts. Yet even harsh critics of megabanks, including MIT's Simon Johnson, suggest that economies of scale are evident in banks with less than $100 billion in assets—which would mean that over six thousand U.S. banks are small enough that they still have plenty of room to grow.

The upshot is that, yes, getting bigger can be bad. Yet as a practical matter, in organizations within every sector and of every size, some leaders and teams handle growth and program expansion well and others do not. In addition, most organizations are small enough that leaders are rightly focused on expanding their footprint as effectively as possible, not on being or getting too big. To us, this means that the key challenges are how to add rules, tools, and people without creating bloated and overbearing bureaucracies, filled with overloaded and irresponsible people. That's what the rest of this chapter is about.

"The Job of the Hierarchy Is to Defeat the Hierarchy"

Plenty of organizations and projects are stifled and stalled by red tape and counterproductive pecking orders. Yet we reject calls by gurus, including Gary Hamel, that "bureaucracy must die" and that top-down control is "toxic." Even small organizations can't function without hierarchies and specialized roles, groups, and divisions. Well-crafted rules and processes create predictability, reduce conflict, facilitate coordination, and reduce cognitive load because people (often with help from computers) are armed with proven responses to routine situations—rather than having to reinvent the wheel each time. It is impossible to grow an organization or spread excellence without such tried-and-true controls, constraints, and building blocks.

Many of us have a hate-love relationship with such bureaucratic trappings. We despise the limits they impose on our freedoms but love what they allow us to accomplish. After reviewing a mountain of studies, psychologists Deborah Gruenfeld and Larissa Tiedens concluded that people are especially ambivalent about hierarchies. Most employees say they prefer participative and democratic organizations and bad-mouth workplaces where a few members wield power over the rest. Yet teams and organizations can't seem to operate without pecking orders. These studies also show that, although people say they dislike hierarchies, they are happier, calmer, and more productive when power and status differences are present and well understood.

Human (and animal) groups can't avoid hierarchies because power and status differences enhance collective effectiveness in so many ways. Hierarchies clear up confusion about who makes decisions and who does not, when decisions are final, and thousands of details such as where to sit, who talks more and less, what to wear, and when meetings start and end. Consider a failed experiment by Google cofounder and CEO Larry Page, who has long been "obsessed with making Google work like a smaller company." In 2001, when Google grew to about four hundred people, Page decided that middle managers were creating needless complexity and friction. So he got rid of all of them, and more than one hundred engineers reported to a single overwhelmed executive. Frustration and confusion were rampant. Without those middle managers, it was nearly impossible for engineers to do their work and for executives to grasp and influence what happened at Google. Page learned the hard way that a hierarchy can be too flat and that middle managers are often a necessary complexity.

The challenge, then, is weaving such complexity into a system that does as much good and as little harm as possible. Chris

Fry and Steve Greene followed an intriguing motto during the years they helped scale Salesforce.com's software development organization—from forty to six hundred people. It sounded a bit crazy to us at first: "The job of the hierarchy is to defeat the hierarchy." Yet as we listened to their story, it made sense: these executives used Salesforce's hierarchy to repair its bureaucracy. In Greene's words, they used it to build a "better organizational operating system."

In 2006, even though their forty engineers were very talented and were still building great products, the Salesforce development organization was facing severe challenges: according to Fry, "We started to see that the progress that teams were making was getting slower and slower and slower, so the number of releases that we were pushing out the door started getting further and further apart. Our ability to respond to customers was getting worse and worse. These are typical things that happen to a lot of companies as they grow."

Fry and Greene believed a big part of the problem was that the system focused most of the control (and blame and credit) on a few senior executives. An unfortunate side effect was that most software engineers had little influence on or personal responsibility for the software that Salesforce developed. Fry and Greene replaced this system with one that used smaller teams and held team leaders and engineers to high levels of accountability. Each development team was expected to complete a new "software demo" (a working prototype) every thirty days, and the entire company released a new product every four months (a goal missed just once in six years). Fry and Greene also created an open internal job market that amplified accountability. Every engineer was free to move to a new team without getting permission from his or her boss. About 20 percent of the engineers chose to switch teams every year, which encouraged leaders to treat people well and develop good reputations, exposed leaders who couldn't keep good people, and put the onus on engineers to find teams that fit their temperament and talent.

This chapter builds on Fry and Greene's view that hierarchy is both a cause and a cure for maladies generated by scaling. We provide five tactics for building better organizational operating systems. Much of this advice builds on our mantra in chapter 1: scaling is a problem of *more* and of *less* because, as more is added, subtraction (and division) help counteract and contain the necessary complexity. Beware, however, of the temptation to oversimplify—to cut out useful muscle and bone. Scaling requires a penchant for parsimony, for understanding the nuances of an organization and its people so you can make things as simple as possible—but no simpler.

1. Subtraction as a Way of Life

Renowned American novelist Ernest Hemingway said the most essential gift for a good writer is "a built-in shock-proof shit detector," the ability to spot bad or unnecessary text, the skill to fix what is salvageable, and the will to throw away what is beyond repair or unnecessary. Leaders and teams that spread excellence act the same way, ruthlessly spotting and removing crummy or useless rules, tools, and fools that clog up the works and cloud people's minds.

IDEO's David Kelley told us a great old story about how Steve Jobs lived the subtraction mindset. In the 1980s, Apple hired Kelley's innovation firm to help design their first mouse. Kelley's designers were on hand when Jobs decided the mouse would have one button rather two. Apple's engineers argued vehemently for two buttons because users could do so many more things than with one. Those engineers weren't pleased when Jobs was swayed by the technical writer instead, who was probably the lowest-paid person in the room: she said it would be a lot easier to write a simple instruction manual if the mouse had just one button—and far easier for customers to learn and use.

This decision dovetails with Jobs's lifelong quest to cut cognitive load and simplify experiences for Apple customers and employees—a mindset that endures at the company. Author Adam Lashinsky, who has tracked Apple for years, observes, "In the rest of the corporate world to say one manages a profit-and-loss statement is to proclaim one's domain." Lashinsky's words inspired us ask the top sixty executives of one big beverage company: "How many of you have P&L responsibilities?" More than fifty raised hands. In contrast, despite Apple's massive market value and cash reserves, Lashinsky reports that only one executive has P&L responsibilities—Chief Financial Officer Peter Oppenheimer—because removing such tasks enables other executives to "focus on their strengths."

Subtraction isn't just for senior executives. The best managers and teams routinely identify unnecessary impediments and get rid of them—as Marketing Manager Dan Markovitz did when he led a seven-person team in a big company. In Matthew May's book *The Laws of Subtraction,* Markovitz describes how his team was burdened and annoyed by a convoluted HR system for managing vacation requests. He decided to ignore it and told his team "as long as they got their jobs done, I didn't care how many vacation days they took each year." It worked beautifully—he stopped wasting time on paperwork, his team felt respected, and they stopped gaming the system: "The number of vacation days that they took actually *decreased.*" Markovitz's experiment succeeded because it created accountability. "My team's focus shifted from figuring out how to beat the system to figuring out how to live up to the responsibility placed upon them."

Subtraction experiments also happen on a larger scale. Executives at Adobe conducted one in 2012 that affected all eleven thousand employees of this firm, which is known for software including Photoshop, Acrobat, Creative Cloud, and the Digital Marketing Suite. They killed one of the most sacred of corporate cows: traditional yearly performance reviews. Management experts have questioned the value of such reviews for decades. Quality guru W. Edwards Deming blasted away: "It nourishes short-term performance, annihilates long-term planning, builds fear, demolishes teamwork, nourishes rivalry and politics." UCLA's Sam Culbert called them bogus and urged companies to abolish them. We sometimes joke that, if the performance review (as usually done) was a drug, it wouldn't be approved by the U.S. Food and Drug Administration because it is often so ineffective and has so many vile side effects.

Despite such blistering critiques, Adobe has been one of the few companies with the guts and gumption to abandon them: in 2012, they moved from yearly performance rankings to frequent "check-ins" where managers provide employees targeted coaching and advice. There is no prescribed format or frequency for these conversations, and managers don't complete any forms or use any technologies to guide or document what happens during such conversations. They are simply expected to have regular check-ins to convey what is expected of employees, give and get feedback, and help employees with their growth and development plans. The aim is to give people information when they need it rather than months after teachable moments have passed. Once a year, managers make adjustments in employee compensation. Managers have far more discretion over such decisions than in the past: they have nearly complete authority to allocate their budget among their charges as they see fit. In addition, employees are now compensated based on how well they have met their goals—forced rankings have been abolished. As part of the rollout, managers were trained in the nuances of giving and receiving feedback and other difficult conversations through lectures and role playing, where they practiced challenging scenarios.

Donna Morris, Adobe's senior vice president for People and Places, explained the motivation for these changes to us. Adobe's leaders decided that the all-too-familiar drawbacks of their old evaluation system just weren't acceptable. The complex infrastructure required for supporting the system and the time it extracted from Adobe's busy people every January and February were bad enough. Morris' team calculated that annual reviews required 80,000 hours of time from the 2,000 managers at Adobe each year, the equivalent of 40 full-time employees. After all that effort, internal surveys revealed that employees felt less inspired and motivated afterwards—and turnover increased.

So Morris and her colleagues decided it was time for a disruptive change. She emphasized that the new "check-in" system where managers and direct reports have regular conversations about performance and other issues (instead of going through a formal process once a year) is part of a broader initiative to instill stronger accountability throughout Adobe. Managers, for example, are now given far more say in their people's salaries and merit increases. Adobe's aim is to give managers the skills, authority, and responsibility so they can act much as if they were running their own businesses. Accountability is amplified by an ongoing "pulse survey" given to a random sample of Adobe employees: it includes measures of how well each manager sets expectations, gives and receives feedback, and helps people with their growth and development. In addition, Morris emphasized that one of her main goals was to subtract technology from the feedback process—she didn't want managers to hide behind forms and computers. Instead, she wanted managers to have candid and unstilted conversations with the people they led.

Morris gave us an update in August 2013—about fifteen months after the change. Adobe's bold move seems to be working. One employee reported to Morris's team that a feeling of relief has spread throughout the company because the old annual review system was "a soul-less and soul-crushing exercise." The pulse survey indicates that most Adobe managers and employees find the new system to be less cumbersome and more effective than the old stack-ranking system. For example, 78 percent of employees report that their manager is open to feedback from them, a sizeable improvement over past surveys. As Morris and her team had hoped, by eliminating a system that required managers to discuss performance issues with employees only once a year, and moving to one that involves regular check-ins, strong managers are honing their skills. Equally important, many weak managers have learned how to talk with their direct reports about what is expected of them, how they are performing, and what they can do to become more effective.

The shift in Adobe's attrition is especially telling. Since the new system was implemented, involuntary departures have increased by 50 percent: this is because, as Morris explained, the new system requires executives and managers to have regular "tough discussions" with employees who are struggling with performance issues—rather than putting them off until the next performance review cycle comes around. In contrast, voluntary attrition at Adobe has dropped 30 percent since the "check-ins" were introduced; not only that, of those employees who opt to leave the company, a higher percentage of them are "non-regrettable" departures.

In short, Adobe's subtraction experiment appears to be having the desired effect. It is reducing unnecessary cognitive load, while at the same time, nudging managers to engage more often and more candidly with direct reports to help them develop their skills and plan their careers. The new system amplifies the feeling that "I own the place, and the place owns me"—because it places the onus on managers and their employees to make regular adjustments that improve individual and team performance. It also bolsters accountability because managers have far more responsibility for setting employee compensation than under the old system. As Morris explained, the old excuse that "you deserve a bigger raise, but HR wouldn't let me" doesn't work any longer.

Despite this promising start, even if this experiment does not succeed, we applaud Morris and her colleagues for summoning the courage to kill this maligned—yet somehow still sacred—practice. In the end, check-ins may prove worse than traditional reviews. But without trying experiments such as this, organizations risk becoming imprisoned by faulty assumptions and destructive practices even when there is a better way.

We don't advocate unbridled subtraction or a mindless quest for simplicity. As scaling unfolds, it is sometimes necessary to inject a big dose of complexity to get through certain phases—and then cart it away when it is no longer needed. Much like the scaffolding that workers use to construct or repair buildings, although once essential, it eventually must be removed. Complexity and confusion are often unavoidable in the early stages when you aren't sure what to scale or how to scale it. Psychologist William Schutz observed that "understanding evolves through three phases: simplistic, complex, and profoundly simple." As people who scale excellence learn what works and what doesn't, and what is most and least crucial, they move toward "profound simplicity," where much of the once necessary complexity—like scaffolding—is in the way and can be removed.

Kaaren Hanson, Intuit's vice president for design innovation, led her team through such a process during a "Design for Delight" (D4D) scaling effort at this financial software firm. Hanson and Scott Cook (founding CEO of Intuit and chairman of the Executive Committee) launched D4D to help employees become more creative, develop user-friendly products and services, and speed them to market. Hanson's team started with what they now see as an overly complex D4D model. It was filled with boxes and arrows and contained over 150 words. Even the title was convoluted:

"Evoking positive emotion by going beyond customer expectations in ease and benefit delivery throughout the customer journey."

After spending a year or so using this model to train and coach Intuit employees, Hanson's team realized that the complexity was getting in the way. They replaced it with a drastically simpler model (see figure 1). It has only thirteen words, including a one-word title: "Delight." It highlights just three D4D methods with the remaining twelve words: Deep Customer Empathy, Go Broad to Go Narrow, and Rapid Experiments with Customers. After Hanson's team simplified the principles—and made related changes in coaching and training—the number of people doing D4D at Intuit jumped from dozens to thousands. More important, a host of new products are being developed with D4D methods. *Macworld* magazine raved that one of these products, SnapTax, works "almost perfectly" to massively speed up tax preparation for "59 million Americans whose tax returns are simple enough that they can file either a 1040A or 1040EZ." Instead of spending hours in front of a computer, customers file their taxes from their mobile device in less than ten minutes, using the camera to take a picture of their tax documents.

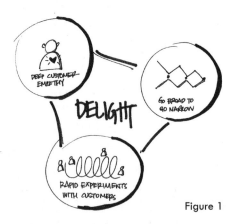

Figure 1

In retrospect, it is easy to fault Hanson's team for that convoluted first model, and indeed Hanson is a bit self-deprecating when she tells her story. Yet her team needed that first model to travel through the "complex" phase of Schutz's journey before reaching "profound simplicity." They couldn't know what was "scaffolding" versus "building" when they first started down the D4D road. After working with the model for a while, however, they learned which parts of the D4D mindset packed the biggest wallop and were easiest to scale. In fact, their own journey reflects five of their thirteen remaining words: "Go Broad to Go Narrow."

We admire and often repeat Procter & Gamble CEO A. G. Lafley's advice to keep things "Sesame Street Simple." But Hanson's journey adds a crucial twist: achieving such "profound simplicity" often requires slogging through some mighty messy complexity along the way.

2. Make People Squirm

We have a rule of thumb for practicing subtraction: if you aren't upsetting people, you aren't pushing hard enough. Remember how upset those Apple engineers got when the technical writer wanted to remove the second button on that mouse? That was a promising sign. Subtraction often entails removing the old and familiar and replacing it with something new and strange (or nothing at all). Subtraction is jarring because we humans have positive emotional reactions to the familiar and negative reactions to the unfamiliar.

The late Robert Zajonc, a renowned psychologist, uncovered hundreds of studies showing that "liking for the stimulus will grow with repeated exposures and will grow algorithmically." This "mere exposure effect" is evident before birth: heart rates of fetuses in the womb rise when they hear their mothers' voices and fall when they hear strangers' voices. In addition, work by Nobel Prize winner Daniel Kahneman on "prospect theory" found that people become risk averse and distraught at the "prospect" of losing something they already have, even if they get something more valuable instead. These negative reactions to losing something familiar are magnified when people invest time and effort in something—be it a product feature, a customer experience, or a corporate ritual. After all, they've done all that work and don't want it thrown on the scrap heap.

During the years we've taught and studied creative teams at Stanford, IDEO, HP, Interval Research, SAP, and elsewhere, we've seen numerous blunders where a person or team puts so much into an idea that they can't bring themselves to kill it—even when it doesn't work, many users or experts tells them it sucks, or it is okay but just isn't worth the added cost or complexity. We sometimes ask if they need help from us or others because, as writer Stephen King said, "It's always easier to kill someone else's darlings than it is to kill your own." This process is never easy or fun. No matter how gentle we try to be, people sometimes get mad at us or others who want to discard their beloved creations. But the best people and teams learn to accept defeat gracefully—or at least grudgingly.

Pixar's Brad Bird, the Academy Award–winning director of *The Incredibles* and *Ratatouille*, is admired by his colleagues for balancing his strong opinions with openness to constructive criticism, especially in his constant but warm arguments with producer John Walker. During the films they've made together, Walker has often helped Bird realize that one of his pet ideas, one that everyone loved and laughed at, had to go for the good of the film. When they made *The Incredibles*, Bird was smitten with a scene where Jack-Jack, the superhero baby, turns to goo in a series of transformations that are witnessed only by the story's villain. Walker explained to us that, although Bird loved the scene, Walker and others at Pixar eventually convinced him that the goo had to go—it would require so much money and time that other, more crucial scenes would suffer. When they make a film together,

Bird and Walker argue every day, and part of Walker's job is to challenge Bird's ideas, make him squirm over things that might not work, are too expensive, or will take too long to finish—to help Bird kill off some of his darlings.

3. Bring on the Load Busters: Subtraction by Addition

The writer Austin O'Malley said, "Memory is a crazy old woman who hoards colored rags and throws away food." Not only do human beings have lousy memories, but the things that we do recall, ruminate over, and act on are often trivial and useless—"colored rags" that clog our consciousness, sapping our capacity to remember and act on more crucial concerns. Fortunately, there are ways to short-circuit these failings. Many are simple additions—objects, activities, and technologies—that cut cognitive load, often by turning attention to what matters most and away from what matters least. Some researchers call these affordances; we call them load busters.

Denis Bugrov, senior vice president at Sberbank, told us about an inspired load buster that helped his employees focus attention and scale excellence. Sberbank is the largest commercial bank in Russia and Eastern Europe; it has nineteen thousand branches, 100 million customers, and 240,000 employees. The bank started a program to improve the customer experience, which, Bugrov confessed, was historically "really bad." Bank executives selected forty "lab branches" and trained their management and staff in innovation, efficiency, and customer service techniques. Each branch was assigned a coach and encouraged to experiment with approaches that weren't in the company's rule book. Each lab branch was linked to ten to fifteen "test branches" so that when they developed a promising idea they could test it, develop ways to roll it out, and get input about making it better. If the test succeeded, the idea was then spread to many more branches.

One big success was the "traffic light system" invented by the lab branch in Norlisk—a Russian mining town north of the Arctic Circle. In response to the CEO's call for reduced customer waiting times and better sales and service, the branch experimented with "varying standard procedures depending on how many customers were waiting in line." They started with a paper mock-up and later developed green, yellow, and red lights that appear on tellers' computer screens. Branch managers activate the green light when lines are short—at such times, tellers are expected to explain things carefully, answer questions completely, and cross-sell services. A yellow light means things are getting busy and tellers should hurry customers a bit and do less cross-selling. A red light means "all hell has broken loose." Bugrov explained: "The standard time to serve a customer is greatly reduced. All customers with 'long' transactions get transferred to a dedicated teller. The tellers are forbidden to cross-sell and discouraged from answering questions in a lengthy manner—customers are given a brochure or directed to the website or call center."

This simple innovation reduced load on all employees and dampened friction between tellers and managers because it reduced clashing messages about how to treat customers. In particular, the "red light" procedures reduced stress on tellers, cut labor costs, and pleased customers with faster service. The Norlisk invention was tried and refined in fifteen test branches a week or so after it was created. It then took only two months to "cascade it out" to several thousand branches. This load buster reduced waiting time by 35 percent during peak times and added "negligible incremental costs." Traffic lights were one of many service innovations developed, tested, and scaled via the "lab" and "test" branches. Bugrov told us that these changes saved Sberbank nearly a billion dollars a year and, according to internal surveys, led to upswings in customer and employee satisfaction.

The traffic lights function like other load busters: they turn attention to what matters most when mental demands are high, priorities clash, and key information is easy to lose or overlook. Psychologist Karl Weick shows how the right load busters are especially crucial during taxing "handoffs"—junctures in organizational life where a task is transferred from one person or group to another. Weick studied handoffs between firefighting crews in the U.S. Forest Service, which often struggles with overload and unclear priorities when a crew that has been battling a fire is relieved by a new one. Crew chiefs have developed a briefing protocol for such exchanges to help pass along the essentials of the "big story." Reminiscent of the checklists that pilots use during takeoffs and landings and that doctors and nurses use during surgery—it dramatically reduces errors. During forest fires, the outgoing crew chief is responsible for five steps during his or her conversation with the incoming chief:

1. Here's what I think we face.
2. Here's what I think we should do.
3. Here's why.
4. Here's what I think we should keep an eye on.
5. Now talk to me (i.e., tell me if you [a] don't understand, [b] cannot do it, [c] see something that I do not).

This last step places responsibility on the chiefs to make sure that messages are received (not just sent) and to resolve clashing perceptions and opinions. In addition, crews "never hand over a fire in the heat of the day," a lesson learned the hard way. During the "Dude" fire in Payson, Arizona, in 1990, six firefighters were burned to death after a botched change of command "at 1:00 p.m. on a hot windy day with temperatures in the high nineties while the fire was making spectacular runs." Crews now do handoffs at night, when "low winds, high humidity, and cool temperatures stabilize the fire and make it most predictable" and it is easier to see fires. Night handoffs give crews time to make sense of the situation, are less likely to thrust them into overwhelming and dangerous fires, and give them a clearer picture of the challenges they face.

4. Divide and Conquer

We've seen how dividing organizations into smaller groups led to improved coordination and accountability and enhanced personal bonds for the U.S. Marines, Pulse News, and Salesforce.com. Harvard's Melissa Valentine and Amy Edmondson dissected a change project at a big hospital that reveals how and why breaking organizations into smaller pieces can have striking benefits.

Before the change at "City Emergency Department," at any given time, twenty-five or so health care workers staffed this hospital unit. These nurses, residents (physicians in training), and attendings (physicians in charge) worked in one big and often discombobulated mob. The classic symptoms of a group that is too big—coordination snafus and weak social bonds—were amplified because doctors and nurses worked four- to twelve-hour shifts and had flexible schedules. This meant that the cast of characters was in constant flux. Each of the three hundred or so patients that City served throughout the day was assigned a nurse or two, a resident, and an attending from the group on hand at the moment. Confusion and inefficiencies were rampant as doctors forgot which nurses were working on which cases—or no one informed them (or the patient) that a nurse who had started on a case had left and been replaced by another. The chaos was even harder on nurses because they had less prestige and authority than doctors. They felt uncomfortable interrupting or imposing on doctors—even when they had pressing questions about patient care or needed to pass along key updates.

Then, following a practice that began spreading among U.S. hospitals during the last decade, executives split City Emergency

Department into four "pods": each had a dedicated physical location containing its own computers, counters, supplies, patient beds, and "crash rooms" where teams worked on patients. Each patient was assigned to a pod for his or her stay. Each pod was staffed by three nurses, a resident or two, and an attending physician. When doctors or nurses came to work, they didn't know whom they would work with—each was assigned a pod for their shift when they arrived. The pods were "stable structures that persisted over time," but, as Valentine and Edmondson explain, "within as little as five hours, all of the individuals staffing a pod could change (but not simultaneously) as a result of shift changes staggered across roles."

The pods had big positive effects. Doctors and nurses reported having more and better information about each case. Patients were kept in a smaller physical area, which made it easier for "podmates" to observe and serve them. Smaller teams reduced confusion and discomfort about whom to ask for help and updates. According to one nurse, before the pods, "You had to walk across the ED all timid" and get up a bit of courage and say to the doctor, "Uh, excuse me?" With the pods, "Now they are in the trenches with us." It was also easier to discern which "podmates" were responsible for particular chores and deserved credit or blame when things went well or badly. As a result, doctors and nurses told Valentine and Edmondson that accountability had increased. One nurse explained,

> Now there is much more of a sense of ownership of each other. I'll say, "My pod isn't running well. Where is my doctor?" And he'll be accountable to me. And the doctors will say, "Where are my nurses, who do I have today?" People rarely, if ever, claimed each other in this way before the pods were implemented even if they were working together on many shared cases. A resident would have used more detached language like, "Who is this patient's

nurse?"—ignoring that the nurse had any relationship to *him*—rather than "Where are my nurses?"

The pods produced big efficiency gains. Valentine and Edmondson analyzed data on 160,000 patients served by the department during the six months before the pods were created and the year after. After the pods, patient throughput time in the Emergency Department plummeted by about 40 percent, from about eight hours (8.34) to five hours (5.29) per patient. This drop reflects not only more efficient use of staff but also a better patient experience: five hours at the hospital sucks a lot less than eight.

The change was effective, in part, because it reduced the need for doctors and nurses in each pod to deal with the other three pods. Yet, as Melissa Valentine wrote to us, in each pod, "Their work involved coordinating with other groups pretty heavily . . . because most patients had lab tests, imaging, or both. So pod staffers were constantly on the phone with those departments to see if they could rush one, where the delay was, and to get more information about results." And when patients needed a bed "upstairs" in a nursing unit, pod staffers had to coordinate and negotiate with those units to find them a place in the overcrowded hospital. The pods' efficiency actually made this overcrowding worse: the Emergency Department was processing patients faster (including those who needed beds), but the rest of the hospital wasn't any more efficient.

As always, once organizations are divided into roles, teams, levels, departments, locations, and so on, the challenge of coordinating and integrating the work rears its ugly head. Recall how, as we saw in chapter 3, the weak integration of different groups and systems at JetBlue led to the Valentine's Day fiasco in 2007, when thousands of passengers were trapped on planes for hours. Bonny Simi's "wisdom of the crowds" approach to "irregular operations" enabled people from different parts of the company to map how the system fit together, identify weak connections and handoffs (with pink Post-its), and weave together actions throughout Jet-Blue.

The division of labor always creates demands for integration, especially when—as at JetBlue—multiple teams and departments in different locations must mesh activities together in tight and timely ways. Even when coordination is less daunting, every team and organization depends on people with enough general knowledge to grasp how the system fits together *and* enough particular knowledge about each part to do specific tasks well. This ever-present challenge is one reason that Facebook devotes massive effort to "Bootcamp" for engineers. After working on ten or twelve projects for diverse teams, an engineer understands a lot about how the work that he or she is doing at the moment fits into the code base, as well as its place in Facebook's overall business strategy.

The approaches taken by JetBlue and Facebook also reduce a related and equally vexing problem: the "going native" or "local optimization" disease, in which, after being schooled in some specialty or working in a function such as finance or R&D, people start believing that their little corner of the world is all that counts and they lose sight of what is best for the organization or project. This instinct can be healthy when the resulting competitive spirit spurs effort and doesn't destroy cooperation and information sharing. But the urge to view people in other groups and departments as enemies to defeat (rather than friends to work and win with) is one that every leader and organization must be vigilant about tamping down.

Organizations use varied antidotes. Money is one: paying people for the overall success of an effort, not just for individual or local performance, can motivate individuals and teams to cooperate, coordinate, and help each other learn and do better work. Incentives help explain why people in start-ups such as Pulse News often cooperate so well: every employee gets stock, so all have a stake in the company's overall success. Another approach, as we saw at JetBlue, is to give people challenges that require them to cooperate with other groups and departments, which helps create the feeling that "we are all on the same team." Another antidote is to name a common enemy and rally troops from different teams to band together to battle the forces of evil. As we saw in chapter 3, that's exactly what Steve Jobs did when he bad-mouthed Michael Dell just after returning to Apple in the 1990s.

Venture capitalist Ben Horowitz's "Freaky Friday Management Technique" is perhaps the weirdest and most entertaining antidote. He once led a company where the customer support and sales engineering organizations were at war. They wouldn't cooperate, undermined each other's work, and "genuinely did not like each other." He was perplexed because both teams had talented people, so he didn't want to fire anyone, but the company's success depended on their cooperation. Then he saw the film *Freaky Friday,* starring Barbara Harris and Jodie Foster, where "mother and daughter grow completely frustrated with each other's lack of understanding and wish that they could switch places and they do. By being inside each other's bodies, both characters develop an excellent understanding of the challenges that the other faces. As a result, the two women become great friends when they switch back." Horowitz decided to apply the technique: "The very next day I informed the head of Sales Engineering and the head of Customer Support that they would be switching jobs. I explained that, like Jodie Foster and Barbara Harris, they would keep their minds, but get new bodies. Permanently."

Both managers were outraged at first. But Freaky Friday worked like magic: "After just one week walking in the other's moccasins, both executives quickly diagnosed the core issues causing the conflict. They then swiftly acted to implement a simple set of processes that cleared up the combat and got the teams working harmoniously." From that day forward, these two organizations had magnificent cooperation.

5. Bolster Collective Brainpower: Increase Cognitive Capacity Instead of Adding More People

Organizational designers sometimes assume that bringing in "new blood" propels innovation and performance. There are times when outsiders bring fresh ideas that help broken organizations and projects abandon obsolete and destructive mindsets. Outsider Lew Gerstner transformed IBM in the 1990s. After General Motors went bankrupt in 2009, former AT&T CEO Ed Whitacre devoted eighteen crucial months to cleaning up the place. Whitacre subtracted like crazy: he got rid of the Saturn and Saab brands and slashed the number of routine reports generated by the R&D organization from ninety-four to four. He attacked GM's infamous "No we can't" culture and pushed accountability down the hierarchy. The *Financial Times* reported, "When subordinates request money for a new initiative, his response is typically to ask whether the amount is within their existing budgets. If so, they are told that the decision whether to spend it is theirs."

Yet too many tales of outsiders who gallop in to save the day don't have happy endings. Organizations and teams that juggle a constant influx of strangers are prone to the same coordination problems, weak social bonds, bitter conflict, and related ugliness we've seen in those that are too big. Yes, as we saw at City Emergency Department, there are ways to enhance performance even when group membership is in constant flux. But it is better to avoid such instability when possible. Whether you are selecting a leader, scaling up a new team or organization, or running an existing project team, sticking with savvy insiders and stable teams and blending people who have worked together before are better paths. Stable teams are more adept at drawing on each other's strengths and countering their weaknesses, and they mesh together their ideas and actions more efficiently and reliably.

As we said earlier, J. Richard Hackman devoted nearly fifty years to studying team effectiveness. He rejected the "myth" that "it's good to mix it up" because "the longer members stay together as an intact group, the better they do. As unreasonable as this may seem, the research evidence is unambiguous." This finding holds, for example, in string quartets, airplane cockpit crews, basketball teams, product development teams, architecture projects, and surgical teams. If you want to increase the odds that your heart surgery will turn out well, pick a surgeon who does many operations in the hospital where your procedure will be done and who has done many operations with the other surgeons and anesthesiologists on the team. Fortunately, as Hackman points out, the designers of some of the most potentially powerful and destructive teams on the planet understand the virtues of stable teams. The U.S. Strategic Air Command (SAC) mandates that the airplanes carrying nuclear bombs are to be maintained and flown by intact or "hard" teams. Their members constantly train, work, and fly together, which enables them to perform better on a host of metrics, including dropping bombs on targets during training exercises.

If you are forming a new team, or fixing an old one, try to bring in at least two or three people who have worked together effectively before. Our Stanford colleague Kathleen Eisenhardt tracked ninety-eight semiconductor start-ups for seven years: the most successful firms typically had top teams with two or three members who had worked together in the past. A similar story emerged when Harvard's Boris Groysberg and his colleagues examined the fate of former General Electric executives who were hired as CEOs of twenty other companies. Three years after these GE alumni took charge, on average, their companies performed about 20 percent worse than competitors (which were led mostly by insiders). Yet this pattern was reversed when new CEOs stocked their senior teams with former colleagues. CEOs who recruited two or more GE alumni to join them led companies that performed about 16 percent above the industry average.

Enduring relationships have underpinned many successes. Microsoft founders Bill Gates and Paul Allen were close friends in high school, as were Apple's Steve Jobs and Steve Wozniak. The two founders of Pulse News, Ankit Gupta and Akshay Kothari, decided they wanted to start a company because they enjoyed doing projects together so much in their Stanford engineering classes. Warren Buffett and Berkshire Hathaway Vice-Chairman Charlie Munger have worked together nearly fifty years. As Buffett sees it, "One plus one with Charlie and me certainly adds up to more than two." Stability was also crucial to the U.S. women's national soccer team, which won numerous championships—including two of four World Cups and two of three Olympic tournaments—between 1991 and 2004. The team had talented players, including Mia Hamm, Brandi Chastain, Kristine Lilly, Julie Foudy, and Joy Fawcett. Yet each believes that the driving factors behind their success were the communication, knowledge of one another's strengths and weaknesses, respect, and ability to play together that they developed during all those years the core group stuck together.

Speaking of talented women, if you want a smarter team, make sure that it has a lot of them. Carnegie Mellon's Anita Williams Woolley and her colleagues studied 669 people in groups that had two to five members. Groups with higher percentages of women had greater "collective intelligence," performing better on cognitively demanding tasks, from "visual puzzles to negotiations, brainstorming, games and complex rule-based design assignments." Woolley's research team set out to study collective intelligence, not gender. But they kept finding that groups with more women performed better on "collective intelligence" tests. Groups with more women typically had superior social sensitivity and thus members cooperated and wove together their talents more effectively. Women were more in tune than men with others' emotions. They listened more carefully, they allowed others to take turns speaking, and their groups weren't stifled by one or two overbearing members—increasing their capacity to perform complex and difficult tasks. These researchers also found that "having a bunch of smart people in a group doesn't necessarily make the group smart" because the "average and maximum intelligence" of individual members isn't linked to performance. Socially sensitive men also help make teams smarter. But if you can't test for this trait before forming a group or adding new members, remember that men are typically the weaker sex in this regard.

You can also magnify collective brainpower by enlisting people who are usually treated as bystanders or passive recipients. The Institute for Health Improvement's 100,000 Lives Campaign used load busters with just this effect. Keeping a patient's head elevated at least 45 degrees reduces the risk of pneumonia when he or she is on a ventilator. In many hospitals, staff drew a line or put tape on the wall behind ventilator patients at the 45-degree mark. Staff told everyone—families, janitors, fellow patients, and patients too—that if the patient's head dipped below the line, they should ask someone to raise the bed or do it themselves. The obligation to notice and prevent this dangerous error no longer fell entirely on doctors and nurses; people once treated as passive, even invisible bystanders were recruited to do the right thing and to encourage others to do so as well.

People also have a greater capacity when they aren't worn down by work and worry. When people get enough sleep, they are more adept at difficult tasks, are more interpersonally sensitive, make better decisions, and are less likely to turn nasty. Certainly, there are times when emergencies and harsh deadlines render sleep impossible. But scaling is a marathon, not a sprint. The humans who propel it will be smarter and nicer if they get enough sleep and even nap at work. British Prime Minister Winston Churchill praised naps: "Nature had not intended mankind to work from eight in the morning until midnight without that refreshment of blessed oblivion which, even if it only lasts twenty minutes, is sufficient to renew all the vital forces." Much research supports Churchill's claim: A fifteen- to sixty-minute nap bolsters alertness, error detection, and mood. For example, researcher Mark Rosekind summarized a NASA study he led this way: "While two pilots flew the plane, the third would have 40 minutes to nap. We found they would sleep for [an average of] 26 minutes, which boosted their performance by 34% and their alertness by 54%."

If you can't bring yourself to encourage employees to lie down on the job, at least give them plenty of breaks. The ordinary fatigue most of us feel during the workday makes us grouchier—and dumber—as the hours go by. Psychologist Shai Danziger and his colleagues studied 1,112 parole decisions made by eight Israeli judges. Prisoners who appeared in front of these judges first thing in the morning had about a 65 percent chance of being granted parole. By the time the judges' midmorning break rolled around, the percentage of prisoners pardoned dropped to nearly zero, even though the mix of cases hadn't changed (i.e., time served and severity of crimes). This pattern recurred throughout the day. Right after their thirty-minute morning snack break, the judges again pardoned about 65 percent of prisoners; that percentage fell dramatically as lunch approached. When judges returned from lunch, that 65 percent pardon rate returned, but it declined as the afternoon wore on—plummeting to nearly zero by day's end.

These findings dovetail with other studies showing that "making repeated judgments or decisions depletes individuals' executive function and mental resources," rendering people prone to simplify, accept the status quo, think less deeply about choices, and perform less well on tasks that "required more mental resources." One reason that those tired judges leaned toward unfavorable rulings was that writing them required less mental effort: on average, favorable rulings ran ninety words long and unfavorable rulings ran forty-eight words.

The implication? If you want to make good decisions as the day wears on, watch for signs of fatigue. Even seemingly trivial levels damage performance. Build in ways for yourself and others to take breaks, whether it's getting a bite to eat or taking a few minutes to stretch your legs. It sounds easy to implement. Yet too many hard-charging leaders and busy teams don't do it.

Give Ground Grudgingly

Scaling requires a balancing act. The aim is to travel forward in the sweet spot between too much and too little complexity as your footprint expands to more people and places—and without swamping people with more load than they can handle.

The risk of adding too little complexity too late is fueled by a well-documented human blind spot. Dubbed "coordination neglect" or "the scaling fallacy," it means that decision makers are prone to underestimate the increasing percentage of time, resources, and staff that are required to orchestrate action as a group or organization expands. Larry Page's effort to banish middle managers is classic: he wanted Google to be just like the good old days when they didn't need many bosses or procedures. Page learned quickly that Google's growth meant that a healthy hierarchy, middle managers and all, was the best hope for defeating the worst elements of bureaucracy. Leaders of growing organizations often resist installing needed processes and technologies because they fear "Big Dumb Company" disease. After Nike's wild growth in the 1990s, in 2001 the sportswear giant was plagued with shortages of some products, oversupply of others, and late deliveries. Founder Philip Knight admitted that this had happened, in part, because they had waited too long to implement a sophisticated supply chain system and that once they started, it was harder to implement than anticipated. As organizations and programs grow, the same superflat hierarchy and lightweight systems that promoted success in the early days can gum up the works.

Sometimes scaling is dragged down by the opposite problem: people are so smitten with process, structure, and grooming that the core work takes a backseat. We saw how the twentieth-century British Navy and twenty-first-century universities ballooned with bureaucratic bloat. The risk of adding too many bosses and bureaucratic trappings too soon can plague organizations that are flush with resources—especially when leaders want a bigger footprint and want it fast. Egon Zehnder's Lindsay Trout told us that "prepopulating the management team" often proves to be irresistible in well-funded start-ups. Trout helps founders build their teams. She warns clients to avoid making the top team too big, too soon, because extra people create unnecessary friction and sap attention from development and sales efforts. Trout says these problems get even worse when a team is "prepopulated" with executives who—on the basis of their experience in big companies—install complex systems for managing supply chains, HR, and other operations years before they are needed.

In short, we advocate "the Goldilocks Theory of Bureaucracy." Much like the children's story, scaling requires injecting just enough structure, hierarchy, and process at the right time. The key challenge, then, is knowing when to add more complexity, when it is "just right," and when to wait a bit longer. Ben Horowitz (whom we've drawn on before) offers advice inspired by American football:

> An offensive lineman's job is to protect the quarterback from onrushing defensive linemen. If the offensive lineman attempts to do this by holding his ground, the defensive lineman will easily run around him and crush the quarterback. As a result, offensive linemen are taught to lose the battle slowly or *to give ground*

grudgingly. They are taught to back up and allow the defensive lineman to advance, but just a little at a time.

When you scale an organization, you will also need to give ground grudgingly. Specialization, organizational structure, and process all complicate things quite a bit and implementing them will feel like you are moving away from common knowledge and quality communication. It is very much like the offensive lineman taking a step backwards. You will lose ground, but you will prevent your company from descending into chaos.

Horowitz explains, for example, that engineers can be jacks-of-all-trades when you have five or ten people "because everybody knows everything and the need to communicate is minimized; there are no complicated handoffs, because there is nobody to hand anything to." As a company expands to thirty or forty, it becomes increasingly difficult for engineers to understand the code base and the thicket of teams, roles, and personalities. When this "supersteep" learning curve makes it too hard for engineers to learn their jobs and the best ones start arguing and screwing up, "you need to specialize." But specialization is like a powerful medicine with nasty side effects: you need to apply it in small doses and take proper precautions. It creates more handoffs to manage (and fumble), fuels conflicts between groups that may focus on what is good for them rather than what is best for all, and creates distance between senior leaders and the rest of the organization.

Horowitz emphasizes that "giving ground" effectively also means first adding processes that stave off as much chaos for as many people as possible. He suggests that the interview process is a good early choice because "it usually runs across organizational boundaries (the hiring group, human resources—or wherever the recruiter lives, and supporting groups), involves people from outside the company (the candidate), and is critically important to the success of the company."

The art of giving ground grudgingly requires biding your time and staying vigilant until clear but less-than-catastrophic problems pop up—a few muffed handoffs, minor screw-ups by good people, or a surprising conflict. We got similar advice from Chris Fry and Steve Greene, those executives who helped scale up Salesforce.com (and now lead Twitter's efforts to build the engineering organization). Greene said, "We like to run it a little hot," to run things on the lean side, but not so "hot" that things explode. Fry told our scaling class that this means adding a bit less structure and process and adding it a bit later than seems necessary: doing so helps people feel less bogged down and encourages them to take personal responsibility—which often results in "organic" and "bottom-up solutions" that negate the need to give ground. In contrast, Fry said when an organization has just a bit too much process and a few too many rules, people feel stymied and frustrated, "like they are walking in mud." Fry and Greene believe that "running a little hot" works because, as an organization expands and ages, it marches forward with an "operating system" that is just barely complex enough—but no more.

Fry and Greene also emphasized that "running a little hot" does not mean pushing employees to their cognitive and emotional limits: running an organization as close to maximum capacity as possible for as long as possible is a recipe for a scaling disaster. This is true, they argued, despite all those experts who are enamored with "100 percent utilization of resources." When you do that, there is no slack. People are already overwhelmed and making questionable judgments. So the smallest surprise or setback can produce mayhem. Here's how Fry framed the problem: everyone knows that this is a bad way to treat a machine—they would never run a computer at 100 percent of capacity day after day because they know it will break. Why shouldn't organizations, large or small, apply the same logic to their people and teams?

CHAPTER 5

THE PEOPLE WHO PROPEL SCALING

*Build Organizations Where
"I Own the Place and the Place Owns Me"*

Our Stanford colleague Perry Klebahn and his wife Annie had a distressing experience on June 30, 2012, when they sent their ten-year-old daughter Phoebe on a United Airlines flight from San Francisco to Chicago—with a transfer to Grand Rapids, Michigan, for summer camp. The Klebahns paid United $99 extra to look after Phoebe because she was traveling as an "unaccompanied minor." No one showed up in Chicago to help Phoebe with the transfer. United outsourced this service, and the employees there "forgot" to show up. Although Phoebe's plane reached Chicago on time, she missed the connection. This happened even though she repeatedly asked United employees to help her. They simply told her to wait. They refused at least three requests from her to use a phone to call her parents and the camp to tell them about the glitch.

When Phoebe didn't reach Grand Rapids, camp officials made

frantic calls to Perry and Annie, who then sought help from United Airlines. Perry and Annie manned different phones and each begged multiple employees to help find their daughter—but all refused to help. Finally, an employee in Chicago told Perry that she was going off her shift and didn't have time to help. Perry asked her if she was a mother. She answered yes. Then he asked, "If you were missing your child for forty-five minutes, what would you do?" That question provoked her to act, and she found Phoebe within fifteen minutes. In her role as a United employee, she wouldn't help; she did the right thing only after being reminded of her role as a mother.

When Sutton posted this story on his blog on August 13, 2012, it provoked a storm of media interest and individual outrage against United. The Klebahns were besieged with journalists from shows including *Good Morning America*, *The Today Show*, *CBS This Morning*, and *Fox News*, and from dozens more radio and television stations; they also received over one hundred inquiries from newspapers and magazines. Variations of their story appeared in over two hundred media outlets. The Klebahns did a single interview with NBC's Diane Dwyer and declined the rest. The feeding frenzy ended for them in a week or so, but United's woes continued as the U.S. Transportation Department ranked them dead last in customer service among the largest fifteen U.S. carriers (with more customer complaints in July 2012 than the other fourteen airlines combined). News also spread about a golden retriever named Bea that had died under United's care. The owner, fashion model Maggie Rizer, reported that United Airlines had demonstrated extreme indifference and insensitivity. When she asked where her two dogs were, an "emotionless worker who seemed more interested in his text messages" answered, "One of them is dead."

Many of the ninety-three comments on Sutton's blog and the hundreds of e-mails he got were from outraged customers with tales of United's poor service. But the most troubling were from people who said they were current or former United employees—especially a comment on the blog from a person who left no name but reported that he was an active pilot:

> I used to be the Captain who ran downstairs to make sure the jetway air conditioning was cold and properly hooked up. Who helped the mechanic with the cowling and held the flashlight for him. I used to write notes to MY guests, and thank them for their business. I wrote reports, hundreds of reports, on everything from bad coffee to more efficient taxi techniques. No more. I have been told to do my job, and I do my job. My love for aviation has been ground into dust. After 15 years of being lied to, deceived, ignored, blamed falsely, and watching the same mistakes being made over and over again by a "professional management" that never seems to learn from the copious reports of our new "watchers," I give up.
>
> It's not an easy thing to do. I am an Eagle Scout, an entrepreneur, and a retired Air Force Officer with over 22 years of service.

Sutton's reaction was 'Painful, isn't it? 'I used to be . . . I used to be . . . I used to be.'" The pilot's words, the Klebahns' story, the owner of that dead dog, and the Transportation Department evidence show what happens when accountability evaporates—even well-meaning and talented people lapse into silence, lay low, dodge responsibility, turn a cold shoulder to clients and colleagues, and don't step up to do the right thing because the system has beaten them down.

It doesn't have to be this way, even given the financial pressures on big airlines. Remember Bonny Simi, who led JetBlue's IROP Integrity project, which created a better system for dealing with "irregular operations" during bad weather? Simi's view is that spreading accountability is a big part of her job at JetBlue. Whether Simi is piloting a JetBlue flight (she still flies several days a month) or doing her job as a JetBlue executive (she is currently vice president of talent), her aim is to help JetBlue's people (and herself) feel as if "we're citizens, not consumers, and we take care of the company as if it is our own." The IROP project was a perfect example of this mindset: everyone from gate agents, to flight controllers, to pilots, to flight attendants joined together to solve a problem that improved customer service, saved money, and made them proud of their work and their airline.

The lesson from the IROP project, and other stories and studies here, is that the capacity for effective scaling depends on both bringing in the right talent (people with the right training and skills) and having people who feel compelled to act in the organization's best interests ("accountability") and who press one another to act that way too. Every company, nonprofit, government organization, foundation, or team that aims to spread better practices, open new locations, or crank out superior products and services needs to create these two conditions.

We talked about what it takes to scale up accountability with Paul Purcell, the CEO of Baird—a successful and rapidly expanding financial services firm headquartered in Milwaukee that has been on *Fortune*'s list of 100 "Best Companies to Work For" since 2004. Purcell emphasized that hiring the most talented people isn't enough. When employees put their needs ahead of clients, colleagues, and the company—whether this results from personality, bad role models, or bad incentives—excellence suffers because they feel no obligation to mentor newcomers or help colleagues do great work. This point was brought home by Leslie Dixon, Baird's chief human capital officer. When we asked what behaviors were "sacred" at the company, she answered: "We believe work is a team sport. We don't make individuality too vivid." When we asked about the "taboos," she answered: "Acting like an individual sportsman. Greed. We have a no asshole rule."

Just talent or accountability alone isn't enough: without healthy doses of both, pockets of excellence can't survive—as we saw with that talented but demoralized United pilot. Arguing over which is more important—employees with the right skills and experience or employees who hold themselves accountable to colleagues and the organization—is futile. It is like asking which is more important for staying alive, your heart or your brain. Both have to function well if you are to lead a healthy life. And there are many paths to achieving this one-two punch.

Talent Density—
Stars in Every Position at Netflix

Netflix CEO Reed Hastings strives for high "talent density" at his company. Hastings believes that the company's devotion to putting highly skilled people in every position who take personal ownership for doing great work that helps the company, not just themselves, is the key reason that Netflix persists as a dominant provider of films and TV shows. Netflix makes clear to employees from day one that merely "adequate performance" results in a "generous severance package." Netflix's unwavering commitment to hiring people who deliver star performances day after day—and quickly firing those who don't meet these exacting standards— has propelled fast, smart, and reliable scaling: the company grew from a small founding team in 1997 to roughly 2,500 employees in 2013.

Hastings sees Netflix as akin to a professional sports team. He wants stars in every position and spends the money to get and keep them. Netflix pays top-of-the-market salaries, even for Silicon Valley, and adjusts compensation so that the company stays at the top. Annual compensation reviews are treated as rehiring decisions. Managers ask: What would the person get elsewhere? Is this person so good that he or she would be difficult or impossible to replace? What would we pay for his or her replacement? What would we pay to keep the person? As a result, when the war for talent rages in Silicon Valley, Netflix employees get big raises without having to interview for jobs outside the company or drum up offers. A Netflix executive explained to us how this works: he offered a new engineer from the East Coast about $150,000 per year, which he accepted. Before the engineer arrived in California for the job, however, a market survey indicated that he was paid below the top of the market. So Netflix raised his pay to about $250,000.

The company abhors micromanagement: Hastings's philosophy is that talent density—having a roster of stars who are also team players—means that fewer rules and bosses are needed than at places that don't focus on hiring the best of the best. This commitment persists even as the company continues to grow. Here is Netflix's entire policy on expensing, entertainment, travel, and gifts: "Act in Netflix's best interests." This minimalist approach to management fuels a virtuous cycle. Employees with impressive skill and motivation are attracted by the pay. Then they stay—and work like dogs—because of the autonomy, pride in their work, and lack of friction.

The downside for employees is that there is rarely a drawn-out evaluation and rehabilitation process when someone isn't cutting it—he or she is promptly sent packing. The same Netflix executive who gave the new hire a $100,000 raise described how this Darwinian approach played out in his group. In the prior twenty-four months, twenty-five of his seventy-five-person team had been shown the door. People were rarely let go for weak technical skills. They were fired for "lack of personal characteristics," which included "not proactive enough, they simply take orders but don't contribute their own ideas, or they don't show enough curiosity to question the status quo." This executive's aim was to lead seventy-five people who all felt compelled to push themselves and their colleagues to the highest levels of performance.

High School Dropouts at Tamago-Ya

The Netflix system won't work in most places; for starters, few organizations have the money to attract the best of the best. Most leaders are unwilling (or unable) to get rid of imperfect employees so rapidly, especially without first trying to correct their weaknesses and develop their skills. Many, perhaps most, organizations that scale effectively get the job done by depending less on hiring fully formed superstars and more on selecting promising people—and then teaching and motivating them to do exceptional work.

Tamago-Ya ("Egg-House"), for example, takes a drastically different approach to hiring and developing people than Netflix. This Japanese company produces organic box lunches and sells them to Tokyo office workers for about $4. Tamago-Ya assembles their lunches near the Haneda Airport, a sixty- to ninety-minute drive from their customers in the Shinjuku business area in downtown Tokyo. The typical order comes from a workgroup that buys twenty to forty lunches every weekday. Each lunch box contains six or more items, and customers have a fairly long list of options. Each lunch is made fresh that morning and delivered warm. Examples of food items include stir-fried beef with oyster sauce, boiled spinach with sesame dressing, coleslaw, and steamed rice. The company takes orders between 9 a.m. and 10:30 a.m. each day. The lunches are delivered by noon that same day—so there is little margin for error in assembly or delivery. Of the sixty thousand to seventy-five thousand lunches that Tamago-Ya delivers each day, late orders are rare and fewer than fifty are wasted (they have a .006 percent failure rate).

Stanford's Jin Whang, an expert in supply chain management, asked founder Isatsugu Sugahara if his company had a sophisticated computer system for forecasting demand and scheduling. Sugahara explained that Tamago-Ya was decidedly low-tech. The company relies on market intelligence from van drivers—mostly high school dropouts, many of whom were arrested in their youth. These drivers interview and choose the customers in their territories. They reject customers when it will be too difficult to deliver lunches on time—such as someone in a location that requires a difficult U-turn on a busy road. Each driver owns his or her route, and drivers' compensation depends on how many lunches their customers buy and whether they can keep waste low—they earn as much as $80,000 a year.

Boxed lunches are delivered in reusable containers that drivers collect at about 2:00 p.m., which gives them the chance to find out what customers liked and didn't like that day—and to get an idea of what customers will order the next day. Every evening, each driver talks to the area manager overseeing his or her team. Forecasts from these conversations are sent to the central office so they can plan the next day's production. Suppliers deliver raw materials such as spinach, fish, and eggs to the Haneda facility by 5:00 a.m. the next morning—the order is an educated guess based on intelligence from the drivers the previous evening and past experience with what and how much customers order at different times of the year and days of the week and in different weather. Customers order more lunches when it is raining, for example. Tamago-Ya also relies on these estimates to start making lunches and loading vans even before orders start arriving at 9:00 a.m.—shortly thereafter, the vans start leaving for Tokyo. The first vans start arriving before 10:30 a.m., and vans with extra lunches are positioned in Tokyo to allow for last-minute adjustments. If more lunches are ordered than anticipated, suppliers rush in the needed ingredients and Tamago-Ya quickly assembles and delivers them.

Tamago-Ya's founder was a high school dropout himself. He is convinced that the methods his company uses to motivate and instill accountability in workers, especially among those crucial drivers, explain why his company has grown and performs so well. By getting to know customers' needs and personal quirks, drivers have the knowledge required to give them superb service. Drivers also feel beholden to the company: they are paid well and strive to reciprocate Sugahara's faith in them by turning in superior performance.

Accountability:
I Own the Place and the Place Owns Me

As Netflix and Tamago-Ya show, accountability works best when it is a two-way street. On the one hand, as David Novak, the CEO of Yum!, puts it, each employee ought to feel and act "like you own the place." On the other hand, employees ought to feel like the place owns them too. A tug of mutual obligation is created because being "owners" entitles and encourages employees to push themselves, peers, bosses, subordinates, suppliers, and sometimes clients to support exceptional performance. And being "owned" means that employees expect, accept, and work hard to meet high standards held and enforced by superiors, peers, clients, and customers. At Netflix, stars have considerable autonomy—they own how they do the work. But they are owned by the company as well, because they are paid so much and are expected to satisfy such exacting standards. At Tamago-Ya, drivers feel and act like owners—like independent contractors—because *they* choose customers and routes. At the same time, they feel obliged to customers, peers, their area manager, and, of course, CEO Sugahara, who gave many a chance to rebuild their lives.

Netflix may seem more cutthroat than Tamago-Ya. After all, you are fired rapidly at Netflix for merely adequate performance. But you are hired to be a star, to be the best of the best, and you know that walking in the door. You also have great latitude in how you do your work; bosses and peers don't monitor your every move. The company is organized for extremely talented employees who give their all. Netflix makes sure that every employee under-stands the bargain: you are given much and expected to give back much in return—or you are sent packing. Tamago-Ya constrains employees in a different way. Drivers rarely have a moment's re-spite from customers, peers, and superiors. The method used by Tamago-Ya, a system where employees can never escape those prying eyes, can be remarkably effective—and quite stressful.

Research on teams that make the switch from being led by a single supervisor to being "self-managing" is instructive when it comes to such accountability. The term *self-managing* may con-jure up images of employees who slack off because they are free to do as they please. Yet several studies show that people feel more constrained—and accountable—in such systems. The pressures to conform and perform are harder to escape because each worker is beholden to every other team member rather than to a single manager or boss. Researcher James Barker describes how a self-managing team caved in to accountability pressures one Friday afternoon. When their manufacturing plant had a traditional hi-erarchy, if members hadn't finished their work and didn't want to work overtime, they would just ask their boss, who let them leave. When members of this newly self-managing team realized they were running a few hours late, several tried to explain why they had to go home—a dinner, a daughter's school play, and so on. After a lot of groaning and discussion, they concurred: "But we promised Howard Bell [their customer] that we would have these boards out today. It's our responsibility. . . . We're gonna have to stay. We have to do this right."

The leaders and consultants that implemented self-managing teams in this plant didn't fully realize—at first—how sharply effort, quality, and productivity would increase because they had created small worlds where every worker felt obligated to every other. In other words, this change generated that powerful—and sometimes distressing—feeling that "I own the place and the place owns me."

Stacking Up Talent Like Firewood
Isn't Enough

Hiring the right people is crucial for propelling scaling, but it isn't enough. Unfortunately, too many leaders and gurus believe that, if they just buy the most skilled and motivated employees, exceptional performances will inevitably follow. They forget that team and organizational effectiveness requires weaving together people with diverse knowledge and skills—not just gathering a lot of talented people and hoping they can figure out how to work together well. Too many organizations stumble because they devote too little effort to helping people mesh their talents, to developing the skills of employees they hire, and to providing incentives that encourage them to pass along tricks of the trade to colleagues and to pitch in to help one another finish projects.

Trying to scale up excellence by purchasing lots of people who have done stellar work elsewhere is also risky because most stars aren't portable. Harvard's Boris Groysberg and his colleagues spent years tracking top performers, including CEOs, researchers, software developers, and stars in investment banking, advertising, public relations, management consulting, and law firms. Groysberg reports that, again and again, "We found that top performers in all those groups were more like comets than stars. They were blazing successes for a while but quickly faded out when they left one company for another." Consider the evidence they gathered on 1,052 star stock analysts who worked for seventy-eight U.S. investment banks between 1988 and 1996—people who do research and make recommendations about stocks that their firm and its clients ought to buy and sell.

Groysberg found little evidence that these highly paid "stock pickers" were portable. When stars joined a new firm, "their performance plummeted by an average of about 20% and had not climbed back to the old levels even five years later." The performance of the new teams they joined and their new invest-ment firms also suffered. This plummeting performance was probably caused, in part, by what statisticians call regression to the mean or, less kindly, reversion to mediocrity: over time, the odds often catch up to people who enjoy a stretch of exceptional performance—which eventually drifts back down to the perfor-mance levels of their average peers. But other forces also worked against these stars. Groysberg found that when an external star arrives, insiders become demoralized; senior analysts often start looking for jobs elsewhere, and "junior managers take the star's induction as a signal that the organization isn't interested in tap-ping their potential."

The dynamics also degenerate on teams that the outside sav-iors join: "Resentful of the rainmaker (and his pay), other manag-ers avoid the newcomer, cut off information to him, and refuse to cooperate." And while investment firms announce that they have lured superstar analysts with much fanfare, their own investors have the opposite reaction; Groysberg "found that the stock prices of the investment banks we studied fell by 0.74%, on average, and investors lost an average of $24 million each time the firms an-nounced that they had hired a star."

These findings, along with evidence from other industries, led Groysberg's team to urge executives to resist bringing in star saviors from other companies—advice that is bolstered by a 2011 study of a large investment banking business by Matthew Bidwell. He com-pared banking insiders who were promoted to outsiders who were hired for similar positions: outsiders were paid about 20 percent more than insiders but performed worse and were more likely to quit or be fired than insiders. As a result, Groysberg advises lead-ers to spend more time and money on encouraging cooperation and information sharing among existing employees, on developing technologies and procedures that enable exemplary work, and on using training and mentoring to develop their own stars.

In other words, as we see again and again, the quick fix rarely works when it comes to scaling. Yes, having money to spend on talent can be helpful. But beware of spending money as a substitute for doing the deep thinking and demanding work required to instill, spread, and sustain excellence.

A similar lesson emerges from studies of industries that can't pay skilled and motivated workers the big bucks showered on star stock analysts, such as manufacturing and service organizations. Wharton's Peter Cappelli shows that U.S. companies increasingly treat talented workers as something that they can hire fully formed and that ought to require little nurturing, mentoring, or training. This trend has grown stronger over the last thirty years, despite evidence that companies gain a competitive advantage by taking the long view—when they devote time and money to developing employees' skills, keeping them motivated, and nudging them to pass along what they believe and know to their coworkers and other teams.

In the worst organizations that Groysberg and Cappelli describe, employee compensation and prestige are based almost entirely on solo achievements. Employees have little reason to help other employees or teams, let alone to sacrifice their personal glory or success for the greater good. They may work in the same building and under the same banner, but they think and act as if they are free agents—and are ready to jump ship anytime a better offer comes along. There is little or no tug of two-way accountability: the unspoken but all-too-clear operating assumption is "I've got mine and you can't have any of it." Many such organizations don't start out this way but end up there when impatient and ambitious leaders give in to the dangerous temptation to scale up the organization on the backs of self-centered superstars.

The unraveling of Dewey & LeBoeuf provides a cautionary tale. The 2007 merger of two once proud law firms—Dewey Ballantine and LeBoeuf, Lamb, Greene & MacRae—reflected a lust by leaders and partners to create a bigger footprint in the world of corporate law, to make it fast, and to make bigger bucks right away. The newly named Dewey & LeBoeuf did have a bigger footprint, with twenty-six offices and 2,500 lawyers. But the timing turned out to be awful because the financial meltdown of 2008 was starting to hit. Dewey's leaders decided that the best way through this crisis was to poach stars with fat books of client business from other firms and throw wads of cash at their own top rainmakers. About one hundred stars received outsized multiyear, multi-million-dollar guarantees; several exceeded $5 million a year. According to the *American Lawyer*, these were gifts that the most senior and powerful Dewey partners gave themselves "at the expense of younger partners." The theory was that these big juicy carrots would propel profits skyward. The tough economic times wrecked this plan, but the firm was still obligated to pay those stars. Not only was Dewey teeming with partners who had little or no emotional investment in the greater good, the vast pay gaps between these stars and hundreds of lower-paid "service partners" further eroded loyalty throughout the firm. Service partners don't land many lucrative clients, but it is impossible to complete the work that rainmakers generate without them. The resulting mess meant the firm couldn't pay its bills. News of the firm's financial distress spooked clients, and both star partners and service partners scurried to defect to rival law firms: 75 percent of the three hundred partners left before Dewey declared bankruptcy under Chapter 11 on May 28, 2012.

Every other large law firm struggled to navigate the financial meltdown. Many relied on hiring stars from other firms as part of their survival strategy. But Dewey was perhaps the most extreme. They stacked up pricey talent like firewood and created a system that fueled inequality and resentment. Despite efforts by a few valiant leaders to reverse the tide, Dewey's partners knew that any talk of loyalty and responsibility to the firm was largely lip service. The firm's greed for money was the primary social glue. As a former partner put it, Dewey chair Steve Davis and executive director Stephen DiCarmine "understood that the firm was all about money. . . . What they could never understand is, if that's all that holds a firm together, you've got nothing left when the money runs out."

After giving a speech about scaling up excellence at another large law firm in 2013, Sutton met several attorneys there who had jumped ship for the Dewey dollars—and had then returned to their previous firm after the collapse. These attorneys explained that, while money is still an important part of the equation for them, they now call themselves "The Grass Is Browner Club" because they have greater appreciation for their supportive colleagues and the sense of shared accountability that pervades their firm. One partner said that he now praises the same pressure to act in the firm's best interests (even if it isn't best for him) that "pissed me off so much" before he lived through the Dewey debacle.

Talent x Accountability = Scaling Capacity

The question, then, is how to scale up organizations and projects that are filled with talented people who feel and act as if they own the place and it owns them—and where the bonds between them are strong and resilient. Our research led us to identify seven means for doing so.

1. Squelch Free Riding

When people feel accountable to their colleagues and customers, they feel obliged to expend extra effort and make sacrifices for the greater good. Making this happen, and keeping it going, isn't easy. Economist Mancur Olson Jr. identifies powerful "perverse incentives" that undermine such "collective action." The problem is that whether or not a single person acts unselfishly usually has a small—often miniscule—impact on the overall performance of most social systems. As a result, each member of an organization or project has a relatively small incentive to work hard and make personal sacrifices—and a big incentive to get a "free ride" on others' effort. Olson shows that, even when everyone in the system benefits, it is often rational for each person to contribute nothing, or at least far less than he or she is capable of, because the personal costs of action outweigh the personal benefits.

Economists call this the free-rider problem. The more people who must band together, the tougher it is to overcome. If you are one of 2 million Walmart employees, for example, no matter how hard you work or how much you assist coworkers, your impact on Walmart's bottom line, overall reputation, and culture is negligible. Similarly, national or statewide elections are for the greater good, but the effect of any one vote is trivial, so economists including Patricia Funk argue that "a rational individual should abstain from voting." Even in small projects, teams, and organizations, free riding rears its ugly head. Our Stanford colleague and venture capitalist Michael Dearing has funded more than sixty start-ups since 2006. He observes that once a start-up grows to about twenty people, if the right precautions aren't taken, newcomers start "feeling like just employees rather than owners."

If you don't find ways to offset and reverse free riding, be ready for a blight of that "I don't care and neither do most of my colleagues" mindset we saw at United Airlines and Dewey & LeBoeuf. Savvy leaders and teams stock their tool kit with every incentive they can find, borrow, and invent—and blend them to spur collective action and squelch free riding. Money isn't the only tool for boosting accountability, but it helps—especially when reinforced by hiring, firing, and promotion practices.

Netflix's leaders are keenly aware of free riding, and they

channel those big bucks that they pay employees to stop this malady. Netflix insists that, to be a star, an employee must "seek what is best for Netflix, rather than best for yourself or your group" and "make time to help colleagues." Netflix also emphasizes that every employee must comply with this taboo against free riding and related sins such as "cutthroat" and "sink or swim behavior" that get in the way of helping "each other be great." We were skeptical when we first read these claims; mouthing the words is far easier than living them. But after extensive conversations with that Netflix executive about how they make hiring, firing, and promotion decisions—and multiple conversations with former Netflix engineers who had been fired (despite strong technical skills) because of their inability or unwillingness to contribute to the greater good (some of whom were still angry about it)—we realized it wasn't hollow talk. At Netflix, when CEO Reed Hastings says, "We have stars in every position," it doesn't mean that his company encourages or even tolerates selfish solo acts; it means that they have people who do great work and help everyone around them do great work too.

We've encountered similar definitions of star employees—along with supportive reward systems—in dozens of organizations that consistently drive out free riding and breed accountability, including McKinsey, Google, Yum!, Pixar, IDEO, JetBlue, Procter & Gamble, and General Electric. P&G's CEO A. G. Lafley doesn't use a complicated system to link pay to employee collaboration; as *Fortune* magazine reported, "Managers who fail to share ideas simply do not get promoted." McKinsey and IDEO use the same standard when making decisions about which consultants to offer a financial stake, a partnership, in their firm.

Susan Peters, GE's vice president for executive development, explained to us how GE bolsters accountability throughout the company. GE evaluates all employees on both their performance and their leadership. Leadership includes supporting the GE culture and other factors that are essential to business success. The five main evaluation categories are external focus, inclusiveness, clear thinking, expertise, and imagination and courage. The nuances of the behavior expected under each category are frequently updated to fit changes in the marketplace and GE's strategy. The standards applied also depend on an employee's role: different things are expected of a twenty-seven-year-old management trainee than of a senior executive who runs one of GE's big businesses.

Peters made two especially instructive points. First, when we asked if GE emphasizes performance or leadership more strongly when they evaluate people, Peters reframed the question. Her view was that the two categories are so intertwined and self-reinforcing that it is usually impossible to separate them. When a GE leader, for example, keeps coming up with promising ideas but doesn't have sufficient courage (and persistence) to turn them into products or services, then performance suffers. In contrast, as we saw with the Adventure Series for kids that GE's Doug Dietz and his colleagues developed, when leaders have both imagination and courage, then success follows. Second, Peters emphasized that leadership at GE is not just for senior executives. GE employees at all levels are "expected to own the responsibility" for constantly improving their skills and updating how they lead in response to changes in their jobs and the business environment. In addition, leadership at GE means encouraging and guiding your peers and the people you manage to take such ownership as well. Once again, we see that accountability to others plays a central role in scaling up excellence.

Exceptional financial incentives aren't required to squelch free riding and create accountability; they just need to be big enough to motivate employees given their needs and other job options. Cofounder Shannon May (whom we met in chapter 1) explained to us how Bridge International Academies' modest pay helps motivate more than a thousand teachers in over 210 schools in Africa. Bridge carefully screens and trains applicants to ensure that they have the skills required to teach their (highly standardized) materials to elementary school students, as well as maintain classroom control. Bridge also uses intensive monitoring—including measuring teacher and student performance and regular observation of teachers—to ensure that each teacher puts the needs of students and Bridge first.

Students' families pay Bridge only about $5 per month, so the company cannot afford to pay big salaries to teachers or school managers. But Bridge does pay the legal minimum wage and also pays into the national health care system in each country for each employee—which many other employers don't do in the countries where Bridge operates. Teachers and school managers are also motivated by performance-based bonuses. One of Bridge's key metrics, in addition to student performance, is "time on task": the number of hours that pupils are in the classroom and learning (which averages about forty-two hours a week). These are hard jobs for teachers: in addition to the exacting standards that Bridge requires them to meet, students are at school from 7:30 a.m. to 5:00 p.m. each weekday and half a day on Saturday. Yet Bridge's teachers are enormously proud of their jobs, and voluntary turnover is low, in part, because Bridge is a more attractive employment option than most have in these poor countries.

Bridge's "Academy-in-a-Box" Starbucks-style approach is a radical departure from traditional schools. Yet this for-profit company seems to be working and has scaled at breakneck speed (from eight schools in 2009 to over 210 in 2013). And Bridge has attracted millions of dollars in venture capital funds. It is already Africa's largest chain of private schools. According to standardized tests administered by an independent evaluation group, Bridge students outperformed students at peer schools by big margins, from 24 percent (on addition skills) to 205 percent (in reading fluency).

Financial rewards are most effective when they dovetail with hiring and firing practices. Hiring the right people is crucial, as we've just seen at Bridge. But so is moving out the bad hires. Mancur Olson Jr. emphasizes that even a few free riders can undermine their colleagues' willingness to work and make sacrifices for the common good. When even a few people ride on the coattails of colleagues and keep getting away with it, hardworking and unselfish members feel like suckers. When that happens, selfishness and greed can spread like wildfire. At Bridge, Shannon May emphasized that, if a teacher isn't carrying his or her weight (which does not happen often), her leadership team moves that teacher out quickly because slacking off can infect other teachers so quickly. The same philosophy is applied at Netflix and Baird. When Sutton first interviewed Baird's CEO Paul Purcell in 2008, he asked how the company enforced their no-asshole rule—the taboo against putting one's own needs ahead of colleagues, clients, and the company: "Paul said that most jerks were screened-out via background checks and interviews before they met him. But he did his own filtering too. 'During the interview, I look them in the eye, and tell them, "If I discover that you are an asshole, I am going to fire you."'"

2. Inject Pride and Righteous Anger

Mancur Olson Jr. emphasizes that collective pride and aggressiveness (especially toward outsiders who deride and can undermine a group) are effective countermeasures to free riding. These emotions turn people's attention toward concerns that are larger than themselves, bind group or organization members together, and are contagious. When people are surrounded by others who feel and act proud about scaling something great, are angry at others who are—or might—impede their righteous efforts, or experience both feelings at once, they think and worry less about their selfish desires and concerns. And they are also more willing to take difficult, even personally risky, actions for the greater good.

Netflix blends those handsome financial incentives with pride and aggressiveness, treating the company like a sports team, not a family, to focus employees on winning and beating the competition. Aggressiveness—especially that righteous anger at some real or imagined foe—can stir up competitive juices when blended with other incentives. Executives from British Petroleum's retail division told Rao how they used such an approach. They wanted to shift internal teams from focusing on "beating each other up" to besting their competitor Shell Oil. So they developed a memorable motto: "Slam the clam," which referred to Shell's clamshell logo. They insisted that every resource decision—building gas stations, allocating R&D staff, advertising dollars, whatever—be steered toward "slamming the clam." Every action that they took was going toward competing against and besting Shell Oil.

General Matthew Ridgway's turnaround of the U.S. Army during the Korean War demonstrates how injecting pride and aggressiveness helped turn his soldiers' attention to something larger than themselves, gave them courage, and restored their lost morale. When Ridgway took command of the U.S. troops in late 1950, the situation was desperate. His forces had just completed a massive retreat in the face of a huge Chinese offensive. His men were frightened and confused. Soldiers and their field commanders huddled in their bunkers. Generals had no coherent plans to battle the enemy, and there was serious talk of a "Dunkirk-style" evacuation, where all U.S. forces would flee Korea at once in defeat and panic. Ridgway did not have the luxury of replacing his exhausted and emotionally defeated troops. He couldn't pay them more to be braver and prouder. Yet somehow he had to revitalize his beleaguered army. His goal was to avoid a shameful evacuation of U.S. troops, turn back the North Korean and Chinese advance, and bring the Chinese and North Koreans to the negotiating table.

Ridgway's immediate challenge was to restore his soldiers'

pride and amplify their courage—to compel them to stand up for themselves and their country. One of his first steps was to fly over the territory where they fought. He squeezed into the clear Plexiglass nose of a B-17 bomber, opened a map on his lap, and ordered the pilot to fly low and slow over the terrain so he could learn firsthand what his forces were up against. Over the next forty-eight hours, he visited each of his commanders. Ridgway discovered that many senior officers did not understand the terrain; they didn't know the names of rivers or heights of mountains. As a result of their ignorance, they placed troops on roads rather than on strategically advantageous ridges. In one of his first such meetings, he listened to Col. John Jeter give a long presentation about planned defensive positions as troops retreated further. Ridgway asked, "What are your attack plans?" Jeter had none. He said, "Sir, we are withdrawing." Ridgway relieved him of his command on the spot—a move meant to signal to other officers that he wouldn't tolerate timid or poorly informed leaders. Ridgway wrote his superiors, "Can't execute my future plans with present leaders" and went on to remove five of his six division commanders and fourteen of his nineteen regimental commanders because, in his view, they lacked confidence and competence.

When Ridgway visited the front lines, and troops showed him maps of enemy positions, he discovered that they were based on reports that were several days old. The maps were outdated because soldiers were afraid to go out on foot patrols to gather new intel. Ridgway knew that old information led to bad decisions about where to deploy troops. The soldiers lacked the confidence to risk their skins for the greater good of the U.S. forces. He pressed them to conduct more frequent patrols instead of hunkering down in bunkers. The patrols generated better information, which enabled combat leaders at all levels to develop better battle plans. As a result, not only did soldiers feel greater pride and courage, they also had greater confidence in orders from on high about how to fight the enemy.

Ridgway rescinded an order to hold ground "at all costs" so his troops would know that he cared about their safety and didn't want needless casualties. He repeatedly toured the front lines and assured troops that no unit would be abandoned in the face of a Chinese attack. He was exposed to enemy fire almost every day. He visited hospitals to make sure that the injured were treated well and traveled with extra pairs of gloves (so he could give them to soldiers with freezing hands). He moved his command post closer to the front, drove in an open jeep in the intense cold, and insisted that his commanders do so as well. Ridgway symbolized the new attitude of courage and compassion by strapping a hand grenade and a first aid kit to his back.

As Ridgway explained, "Before going on the offensive, we had work to do, weaknesses to shore up, mistakes to learn from, faulty procedures to correct, and a sense of pride to restore." By spring of 1951, the same army that had fled from the Chinese a few months earlier drove them north of the thirty-eighth parallel—which remains the border between North and South Korea to this day. Walter Winton, Ridgway's aide, summarized his boss's approach: "He did not turn the Eighth Army around by being mean to people, by shooting people, by relieving people, by chopping their heads off, or striking fear. He breathed humanity into the operation and saw to it that his men were warm, properly fed and properly led."

Ridgway faced the challenge of restoring excellence that had been destroyed by a spate of bad decisions and weak leaders. By insisting that his soldiers be more aggressive, replacing demoralized and incompetent leaders, and personally displaying the courage he expected from every soldier, Ridgway restored his troops' confidence and pride. In doing so, he was able to scale up accountability throughout the U.S. forces.

3. Bring in Guilt-Prone Leaders

When Ridgway moved out weak officers, he made sure that their replacements always put their troops' well-being first. The reason, Ridgway explained, was that "the hard decisions are not the ones you make in the heat of battle. Far harder to make are those involved in speaking your mind about some hare-brained scheme which proposes to commit troops to action under conditions where failure is almost certain, and the only results will be the needless sacrifice of priceless lives."

A 2012 study suggests that, when leaders are prone to feeling guilty, they are especially likely to display concern for others and to put the greater good ahead of their personal goals and glory. Stanford's Becky Schaumburg and Francis Flynn found that guilt-prone leaders have a strong sense of personal responsibility for their actions and are attuned to the impact of their decisions on others. They feel especially bad about past mistakes and worry constantly about messing up in the future, which they compensate for by being action oriented, constantly taking preventive measures to avoid future mistakes and steps to repair the damage done by their past errors. Schaumburg and Flynn propose that guilt-prone people often emerge as leaders because—to avoid feeling bad about not meeting their responsibilities or hurting others—they work hard and selflessly to help their groups and organizations achieve goals. Shame-prone leaders are different: when they make mistakes, they feel sorry for themselves, are filled with and frozen by worries that they are bad people, and run from the messes they make.

Schaumburg and Flynn did a series of studies that confirmed guilt-prone people are more likely to emerge as leaders and to be more effective leaders than others. In one study, these researchers assessed 144 university students and staff members for proneness to shame and guilt and then put them in three- or four-person groups without designated leaders. The groups then spent about an hour working on group decision-making exercises, such as developing a marketing campaign for products from the "As Seen on TV" website. After the exercises ended, group members consistently reported that guilt-prone teammates had become their leaders. In fact, "Guilt proneness predicted emerging leadership even more than did extraversion, a well-known marker of leadership." Members didn't use guilt proneness itself as a sign of leadership potential; rather, they admired the deeds that flowed from it—especially the concern that such leaders had for others. For example, guilt-prone members worried about colleagues who might feel ignored or disrespected, so they made sure that every member's opinion was heard.

Schaumburg and Flynn also did a follow-up study with 141 first-year M.B.A. students. The students' leadership abilities were rated by former supervisors, peers, direct reports, and clients. Guilt proneness was a hallmark of those who were rated as the most effective leaders. Schaumburg and Flynn's analysis shows that the students' strong sense of responsibility for others was a big reason that such leaders were portrayed in glowing terms such as "exceeds expected results," "provides an excellent role model for others," "tailors message to effectively communicate with diverse audiences," and "expresses emotions productively." Guilt proneness appears to be a vaccine against the brazen self-interest that can plague leaders. Many studies show that when people gain power they tend to put their own needs first. They ignore others' needs, act impulsively, and act as if rules are for "the little people," not them. Guilt-ridden leaders are less likely to display such "power poisoning": doing so would make them feel bad about themselves.

Veteran Pixar employee Craig Good told a story to Sutton that demonstrates how guilt-prone leaders act, why they are so admired, and how they create loyalty and the tug of obligation in others. In 1985, Ed Catmull and Alvy Ray Smith led the Computer Division at Lucasfilm—the group that ultimately evolved into Pixar. Catmull and Smith had great faith in the computer animation work that their group did; they hoped and believed it would eventually enable filmmakers to make quality films reminiscent of Disney classics such as *Dumbo* and *Snow White*. George Lucas, creator of the *Star Wars* films (and founder of Lucasfilm), was skeptical of the economics of the Computer Division but tolerated it because he found their work intriguing and his firm was flush with cash. But after Lucasfilm hit a rough patch and was under financial pressure in 1985, Lucas appointed Doug Norby as president to rein in expenses. Norby demanded deep layoffs at the Computer Division. Catmull and Smith tried to make a financial case for keeping the group intact, arguing that if Lucasfilm eventually sold it the value would be diminished if the division lost technical talent. Norby wasn't swayed. As Craig Good tells it: "He was pestering Ed and Alvy for a list of names from the Computer Division to lay off, and Ed and Alvy kept blowing him off. Finally came the order: You *will* be in my office tomorrow morning at nine with a list of names."

The next day, Catmull and Smith presented Norby a list with just two names: Ed Catmull and Alvy Ray Smith. Even more than twenty-five years later, Craig Good is still grateful. "We all kept our jobs. Even me, the low man on the totem pole. When word got out, we employees pooled money to send Ed, Alvy, and their wives on a thank-you night on the town." After this, Pixar was sold to Steve Jobs, and the rest, as they say, is history. Catmull and Smith did what guilt-prone leaders do: even if it hurts them, they put others first and do what is best for the greater good. Catmull is still Pixar's president; Smith left after a few years but played a crucial role as an early leader and technical genius.

The Lucasfilm story is one of many we've heard about Catmull's penchant to worry about others and put their needs ahead of his own. They are staples of our interviews and informal conversations with Pixar's people over the years. Catmull's actions reflect and reinforce Pixar's mindset, creating feelings of accountability among employees from Academy Award–winning film directors on down to return the favor with their own extra effort and self-sacrifice (of course, Catmull sometimes feels guilty about this!). During our visits to Pixar, we always notice the feelings of owner-ship and pride that permeate the place, evident in everyone from receptionists and executive assistants, to animators, to directors and senior executives.

In 2011, when Sutton asked Catmull to check the Lucasfilm story for accuracy, Catmull emphasized he is not opposed to all layoffs; sometimes they must be done for the greater good. This foreshadowed another finding from Schaumberg and Flynn's re-search: "Guilt prone managers were more likely to support layoffs to keep a company profitable than were those who are less guilt prone." Of course, guilt-prone leaders feel bad about doing layoffs. But as Schaumberg explains, "If people feel guilty toward their or-ganizations, they'll behave in ways that make sure they live up to the organization's expectations . . . [even though] these behaviors might not look like what we usually think of as guilt."

4. "I'll Be Watching You": Use Subtle Cues to Prime Accountability

Our scaling mantra in chapter 1, "Engage all the senses," high-lights how beliefs and behaviors are bolstered by small, seemingly trivial, and often unnoticed cues. Such cues can be harnessed to trigger accountability. For example, some clever studies show that, if people are given subtle reminders that others might be watch-ing, they are prone to do the right thing. Melissa Bateson and her colleagues from Newcastle University uncovered a simple way to encourage the forty-eight employees in their "Division of Psychol-ogy" to pay for their fair share of coffee, tea, and milk. The division had an "honesty box" and a sign asking for voluntary contributions next to the drinks. The researchers randomly alternated two posters behind the "honesty box" over a ten-week period: pretty flowers versus a pair of eyes that stared back at the employees. Those eyes apparently reminded people that they were beholden to others—contributions were three times higher when that poster was on the wall compared to the flower poster. Bateson was also part of a second research team that alternated posters with "eyes" and "flowers" in a large Newcastle University cafeteria. The researchers measured whether people cleared their trays or left them and other litter once they finished meals. Once again, the eyes had it: people were about 50 percent less likely to litter than when pictures of flowers hung on the wall—and the "eyes" had a far stronger impact than signs that urged people, "Please place your trays in the racks provided after you have finished your meal."

The *India Times* describes another visual image that encouraged people to behave less selfishly. Commuters had long complained about men who staggered out of a local bar and urinated on walls outside the Guindy Railway Station, creating an unbearable stench. Then fifty autorickshaw drivers "pooled money and painted the wall with images of all the Hindu gods. That put a stop to people unzipping along the station wall." The drivers' decision to pay for those pictures was also motivated by feelings of accountability. As one explained, "At the end of the day, it is our auto stand. We pay Southern Railway 1,200 to park our vehicles at the entrance of the station, where we get most of our passengers."

5. Create the Right "Gene Pool"

Vinod Khosla was Sun Microsystems' founding CEO and is now one of Silicon Valley's most renowned venture capitalists. Khosla used this experience as fodder for a 2012 paper called "Gene Pool Engineering for Entrepreneurs." His main argument is echoed by academic research on "imprinting," that "a company becomes the people it hires" because founders and first hires create the culture—and thus founders should focus on bringing the right mix of people to tackle the primary risks a company faces. Khosla's assertion that "the people make the place" has been made by everyone from star CEOs, to management gurus, to industrial psychologists, and plenty of evidence shows that who an organization hires has deep and enduring effects on culture and performance.

Michael Dearing, a venture capitalist and our Stanford colleague, has developed strong views on "gene pools" after screening over three thousand founders and funding over sixty companies since 2006. Dearing observed that the most successful founders are prone to certain "cognitive distortions": biased, even objectively inaccurate, ways they think of themselves and filter information that enable them to make quicker and better decisions, bounce back from setbacks, and attract talent. One distortion is "personal exceptionalism," the belief you are "on the top of your cohort" and destined to greatness. Dearing believes exceptionalism helps founders be resilient, persistent, and persuasive when enticing employees, customers, and investors to work with them. Another distortion is "dichotomous thinking," or, as Dearing describes it, "X is shit, Y is genius" thinking. These snap decisions and strong opinions help a start-up team know what to focus on and what to ignore. It stops them from trying to jam in every feature or please every customer. The main risk, Dearing says, is that the accompanying perfectionism that founders often exhibit can be exhausting and exasperating. Steve Jobs drove people crazy this way—for example, refusing to accept ugly bolts that were hidden inside Apple computers or firing sixty-seven nurses before finding three that he liked.

Netflix and Tamago-Ya illustrate how "people make the place" thinking plays out in larger organizations. Netflix CEO Reed Hastings's strategy is to stock the place with brilliant and unselfish talent who need little supervision or training. At Tamago-Ya, founder Isatsugu Sugahara seeks high school dropouts like himself, who are motivated to excel by the performance-based pay and have a desire to reciprocate Sugahara's faith in them. When big organizations or projects attempt to scale up by embracing new mindsets—and discarding old ones—they do something akin to gene pool "reengineering." That can be a good thing. It's exactly what Ridgway did when he replaced senior officers who hurt morale and brought in others who fueled pride and put soldiers first. In chapter 3, we saw how CEO Charlotte Beers hand-picked "the thirsty for change group" to transform Ogilvy & Mather. Their discomfort with the status quo, penchant for long-term thinking, flexibility, and impatience helped the company's seven thousand employees change from feeling beleaguered and acting undisciplined to being "intensely client and brand focused"—fueling a $2 billion increase in billings during Beers's four-year reign.

Yet there are limits to treating an organization's "gene pool" as if human qualities, experience, and skills are fixed. Even when you hire the right people, the experiences and training you provide are crucial for spreading the right beliefs, behaviors, and skills. In other words, the people make the place *and* the place makes the people! Many organizations use formal programs to "build" the people they need. One tried-and-true approach is to rotate "high-potentials" through diverse and increasingly challenging jobs. That's how the upscale department store Neiman Marcus develops potential store managers. The path entails becoming first a master salesperson and then a top merchandise buyer. A Neiman employee can become a store manager only after mastering selling and buying in a given location because each store is operated and stocked to serve its particular market.

Organizations can also be restructured in ways that multiply talent. Consider Tata Consultancy Services, or TCS, an Indian software firm with over 280,000 employees and $11.6 billion in annual revenues. Senior executives were concerned that the company was growing so fast that it wasn't being responsive enough to its top four hundred customers—in particular, customers were often getting mixed messages from different parts of TCS. CEO Natarajan Chandrasekaran (known as Chandra) believed that he needed a "CEO factory" to ensure speed and responsiveness. So he carved the company into sixty industry-focused business units, each of which reports to a president and a CFO (who oversee as many as three units). Each unit starts out employing three thousand to five thousand people and having maximum revenues of $250 million. But it can grow into a billion-dollar business before it is deemed too big and is carved into smaller pieces. Each unit is given considerable autonomy: for example, each can negotiate the price of contracts with vendors and customers without consulting the corporate finance department.

Chandra reports that the new structure has many advantages. As he hoped, TCS customers report that the more nimble and empowered units are responding to their needs more quickly and effectively than under the old structure. The new structure also frees Chandra to focus on broader strategic issues, and, as *Forbes* reported, "Perhaps the next CEO will emerge from this group. It is an excellent way to test their mettle."

Scaling up an organization also requires constantly reconsidering the kinds of talent that you have, need, and ought to hire and incubate. Walgreens was able to open 261 new stores in 2011 because senior executives made a conscious decision to develop deeper and, especially, broader "bench strength" among its managers—so they could hit the ground running and create stores that replicated Walgreens' culture. To improve customer service, Walgreens also revamped what pharmacists do, moving them from the traditional behind-the-counter role of filling prescriptions and wrangling with insurance companies to a new role focusing on helping customers understand, select, and use medicines and other health products. Walgreens also created "health concierges," employees who specialize in helping chronically ill customers. This emphasis on broadening old roles and creating new ones has multiplied the numbers of employees who "get" the customer's perspective, the nuances of running a store, and the Walgreens mindset.

6. Use Other Organizations as Your HR Department

Using other organizations to screen and train talent is a tried-and-true approach. For over seventy-five years, the U.S. military has selected and developed pilots—who are then hired by commercial airlines. The *Air Force Times* reports that "45 percent of the 6,100 pilots at Southwest Airlines are veterans or reservists"; their pilot hiring manager is Rocky Calkins, a former F-15 pilot. In Silicon Valley, many high-tech companies use Stanford University as a kind of HR department. This is not new; after Bill Hewlett and David Packard started HP in 1938 (with a $500 loan from Stanford professor Frederick Terman), HP hired mainly Stanford engineering grads. This trend persists among hundreds of companies. Google founders Larry Page and Sergey Brin, two dropouts from Stanford's computer science PhD program, received early funding from a dropout from the electrical engineering PhD program (Andy Bechtolsheim, cofounder of Sun Microsystems). Google's lead board member is Stanford's president John Hennessy (a computer scientist who did finish his Stanford PhD program).

Google uses the Stanford Engineering School, especially its computer science department, to stock the company with software engineers who have strong technical, interpersonal, and leadership skills. The introductory computer science sequence is one of the most popular courses in engineering. Hundreds of students take "CS 106" each year. It is taught by a team including a head lecturer, two graduate student course assistants called "coordinators," and twenty or so smart undergraduates who teach small "sections." The coordinator role entails interviewing, selecting, and hiring new section leaders, teaching these newcomers a ten-week class on how to teach computer science, and organizing and coaching the section leaders as CS 106 unfolds. Google hires as many of these "coordinators" as possible, a practice that proved especially valuable in the company's early years. One was Marissa Mayer, Google's twentieth employee and its first female engineer. Mayer led many of the company's product development efforts, including Google Maps and Google Mail, and at the age of thirty-seven became CEO of Yahoo!

Other Silicon Valley companies have followed Google's lead. Venture capitalist and former Mozilla CEO John Lilly (another former coordinator) is especially impressed with how "Schrep," Facebook's chief technology officer Mike Schroepfer, has turned recruiting and making the best use of coordinators into "an art form." A few years after graduating, Lilly cofounded a company called Reactivity, which was eventually sold to Cisco for $135 million. Lilly believes that being a coordinator "changed everything" for him. It meant that he "learned how to interview and recruit people. You do over fifty interviews every quarter and hire the best ten to twenty. Coordinators tend to be the best able to scale in an organization after school."

Some U.S. charter school chains use a related recruiting strategy. Charter schools take many forms, but the basic idea is that these typically smaller and more focused schools are freed from many rules and constraints that other schools face (even though most are still beholden to and funded by a state or local government). Charter schools are often held more accountable than traditional public schools for student achievement—on metrics like test scores and the percentage of students who go to college. Charter management organizations, or "nonprofit networks of charters operated by a home office," often run such schools. For example

KIPP (Knowledge Is Power Program) runs over 140 schools in twenty states. YES Prep manages eleven schools in Houston that teach over seven thousand students. Rocketship Education was launched in San Jose in 2006; it now runs seven schools in San Jose and opened Rocketship Milwaukee in September 2013.

All three chains focus on providing students from low-income areas with an alternative to (often troubled and underperforming) traditional public schools. KIPP was founded by Mike Feinberg and Dave Levin in 1994; as KIPP tells the story, "They opened two KIPP middle schools, one in Houston and one in New York City. By 1999, these original KIPP charter schools were among the highest-performing schools in their respective communities." Similarly, YES Prep was started as an alternative to traditional public high schools, and YES leaders report that 100 percent of its graduates have gone on to four-year colleges. Rocketship relies on individualized instruction and tutoring. It boasts that "California state standardized testing results from the 2011–2012 school year" show that "Rocketship Education is the leading public school system for low-income students in the entire state."

Skilled and committed teachers are needed to scale up these chains: all three rely heavily on Teach for America (TFA). This nonprofit was founded in 1990 by Wendy Kopp, based on the undergraduate thesis she had written at Princeton a year earlier. Over twenty-eight thousand teachers have since been recruited by TFA from top colleges and universities, have been given training, and have taught in low-income communities. TFA recruits ambitious students—class presidents, athletes, and the like—who will commit two years to teaching kids who live in poverty. It partners with companies such as Goldman Sachs so that graduates can defer more lucrative job offers and devote two years to teaching. About 75 percent of Rocketship Education's teachers are in TFA or are TFA alums. Founder John Danner sees TFA as his human resources department: TFA screens and trains candidates well, and these entrepreneurial, energetic, and smart teachers transmit the same qualities to their students.

7. Hire People Prewired to Fit Your Mindset

As we've implied throughout this chapter, bringing in people who are prewired with personalities, values, and skills that mesh well with whatever mindset and moves you aim to scale can amplify your odds of successful scaling. The Danish consulting firm Specialisterne (the Specialists) is an extreme case: they've turned high-functioning autism into an advantage. Thorkil Sonne was inspired to start the firm after discovering that his son, who has autism, was adept at memory tasks and had an intense focus that helped him to flawlessly perform repetitive and tedious chores. Sonne realized that people like his son could excel at tasks such as data entry or software testing, even if their communication skills were weak.

So he started this consulting company, which now employs thirty-five high-functioning autistic people to do such exacting work for corporate clients. For example, one client is a cell phone company. Software glitches in new phones are uncovered by testers who execute lengthy scripts containing over two hundred detailed instruction sets; testers often get bored, take shortcuts, and make mistakes. Many, although not all, high-functioning autistic people excel at such tasks. Sonne describes people with disabilities as being prewired to master some tasks that the rest of us find difficult. He offers a lovely analogy: when dandelions pop up on a lawn, we call them weeds; but those same spring greens make for delightful salads. Similarly, some apparent weaknesses of autistic people turn out to be strengths for repetitive tasks that require extreme concentration.

Extreme Accountability:
The Attack on the Taj

On November 26, 2008, the Taj Mahal Intercontinental Hotel in Mumbai, India, was one of the targets of a terrorist strike that killed 175 people across five locations. As the bullets were flying, Unilever board members, executives, and their spouses were dining at the Taj to bid farewell to CEO Patrick Cescau. Taj employees jumped into action to protect their guests. They drew the curtains, separated wives from husbands to reduce the danger to families, and asked guests to lie down under tables and switch off cell phones. They comforted the guests and served them water and snacks until they were rescued the next morning. Mallika Jagad, a twenty-four-year-old banquet manager, led the thirty-five brave Taj employees who protected these guests from Unilever. Elsewhere in the hotel, a telephone operator tipped off Thomas Varghese—a forty-eight-year-old head waiter at the Wasabi by Morimoto restaurant—that the terrorist attack was in progress. Varghese calmly instructed fifty-four hotel guests to lie down and asked other employees to cordon off the guests. All escaped down a staircase the next day—except for Mr. Varghese, who insisted on being the last to leave and was gunned down at the bottom of the staircase.

The Taj's general manager, Karambir Singh Kang, directed operations throughout the hotel—even as his wife and two children died in a fire on the sixth floor. Kang refused to give up his post. After learning the terrible news about his family, he vowed to his father, "If it [the hotel] goes down, I will be the last man out." In the chaos of the terrorist attack, most employees were cut off from their superiors. Yet they took independent initiative without waiting for orders or asking permission to do what they believed was right. Telephone operators elected to stay at their desks, manning the phone lines (even though they sat just a few feet from the terrorists); kitchen staff formed human chains to shield guests as they were evacuated. Such bravery was not limited to a handful of the Taj employees. It permeated the entire organization. The exemplary behavior of the Taj employees helped some 1,500 guests escape on a tragic night when thirty-one people, including eleven hotel employees, were killed by gunfire and twenty-eight people were seriously injured.

Why were these employees inspired to such noble acts during this terrible crisis? How were they able to embrace such an extraordinary level of accountability and to ignore their own safety, far beyond any conventional definition of customer service? It starts and ends with a mindset, one that the Taj Group strives relentlessly to sustain: employees are advocates of the customer, rather than ambassadors of the company—*their job is to look out for the customer first, last, and always.* Can you imagine such a mindset at United Airlines? Here is what happened to that disillusioned United captain we wrote about at the outset of the chapter: "I had the gall to apologize to my 150 passengers for a delay of 45 minutes one day. I was asked to write a letter of apology TO MANAGEMENT for mentioning the problem."

So how does the Taj support the opposite mindset? They start by selecting employees who are predisposed to be customer advocates, young employees from small cities where the common attitude is "The guest is God"—villagers who display respect for elders, consideration for others, and positive energy and who are keen to prove themselves. They look for young employees from humble families who need the income and are eager to make their families proud. In other words, the Taj seeks new hires who are prewired with the values and motivation to embrace and live its mindset.

These new employees are indoctrinated for eighteen months; most hotel chains train newcomers for twelve months or less. Every trainee is taught to make decisions without supervision and told that anything they do (within reason) that "puts guests front and center" will be supported by management. Trainees are especially encouraged to exhibit these values during the forty to forty-five "moments of truth" that occur each day—the typical number of daily interactions that a hotel guest has with Taj employees during a stay. And trainees are surrounded with coworkers who live this mindset, which reinforces and creates social pressure to put the client's interests first.

The Taj's reward system reinforces this mindset. Employees receive points based on compliments from customers and colleagues, self-reports of their accomplishments, and their suggestions for making improvements at the hotel. Every day, the hotel general manager, the HR manager, and department managers review this information and post the points awarded to employees on the intranet. By accumulating points, employees can achieve any of five performance levels ranging from the managing director's club to the silver club—visible and valuable rewards that generate kudos from coworkers and their families. Taj senior executives emphasize to supervisors that "the timing of the reward is more important than the reward itself," that offering it as soon as possible—and doing so in person—is crucial.

In short, those Taj employees didn't see themselves as heroes on November 26, 2008. They just did what they always do—putting the guest first. It is the first order of business for them every day.

The Taj is a place where employees live this mindset because, like other organizations that scale up excellence, it is brimming with people who have the skill to do exemplary work and who feel obligated to do the right things to accomplish some greater good.

CHAPTER 6

CONNECT PEOPLE AND CASCADE EXCELLENCE

Using Social Bonds to Spread the Right Mindset

Ignorance, mediocrity, and mistakes run rampant when organizations fail to link the right people to the right information at the right time. This is true even when everyone involved has the best of intentions and even when someone somewhere knows exactly what to do (but no one has figured out how to get the information to those who need it). During the Iraq war, improvised explosive devices (IEDs) were among the most lethal dangers to U.S. forces. In 2005, Master Sergeant Chad Walker's 172nd Stryker Brigade had been fighting in Iraq for fifteen months when, at the U.S. embassy in Baghdad, he saw "an IED defeat handbook, it was sitting on some guy's desk." The handbook was filled with hard-won lessons that the Center for Army Lessons Learned (CALL) had gathered from numerous combat units. Walker wasn't pleased: "It infuriated me that my soldiers and I were not exposed to the knowledge found in this handbook until the very end of our 16-month deployment."

Fortunately, CALL did get better at "connecting and cascading" as the war progressed. For example, many soldiers perished after their Humvees "overturned in Iraq's many irrigation canals," the doors wedged shut, and the trapped soldiers drowned. In response, Bill Del Solar, a safety officer with the Tenth Mountain Division, cobbled together the cables and hooks that most vehicles already carried to invent "rat claws"—a flat steel hook that rescuers attached to another vehicle and used to rip the doors off overturned or disabled Humvees. CALL quickly spread the news via websites and online forums. CALL analyst Colin Anderson reported, "In a 24-hour period, the feedback we got was really good, because a lot of other units that were in-theater at the time didn't have a clue that it existed. They were able to take it and use it."

Other soldiers used CALL forums to discuss RKG-3 hand grenades that enemies were throwing at army vehicles; they focused on how RKG-3s didn't explode when they hit soft surfaces. That knowledge inspired prototypes that looked like big trampolines and could be mounted on vehicles. Their idea worked. RKG-3s bounced off without blowing up. CALL's deputy director David Bialas explained: "It boiled down to three or four types of designs, then sharing among themselves. They put them on the vehicles right away. . . . In a very short period of time, with the effectiveness of that particular device, the casualties went down tremendously."

The Goal: Domino Chains of Goodness

As CALL's success suggests, scaling hinges on discovering (or creating) pockets of excellence and connecting the people who have it, and their ideas and expertise, to others. When all goes well, a chain reaction occurs where excellence flows from one person, team, or place to the next—much like those "domino chains," where the energy generated by one falling domino creates the energy to topple the next, and then the next, and so on, until all have fallen.

We've seen numerous examples of how such domino chains are built, triggered, and fortified: the efficiency improvements at Wyeth; Facebook's Bootcamp; the growth of Bridge International Academies and Pulse News; Claudia Kotchka's efforts to embed innovation experts in P&G businesses; Andy Papa's crusade to transfer the "athletic mindset" from football to NASCAR pit stops; the rollout of KP HealthConnect; and the 100,000 Lives Campaign. But we want to underline and expand on a theme that pervades these and other successful scaling efforts: a core team was accountable for ensuring that the right links were made and that the right facts and feelings kept flowing through the right connections in every case.

The team that built and coaxed the domino chain to keep cascading during the 100,000 Lives Campaign is especially instructive. In chapter 2, we described how the Institute for Healthcare Improvement (IHI) kicked off the campaign with a hot cause (preventing needless deaths) and cool solutions (six proven practices) and how some 120,000 fewer preventable deaths had occurred in U.S. hospitals by the time this eighteen-month effort was over. But we haven't discussed the "ground war" waged by the small but mighty scaling team led by twenty-eight-year-old Joe McCannon. Although the team never had more than ten full-time young staffers (and IHI never had over one hundred employees), this small band identified and created pockets of excellence in about 3,100 U.S. hospitals and kept those life-saving practices cascading from one "domino" to the next throughout this vast (and otherwise largely disconnected) network.

The team's initial goal was to enlist at least 1,600 hospitals, which they calculated would be enough to prevent one hundred thousand deaths. They were bent on spreading a new mindset:

shifting health care administrators and providers from viewing errors and risks as *inevitable, difficult to prevent,* and thus *unacknowledged* to viewing errors and risks as largely *preventable* and thus best *discussed candidly* and *admitted freely*—because such openness reveals root causes and makes it safe for health care providers to ask for help so they can learn better ways to care for patients. As with other effective scaling efforts, they believed and behaved as if their success depended, above all, on the day-to-day grind of implementation. They borrowed a motto from the U.S. Army: "Amateurs discuss strategy; professionals discuss logistics"—in other words, the nuances of getting things done.

McCannon explained that most hospitals are specialized and tend to excel at a few things, which meant there already were many pockets of existing excellence in the industry. His campaign team focused their logistical prowess on identifying such pockets and helping to pass their expertise along to other hospitals: "If an organization in Oregon is doing very well on providing reliable care for heart attacks, it is our job to connect them to the whole world. The flip side is, when an organization in Oregon is interested how an organization in Massachusetts does well in reducing an infection, we have to clear the pathways and provide channels, so that others know that they can reach out to them. We lean heavily on the participants to teach us and others."

McCannon's team used a number of methods to make and maintain such connections. They had a weekly phone-in "radio-style" program called "Campaign Live," where staff from hundreds of hospitals tuned in to learn about implementing successful evidence-based practices and other pertinent lessons. They maintained websites and provided reports and brochures pertinent to every aspect of the campaign, including research on reducing health errors, the nuances of adopting each practice, and additional archived "Campaign Live" programs. But the team's most important work entailed building networks of hospitals and other medical organizations to help the campaign—and stepping aside once they kicked into gear.

The need for such "outsourcing" became painfully clear just two months into the campaign, when over 1,600 hospitals had already signed up. McCannon's team responded by sending out a strong message that participants should "make the campaign your own." McCannon added, "Getting what we wished for so fast was scary and motivating. We started making a lot of local marriages happen because it was the only way to have the capacity to get it all done." These "marriages" involved mostly "nodes" and "mentor hospitals." The seventy "nodes" lifted the administrative burden off IHI; each helped run the campaign in a given region (usually states) or across key specialties (e.g., rural, academic, children). For example, in Vermont, the Association of Hospitals and Health Systems teamed up with the Northeast Health Care Quality Foundation to form a node to help manage and coordinate the campaign across the state. In particular, they took charge of recruitment—their goal was to convince every hospital in the state to join the campaign.

Although "nodes" carried part of the administrative burden, McCannon's team stayed focused on the nitty-gritty of developing and recruiting some two hundred "mentor hospitals"—the lifeblood of the campaign. These hospitals were experts in at least one of six evidence-based practices that the campaign was focused on spreading:

1. Rapid-response teams: experts who spring into action when a patient's condition deteriorates rapidly
2. Procedures for acute myocardial infarctions (i.e., heart attacks), including rapid administration of aspirin and beta-blockers
3. The "ventilator bundle": practices for patients on ventilators that prevented pneumonia

4. The "central line bundle": practices including checklists to prevent infections related to central venous catheters

5. Prevention of infections at surgical sites through antibiotic use and other practices, including steps to ensure that all health care workers have clean hands

6. "Medication reconciliation": comparing the drugs a patient is prescribed to prevent dangerous interactions

Once McCannon's team discovered that a hospital was adept in one of these areas, or his team had helped a hospital learn one of these "bundles," the staff there was recruited to mentor other hospitals. For example, McCannon's team connected the Contra Costa Regional Medical Center in California with four mentor hospitals that were experts in medical reconciliation. Contra Costa experimented until they developed reconciliation procedures that worked for them; they then became a mentor hospital in medical reconciliation themselves, and McCannon's team connected them with other hospitals that needed their expertise.

As the campaign unfolded, the team spent more and more time in the field: they found that face-to-face contact was even more crucial than they had first realized. So four team members became full-time "harvesters," traveling from hospital to hospital to spot needs, uncover and instill better practices, and create network connections. McCannon and several teammates rented a bus in September of 2005, plastered it with patients' pictures and campaign slogans and facts, and drove it from Boston to Seattle—visiting hospitals in sixteen cities to whip up enthusiasm and spread practices in person. McCannon explained that other methods helped spread key lessons, but nothing worked as well as being there live, in the flesh, to give health care providers "exactly what they need, when they need it."

Despite its idiosyncrasies, this campaign had two hallmarks of the best scaling efforts. First, as we've emphasized, a core team kept the right information, guidance, and motivation flowing in the network. Second, the team continued to find and groom dedicated helpers so that they weren't burdened with every detail of the "connect and cascade" process. IHI especially needed help, given their tiny size and modest $3.3 million budget. Yet, as we saw with the multi-billion-dollar KP HealthConnect rollout, no matter how much money a team has, scaling depends on a chain reaction where—to use the domino analogy—the core team doesn't have to go in and personally push over each tile.

Throughout this chapter, we focus on harnessing the connect-and-cascade process. We begin with an obvious core question that is often forgotten, ignored, or dismissed but that too often comes back to bite those bent on scaling.

Excellence: Got Any?

We run a "take it home" panel during our "Customer-Focused Innovation" executive program, where a group of managers and executives draw on their personal experience to give advice about spreading the practices we teach. Claudia Kotchka, who leads it, pulls in scaling veterans such as GE's Doug Dietz, JetBlue's Bonny Simi, and others, including Hyatt's Dania Duke (general manager of the Santa Clara Regency), and Cybex's Bill Pacheco (director of engineering at this exercise equipment company). During each panel, at least one of the sixty or so program participants in the audience tells pretty much the same story. Their organization has a big innovation effort: workshops, conferences, a well-funded scaling team, the whole shebang. Yet no team or project actually uses the practices that are allegedly being spread to tackle real problems. In one company, executives couldn't name a single project that had ever used design thinking, even though the company had dedicated multiple people and teams to spread design thinking during the past decade.

Researchers have portrayed scaling as a three-stage process: excellence, efficiency, and expansion. To us, that sequence is too linear; scaling usually unfolds in fits and starts that rarely fit this tidy progression. Yet those three orderly stages—and that troubling story managers and executives keep telling us—imply a simple, but critical, lesson that we now highlight during the panel: *"To spread excellence, you need to have some excellence to spread."* Executives often hoot and holler in response to this, because, they tell us, the top dogs at their workplace behave as if this fact of organizational life doesn't apply to them.

This "absence of excellence problem" sometimes rears its head because powerful zealots are determined to scale something they are convinced is marvelous despite precious little evidence that it works. For example, if anyone ever tries to institute handwriting analysis or "graphology" to select employees for your organization, stop them immediately. Graphology is still a common selection practice in France and Israel, but every shred of unbiased evidence shows it is useless for assessing employee traits and potential.

This problem is also a side effect of treating scaling as a pure air war. Leaders and teams that make this blunder often apply a thin and short-acting shellac of insight to vast numbers of people—a quick workshop or two, a few speeches, or online courses. Then they declare victory. To paraphrase former Yahoo! executive Brad Garlinghouse (now CEO of YouSendIt), this is the peanut butter syndrome. In 2006, Garlinghouse wrote what the *Wall Street Journal* dubbed the "Peanut Butter Manifesto," a lament about Yahoo!'s slide toward mediocrity:

I've heard our strategy described as spreading peanut butter across the myriad opportunities that continue to evolve in the online world. The result: a thin layer of investment spread across everything we do and thus we focus on nothing in particular.

I hate peanut butter. We all should.

Similarly, some leaders believe—or pretend to believe—that just by spreading a thin coat of something good, deep pockets of excellence will somehow magically form. But the connect-and-cascade process doesn't work that way. You've got to act as Wyeth did when they rolled out quality and cost control methods to seventeen thousand employees. They started by focusing on a few "minitransformations" in eight plants: each was supported by intensive training, coaching, and feedback from Wyeth's staff and consultants, and each involved extensive experimentation and rehearsal. Once a pocket of true excellence was created, the lessons were cascaded from that minitransformation to the next, as when "Fifi" Haknasar's team at the Pearl River Plant cut change-over time from fourteen to seven hours. This domino chain continued until seventeen thousand employees had changed their ways. It took hard work, lots of money, and eighteen months to finish. But Wyeth saved over $250 million, quality increased in almost every plant, and so did employee accountability and pride.

Yet, as the learning curve research that we introduced in chapter 2 reveals, sometimes even though early pockets are mediocre (or even downright crummy), taking the effort to create them is often worthwhile. Scaling is sometimes led by teams that have limited skill or experience with what they spread—and sometimes no one in their network is very adept at it either. Yet, as the scaling team and the groups and units that they help gain more experience, true excellence can emerge. In the 1990s, Sutton worked with a Hewlett-Packard supply chain group called SPaM (Strategic Planning and Modeling) that traveled down just this path. At first, as SPaM's leader Corey Billington admitted, his consultants knew little more than the HP businesses they served. Little by little, by gaining experience and working alongside experts such as Stanford's Hau Lee, SPaM's ability to spot and solve supply chain problems improved. After crawling up this learning curve for a few years, SPaM built a reputation inside and outside HP for inspired work, especially in HP's massive printer business. SPaM succeeded because they focused on developing and transferring real excellence instead of spreading a thin coat of supply chain peanut butter across HP.

Whom Do You Connect?

It's About Diversity, Not Just Numbers

As we saw in chapter 3, when Bonny Simi assembled that first group to tackle JetBlue's "irregular operations" problems, she invited people from all over the company: baggage handlers, gate agents, reservation agents, mechanics, flight controllers, managers from varied locations and functions, and pilots like her. The group was diverse in other ways: photos and films reveal a mix of men and women, old and young, and Hispanics, Asians, African Americans, and Caucasians. Simi's main motivation was to bring together and blend people with expertise on a broad range of interconnected operations. But studies of persuasion and social networks suggest that starting with a diverse group propels scaling for other reasons. Such breadth means that a team is linked to more "nodes" in the organization's network: to the varied departments, locations, functions, and levels of the pecking order where each member is stationed, as well as to their numerous (and often nonoverlapping) informal friendships, groups, and affiliations. If

Simi's initial IROP group at JetBlue had contained only, say, white male pilots from New York, or Hispanic female gate agents from Long Beach, the new mindset would have cascaded to far fewer people and places.

Another advantage is that early recruits worry less about being taken advantage of when a broad cross section of the organization is involved. They don't feel singled out as guinea pigs for a crazy experiment or, worse, start wondering if some sneaky or overly ambitious executive is setting them up for failure or embarrassment. The breadth also conveys that what you are scaling can help many or most organization members, not just some specialized group. Many organizations are divided into silos of employees with similar skills and backgrounds; people within accounting, engineering, and HR often work side by side and have limited contact with other departments or functions. If people in only one silo, say marketing, are invited at first, others in the organization may conclude that only marketing folks are interested or will benefit from the effort.

Ironically, diversity also propels scaling because of the power of homogeneity, specifically what psychologists call "similarity-attraction" effects. For better and worse, we humans tend to have warmer feelings and spend more time with people who are similar to us. Harvard's Rakesh Khurana jokes that most of us are drawn to people who are just like our favorite person: ourselves. Khurana uses these findings to explain why U.S. corporate boards are composed primarily of white males between fifty and seventy years old: members can't resist reproducing themselves. Even in diverse workplaces, when given the choice, women tend to congregate with women, and men with men, as do people of similar ages and racial backgrounds. The same goes for people from similar professional backgrounds: when, say, engineers, graphic designers, and copywriters work in the same place, if given a choice, they tend to hang out with colleagues like themselves.

This means that, by stocking an initial scaling team with people who mirror the diversity of the larger organization, once the team's members embrace and live a mindset, it will cascade more widely than if you had started with people who all looked alike and thought alike, were all from the same place, and all did similar work. Scaling stalls when you start with a bunch of clones. Early on, you need a team with different, largely nonoverlapping, connections so that when they flock back together with others like them they will influence more parts of the network.

Charles Darwin's "four musketeers" are a classic example of this strategy: these leading scientists defended and spread evolutionary theory after *The Origin of Species* was published in 1859. Each worked in a somewhat different field and thus had ties to many, often nonoverlapping, networks. Charles Lyell was the most famous geologist of his time. Joseph Dalton Hooker was a renowned botanist and director of the Royal Botanical Gardens. Hooker also had broad international contacts because he was an avid explorer: he joined and led expeditions to study and gather plants in Antarctica, the Himalayas, India, Palestine, Morocco, and the western United States. Asa Gray was the most influential American botanist and author of the classic text *Gray's Manual of Botany*. Gray arranged for *The Origin of Species* to be published in the United States, defended the theory in popular and scientific publications, and expanded it in his influential book *Darwiniana*. Finally, Thomas Huxley is most famous as "Darwin's bulldog," battling critics with zeal and skill. This renowned and self-taught zoologist proposed that birds evolved from dinosaurs, now a widely accepted hypothesis. Huxley also devoted a great deal of effort to developing modern scientific education in Britain's schools—which have spread evolutionary theory to millions.

Most leaders who aim to spread a mindset don't have a dream team like Darwin's, but any scaling effort will move faster and farther if you start with a diverse group of evangelists.

Look for Master Multipliers

In chapter 4, we introduced Vice President Kaaren Hanson, who leads Intuit's Design for Delight, or "D4D," efforts, which have changed how thousands of Intuit employees think about and do their work. It took Hanson's team a few years to learn that the greatest solo designers—who keep creating products and services that customers fall in love with and must have—aren't always the best at spreading their talent and enthusiasm to others. You need master multipliers, as we call them, as well. Not only do such people have deep knowledge and enthusiasm about what they spread. They are adept at finding others to help them fuel the connect-and-cascade process. They are skilled at spotting which "students" are most likely to succeed; at giving them the right feedback at the right moment in the right way; at maintaining the highest quality standards; and at having the patience and self-control to allow people to learn from their own mistakes—to resist micromanaging or jumping in and doing it for them.

Hayden Fry, who coached the University of Iowa football team from 1979 to 1998, embodies these qualities. Fry's teams performed well, winning 143 of 238 games and three Big Ten titles. But within football circles, he is most admired for producing more head coaches of top football programs (sixteen) than anyone before or since. Fry recruited certain Iowa players to become coaches. All were, in his lingo, "bell cows": members of the herd that other cows always followed. Each year, Fry took the unusual step of asking several active players with strong leadership skills to coach fellow players. He did so to help them develop coaching skills and to help him decide which of them to offer entry-level coaching jobs. Fry's former assistants report, "He wouldn't hire an assistant unless he believed that assistant was capable of becoming a head coach some day."

Much like the best D4D mentors, Fry didn't micromanage. Bill

Brashier, who coached with Fry for over twenty years, said, "He hired you because he knew you'd do what you were supposed to." As Dan McCarney, a former assistant who became North Texas's head coach, put it, "He knew more about what we could do than we knew. You can't imagine the kind of confidence and motivation that gives you. It makes you feel like you can't let him down." Fry was a master multiplier; he took great pride in his former assistants' success. In 2011, he said: "I think of these guys as my sons and I follow and watch them all." He added, "It makes you feel good, like you really made a difference in people's lives."

Master mentors aren't necessarily as socially skilled as Hayden Fry, but all find ways to pass on their expertise. Dr. William Halsted of Johns Hopkins University, for example, started the first surgical residency training program in the United States in the late nineteenth century: it included an internship, six years as an assistant resident, and two years as a resident surgeon. He trained many of the most prestigious surgeons of the twentieth century, including Hugh Hampton Young (founder of modern urology surgery) and Harvey Williams Cushing and Walter Dandy (founders of modern brain surgery). Halsted's biographer Gerald Imber described him as "direct, severe, and gentlemanly," a man who showed flashes of charisma but taught largely through example rather than words. Halsted focused intensely on his work, devoting hours to studying and thinking about the smallest details of surgery—down to bandaging patients himself after operations. Yet he rarely knew the names of his interns and assistants. He mostly talked to his senior residents, who were expected to pass on his skills to their junior colleagues.

Halsted's system worked, in large part, because he was so dedicated, competent, and inventive. Although he struggled with cocaine and morphine addiction most of his life, he developed and taught many modern surgical methods, including "aseptic technique" and the use of newly discovered anesthetics. He convinced the DuPont company to develop the first thin surgical gloves and then showed that their use during surgery dramatically reduced infections. Halsted pioneered many surgical procedures: he introduced radical mastectomies for breast cancer, performed one of the first gallstone operations (on his mother, at 2:00 a.m. on her kitchen table), and did one of the first blood transfusions, to name just a few.

Despite his addictions, quirks, and tendency to ignore those under him, Halsted fits the profile of a master multiplier. Even if he didn't know their names, Halsted had a sharp eye for talent and didn't hesitate to remove interns and residents who lacked the necessary drive, skill, and temperament. Much like Hayden Fry, Halsted worked only with young surgeons who he believed had potential for greatness—to be a head surgeon in a large hospital. Finally, despite his attention to detail, after he perfected a technique or procedure, Halsted often lost interest in repeating it. His residents were given the autonomy to perform such operations themselves without him breathing down their necks.

It helped, of course, that Halsted was the most talented and inventive surgeon of his time. Although the best mentors aren't always star performers, all must have a deep understanding of their craft in order to be able to pass along true excellence. For example, Phil Jackson is the most successful professional basketball coach in history, winning eleven National Basketball Association (NBA) championships with the Chicago Bulls and Los Angeles Lakers. Jackson started his career as a player and was on two NBA championship teams. But he was a benchwarmer, not a star player. As a coach, Jackson is adept at identifying and developing talent, has a chess master's knowledge of the game, and is renowned for having a light touch with his players—much more so than other coaches. When his teams play badly, rather than hollering at them, calling time out, and making substitutions, Jackson often sits calmly and lets them work through the rough patches—resisting the temptation to micromanage.

Bring On the Energizers

In chapter 1, we described Facebook's Bootcamp for new engineers—a classic connect-and-cascade process. Mentors are assigned to newcomers who help infect them with Facebook's mindset and knowledge of its code base and practices. But beliefs and behaviors aren't the only thing that cascades during Bootcamp. So do emotions, especially positive energy. University of Virginia's Rob Cross and his colleagues show that positive energy is an especially contagious and crucial emotion for spreading excellence in social networks. They use simple questions to measure if a person is an "energizer" or a "de-energizer" such as: "People can affect the energy and enthusiasm we have at work in various ways. Interactions with some people can leave you feeling drained while others can leave you feeling enthused about possibilities. When you interact with each person below, how does it typically affect your energy level?" The possible answers are: 1 = de-energizing; 2 = no effect/neutral; or 3 = energizing.

Cross and his colleagues find that answers to such "energy" questions predict employee performance evaluations, promotions, and the chances that employees will stay or leave. They've also found that successful and innovative organizations have networks that are swarming with interconnected energizers. Their studies show that such networks hum along, in part, because colleagues seek more information from and learn more from energizers (compared to de-energizers). Energizers also are given more ideas and more help from others and are more likely to have their ideas heard and implemented. Energizers aren't necessarily charismatic, entertaining, or bubbly; Cross observes that many are understated or shy and strike new acquaintances as dull. Yet as their relationships unfold and they reveal their true colors they create energy through their optimism about the possibilities ahead. Energizers also have a knack for fully engaging the person in front of them right now, valuing others' ideas, and creating conditions that enable others to make steady progress.

In short, energizers propel the flow of excellence. This insight brings us back to Facebook and Chris Cox, whom we introduced in chapter 1. Sutton first met Cox in 2007, when, at the tender age of twenty-six, he was Facebook's head of human resources. After talking with Cox for half an hour, Sutton realized:

1. This guy is more mature than most Silicon Valley executives twice his age.
2. I feel so energized by his spirit and his ideas.

Cox has held many other roles at Facebook since, including vice president of product. But regardless of his title, Cox has always played the same key role in the company—which he joined when it had about thirty employees. One insider after another, including Chief Technology Officer Mike Schroepfer (or "Schrep"), has emphasized to us what a constructive force Cox has been throughout Facebook's wild ride. He keeps everyone's spirits up, convinces key people to join the company (and not to leave), and makes them feel proud to be at Facebook. Cox has wickedly strong technical skills; but his contagious energy is rarer and even more valued. As of 2013, Cox was still giving the welcoming talk to almost every new employee, offering his take on the company's history, strategy, and mindset, and transmitting that wonderful positive energy.

The upshot? To spread excellence, it helps to hire, spot, and connect energizers. But almost every organization also has its share of talented *de-energizers.* Many are such downers, and so tough on others, that if rehabilitation fails it may be best to send them packing. Rob Cross's research shows that this is often their fate. But some de-energizers are so valuable that they are worth keeping around. In such cases, two kinds of approaches can be useful. The first applies mostly to skilled individual contributors who drag down colleagues. The idea is to leave them on the payroll but to keep interactions with them as infrequent and brief as possible. As the managing partner of one law firm put it, these are people who "aren't cleared for customer contact." In one organization we know, an ornery but talented engineer had a private office with a door—even though the CEO had an open office. And the de-energizers's office was strategically placed in a back corner where few people ventured. It worked. He communicated mostly via e-mail (where he was fairly civilized), and although he emerged to flame his colleagues and their ideas now and then (and was usually right, they confessed), his closed office and relative isolation kept such unpleasantness to a minimum.

This approach, of course, won't work when de-energizers hold key leadership positions. In such cases, colleagues who are epic energizers can help compensate for and repair the damage. This is what happened during the years that the cold and impersonal Dr. William Halsted produced so many skilled surgeons at Johns Hopkins. Several of his peers were renowned energizers, especially Dr. William Osler, one of the "Big Four" credited with creating modern surgical education. Osler was widely beloved for his warmth, stories, and practical jokes (except by Halsted, who saw him as a clown). He was regularly "seen walking the halls with an arm on a resident or a student or intern" and "was the only senior faculty member who regularly socialized with the students." Halsted was a genius, but he ignored others and often brought them down. Osler, on the other hand, as Halsted's biographer put it, was "in the eyes of all, particularly his juniors, the beating heart of the institution."

Activate Dormant Connections

Over 80 percent of women who own businesses in the United States were Girl Scouts, as were nearly 60 percent of current female U.S.

congressional representatives and 70 percent of female senators. Almost every female U.S. astronaut who has flown in space was a Girl Scout, as were all three U.S. female secretaries of state, and all five female governors of U.S. states in 2013. Yet influential women, even if they had a compelling experience in the Girl Scouts and would like to help the girls it serves, are often engrossed in and distracted by the world around them as adults. Marina Park, the CEO of the Girl Scouts of Northern California (and Sutton's wife) realizes this and often uses these facts to rekindle enthusiasm and garner support for the organization. In particular, Park seeks out women who could be great teachers and role models to young girls and works to reconnect them with the Girl Scouts.

In 2008, Park was among the "150 Most Influential Women" honored at a dinner by the *San Francisco Business Times*. Each honoree was asked to offer ten words of advice (or less). Park told the audience, "Raise your hand if you were ever a Girl Scout." About 75 percent of the women in the room waved their hands; many hooted and hollered, and then there was a roar of applause. After their background as Girl Scouts was made public, Park worked the room and talked to potential supporters and mentors. She also later followed up via e-mail with other honorees she didn't get to speak with in person. Park invited a dozen or so accomplished women to come to "Camp CEO" the next summer to spend three days mentoring underserved teenage girls from Northern California—and several accepted. In addition, several more have since volunteered on key Girl Scout committees and projects.

As Park's actions suggest, there are several intertwined ways that leaders can re-engage potential supporters. First, remind them of the dormant connection. Talk to them about their fond memories and, especially, about their pride in what they accomplished as a member, and later, because of what they gained from being part of the organization. That's exactly what Park did. Next, channel those feelings toward action; gently entice and prod people to rekindle old connections and create new ones, as Park and her colleagues did when they invited women to Camp CEO. Third, make it easy for "renewed recruits" to live the excellence you aim to spread, and in turn, to pass it along—to become part of a domino chain of goodness. Many of the women who attended Camp CEO not only served as mentors during this three-day event, they continued to advise and create opportunities for girls they met at camp for years afterwards. A number of the Camp CEO attendees also convinced other colleagues to join them in helping the Girl Scouts; Park herself was so taken by her experiences at Camp CEO that, after twenty-five years as a corporate lawyer, she changed careers to lead the nonprofit Girl Scouts of Northern California in 2007.

Similar methods can be used to reactivate connections among current and future employees. That is what Marissa Mayer did during her first year as Yahoo!'s CEO. In a playful response to Brad Garlinghouse's Peanut Butter Manifesto, Mayer launched PB&J ("Process, Bureaucracy & Jams") a few weeks after taking the job. She urged employees to share suggestions about making Yahoo! more enjoyable, efficient, and innovative, and she pledged to help implement good ideas and make it easier for employees to work together to solve problems. Within a few months, Mayer and her colleagues implemented hundreds of these ideas, often small things such as removing barriers from parking lots and getting rid of useless training in the employee gym. These small changes— along with bigger ones such as giving every employee an iPhone 5—stirred hope inside the struggling company. People started to believe that Yahoo! could be great again if they worked hard and worked together. Another, especially controversial change cranked up pressure to build stronger connections: Mayer forbade employees to work at home. There were many outcries from employees and pundits. But Mayer insisted on making the move because Yahoo! was plagued with weak connections among employees.

When pockets of excellence did exist, that excellence spread haltingly if at all. Many Yahoo! employees felt alienated from the company and each other.

Yahoo! still faces many perils: brutal competition, an evolving strategy, and cumbersome processes. But Mayer's early moves have generated hope and tangible results. The stock price nearly doubled her first year, and there were hints that connections among employees, and pride in the company, were on the upswing: 50 percent fewer employees were leaving voluntarily than before Mayer arrived. Dormant connections were also reactivated: 14 percent of new hires were "boomerangs," former employees who had returned to Yahoo! And many influential former employees (including Brad Garlinghouse) who had remained silent or been openly critical about Yahoo! for years began expressing support for Mayer and optimism about the firm's prospects.

Connect Everybody: Turn Work into a Game That People Like to Play

Let's face it. Many executives are wary, even downright hostile, about the F word: *fun*. Libby Sartain, who was head of "People" at Southwest Airlines, describes how she got in trouble for "cackling" in the hallways when working at Mary Kay Cosmetics. Sartain says that one reason she moved to Southwest was so she could laugh with reckless abandon. Unfortunately, as a small but growing band of researchers, consultants, and pundits argue, if you apply the standards for good computer game design to evaluate most jobs and organizations, "Work is a lousy game." Stanford communications professor Byron Reeves argues that, compared to popular multiplayer games like World of Warcraft, most organizations don't engage people, don't bond them together, and have poorly designed incentives—but do create unnecessary friction and status differences.

Reeves and other "gamification" advocates assert that work-places would be more fun and effective if the principles for designing computer games were applied to designing organizations. They also argue that computer games ought to be designed and woven into the fabric of work to attract and motivate employees and to enable organizations to operate more effectively. In 2011, the research firm Gartner predicted that by 2015 50 percent of organizations would "gamify" their innovation processes and that by 2014 at least 70 percent of the two thousand largest global companies would have at least one "gamified application" as part of their marketing efforts. Only time will tell if gamification is a fad that will soon fade or if it will become a fixture in modern workplaces. And even people who believe in the future of gamification—such as J. P. Rangaswami, chief scientist at Salesforce.com—point out some important limitations. He argues that some workplaces are so inherently boring and stressful that more basic changes are needed than "putting the lipstick of gamification on the pig of work."

We agree that if an organization is fundamentally oppressive and unfair, with nasty politics and soul-crushing jobs, then adding a few silly games won't help and may be seen as hypocritical. But when work isn't broken—when leaders are respected, processes are fair, and people have engaging jobs—then savvy "gamification" is a promising approach for making work more fun, creating stronger bonds among people, and helping them develop and spread excellence.

Consider Rite-Solutions, a 150-person company where the core business is developing and selling software solutions to the U.S. Navy and casinos. CEO Jim Lavoie and COO Joe Marino are committed to making it a fun and engaging place. As author and innovation evangelist Polly LaBarre tells it: "At Rite-Solutions, you start to get the message you matter at 9 a.m. on your first day of work. That's when the company throws you a birthday bash, complete with wrapped presents and cake. While you're being feted by your new colleagues, your family gets a 'welcome wagon' of flowers, gifts, and a personal note delivered at home."

Lavoie and Marino, of course, are in it for the money too, not just for fun. But they wanted to figure how to best engage and link employees to generate ideas that Rite-Solutions could develop or sell to others. They believed that getting people to start generating ideas wouldn't be hard; the problem was saying no to ideas without destroying enthusiasm. Past experience had taught Lavoie and Marino that most new ideas need to be killed because many are bad and others are not feasible right now. It is also wise to kill many good ideas: it is usually smarter, say, to devote enough time and resources to develop one or two ideas well than to spread efforts too thinly across ten or fifteen promising ideas. To kill them off, many firms use "murder boards," committees that not only kill ideas but subject the people who propose them to withering criticism, even ridicule. Colleagues who witness such ugliness tend to keep their ideas to themselves lest they suffer the same fate.

Lavoie and Marino used a "gamification strategy" to entice employees throughout Rite-Solutions to generate a broad swath of ideas, select and develop a few, and kill most of them. Rao and Stanford case writer David Hoyt documented the details of an online game called Mutual Fun, which was designed to make the process of coming up with new ideas for the company—and killing them—fun, motivating, and safe, while at the same time building stronger bonds between people in the company. Rao and Hoyt learned that Mutual Fun was played by 95 percent of Rite-Solutions' employees. As LaBarre says, "It's a colorful, intuitive and immediately engaging platform—think Bloomberg terminal meets Monopoly board." This internal stock market has three categories:

1. "Savings Bonds," ideas that could save the company money or increase efficiency
2. "Bow Jones," ideas that use existing technology to create new products or services
3. "SPAZDAQ," ideas about new technologies

After an employee submits a new idea, it is quickly and lightly screened by a senior engineer and listed in Mutual Fun. Every employee gets $10,000 of play opinion money to invest in their colleagues' "idea stocks." The game also enables employees to discuss ideas and volunteer to work on them (on their own time). Stocks that attract more play money and volunteers move up in value; the firm invests "Adventure Capital" (real money) in the top fifteen stocks. For example, Rebecca Hosch, Lavoie's assistant, proposed an educational tool called "Win/Play/Learn" (WPL) based on a bingo algorithm that Rite-Solutions developed for casinos. WPL "became a hot property on Mutual Fun and was ultimately licensed by toy-maker Hasbro." Stocks that don't attract investors are delisted but often spark new proposals. When an idea saves money or produces revenue, creators and implementers share the gains—with a greater percentage going to implementers.

As of 2011, Mutual Fun had generated more than fifty innovative ideas; fifteen had been launched and accounted for over 20 percent of the firm's revenue. In addition to "Win/Play/Learn," they've sold several other ideas to other companies, including Mutual Fun itself. Mutual Fun helps Rite-Solutions generate strong ideas and kill weak ones, while enabling employees to build bonds with each other and the company. It is one of the reasons that Lavoie and Marino have "cultivated an almost unshakable loyalty among their people" and enjoy "near zero turnover and constant peer referrals of the best and the brightest."

Making Nets Work

When it comes to scaling excellence, network diagrams—and old-fashioned organizational charts—can be a helpful starting point. But drawing and discussing such orderly images can become seductive diversions. Organizational life is messier than those tidy illustrations suggest. For those charged with scaling up an organization, *your job isn't to draw a network diagram; it is to get the "net"—the organization—to work.* Scaling doesn't succeed until the networks you build are buzzing with constructive actions that reflect and reinforce the goodness that you aim to spread.

In this spirit, we offer seven tools for "making nets work," different approaches for configuring and activating domino chains of excellence. But before we describe these tools, we propose two overarching rules: *Once is not enough* and *One is not enough*.

Our first rule is *Once is not enough* because beliefs and behaviors do not spread like contagious diseases—one exposure is rarely enough to infect people. If you want a mindset to stick, you've got to pummel people with multiple messages and exposures to get people to remember, accept, and live it. Antanas Mockus, the brilliant and eccentric former mayor of Bogota, Colombia, applied this rule to nudge, annoy, and embarrass the citizens of his chaotic and dangerous city to drive and walk more safely. He called attention to these problems (and to excessive water usage and crime) by running around the streets in a Superman costume pretending to be a superhero called "Supercitizen." His office distributed 350,000 "thumbs-up" and "thumbs-down" cards and asked citizens to give each other feedback about their driving and behavior as pedestrians. Mockus had shooting stars painted on sidewalks and roads where people died in accidents—reminders to be more careful. Most famously, he hired 420 mimes and sent them out to tease and taunt reckless drivers and pedestrians: his theory was that citizens were more afraid of embarrassment than traffic tickets.

By the time Mockus ended his eight years as mayor in 2003, this pummeling of his citizens' senses was working: traffic accidents had fallen by over 60 percent and fatalities by over 50 percent.

Our second rule, *One is not enough,* follows from the first. Each tool isn't right for every scaling challenge. Nor are all tools mutually exclusive. Using a blend of two or more is usually better than relying on just one. In a company or nonprofit, for example, you might combine a message from the CEO that urges people to reduce energy costs in your organization with a bazaar or trade show–style event where people set up tables or booths and share methods they've used to reduce such costs. The blend of the two methods is likely to be more effective than either alone. Not only do multiple tools increase the rate of polite pummeling, but different people are attracted to and motivated by different tools. Some people might be more strongly influenced by pressure from management or their direct reports, others by exchanging ideas with peers from other parts of the organization in a bazaar. The idea is to provide people with multiple "on-ramps" to get them on the road to embracing and living the mindset you aim to spread.

Here is our menu of seven tools for getting nets to work.

1. The Top-Down Approach

As we saw in chapter 4, although many people are ambivalent about hierarchies, all groups and organizations have them and need them to survive and thrive. Hierarchies come in handy for creating a domino chain reaction that starts from the top and cascades down the pecking order. For example, Denny Strigl, former CEO of Verizon Wireless, was concerned because, a few months after Verizon introduced text messaging, few customers were buying this feature. He also noticed that few Verizon employees were texting. So he decided to cascade this behavior to those he knew and could best influence others—his direct reports. As he put it,

"If our own employees weren't convinced that texting was something useful, there was little likelihood we were going to convince customers of its value." Strigl started by texting each vice president who reported to him. When no one responded, he called each to say "I would be using text messaging a lot, and I expected them to do the same." When he sent the next text, his vice presidents all responded right away. Strigl continued to text each one every day. Most responded immediately; if they didn't, he called them or dropped by their offices to ask them why they hadn't answered. Soon his vice presidents were, in turn, texting their direct reports and following up when their underlings didn't respond. Whenever Strigl spoke to groups of Verizon employees, he asked who had sent a text message that day. At first there were only a few raised hands; soon they all went up. Just about every employee was using text messages at work—which helped them explain it to customers and friends and families too.

This is a textbook example of a behavior rolling down a hierarchy. But for more complex and controversial changes, command-and-demand often isn't enough.

2. Broadcast Your Message Out to One and All

Webinars, brochures, mailings, websites, and gatherings where senior executives make speeches to employees are part of many scaling efforts. They can signal that the ideas leaders and teams aim to spread are important, teach people about the content, and pique interest. But such "air war" tactics alone are rarely enough to persuade people to join on and help expand a movement. The Institute for Health Improvement broadcast *Campaign Live,* a weekly program that people participated in by phone or the Web that was hosted by Madge Kaplan, a former National Public Radio health reporter. When Rao visited IHI's offices in Boston, he sat in on a show where over one thousand listeners from across America posed dozens of questions to a panel about "pressure ulcers"—bedsores and how to reduce them. Yet, as we saw, campaign manager Joe McCannon knew that this and other one-way broadcasts weren't enough to connect hospitals that mastered life-saving practices to other hospitals that wanted to learn such practices. Creating those strong ties required ground war tactics: personal e-mails, phone calls, and especially face-to-face interaction.

Mitchell Baker, the founding CEO (and now chair) of the Mozilla Corporation, writes a blog about the company and related topics that is read by employees and thousands of people in Mozilla's open-source community who write code, do quality control checks, and spread their software. Baker has had a public blog since the company's early days, when she spearheaded the effort to spin out an open-source project "trapped" inside Netscape. It eventually became the Firefox browser, which has generated hundreds of millions of dollars for Mozilla. *Lizard Wrangling—Mitchell on Mozilla & More* is among the most detailed and bluntest blogs we've ever read by a senior executive. Baker presents nuanced financial information, describes changes in senior executives, and talks openly about tough challenges—including the revenue and market share that Firefox has lost as millions of users have switched from personal computers to tablets and smart phones. But Baker would be the first to tell you that—although her broadcasting helps—Mozilla's vast international footprint has spread largely via personal connections made between people who develop, test, and promote Firefox (often via connections formed on the Web between programmers and other supporters who never met in person).

3. Surround Them: Have the Many Teach the Few

One of the most effective—if inefficient—ways to spread new behaviors and beliefs is to take one person, or a small team, and embed them among large numbers of people who already eat, live, and breathe the mindset that you want them to embrace. Everywhere they turn, someone is there to model the right behavior, teach and coach them, and correct them when they aren't saying or doing things that are quite right by local standards. A few years back, Sutton interviewed Captain Nick Gottuso, then a captain in the Hillsborough, California, police department and leader of the twelve-person sniper squad for the local SWAT team. Gottuso explained that the skills required to be on the squad were so difficult to learn, their worldview was so subtle and so strong, and the level of coordination required during hostage crises and other situations where firing their weapons might be necessary was so high that the squad could integrate only one or two new members per year.

4. One on One: The Power of Pairs

This tool is core to most successful scaling efforts: nearly all depend at least partly on dyads where each "domino" topples the next. It was at the heart of the 100,000 Lives Campaign. Once a hospital, for example, became expert in reducing pneumonia for patients on ventilators, its staff changed from being students to teachers—and mentored another hospital. The power of pairs is central to Facebook's Bootcamp: each new engineer has a mentor to provide coaching, answer questions, and link the newcomer to the ten or twelve groups he or she will work with during the six-week program. Pairing teachers and learners is also essential for scaling talent. Zynga, which makes "social" Web-based games such as FarmVille, has a policy that encourages managers to mentor direct reports: you can't get a promotion to the next level unless you "grow your own replacement."

Pairings are also critical for spreading change: not just for teaching new ideas and skills but also for persuading others to support and smooth implementation. A key challenge in using this approach is figuring who is best paired with whom. One strategy is to match "socially similar" people or units. That way, each "teacher" can better empathize with the challenges that each "learner" faces. And those being taught can't complain, "You're so different from me [or us], you couldn't possibly understand." About ten years ago, Sutton and Rao both worked with a fast-food chain that paired high-performing and low-performing franchisees. The high performers then coached low performers. The company provided incentives so that, if the weak store in the pair improved, the franchisee running the strong store was paid a handsome bonus. Because of internal politics, the program never got past the pilot stage. But early results were promising, in large part, because the company formed pairs that were similar in so many ways: in terms of franchisees' personal backgrounds, store employees' backgrounds, customer mix, neighborhoods served (e.g., urban vs. rural, rich vs. poor), sales volume, and so on.

Is it better to pair "persuaders" from a scaling team with individuals who support, reject, or are unsure about the brand of excellence in question? Julie Battilana of Harvard and Tiziana Casciaro of the University of Toronto spent years studying this question. They tracked sixty-eight diverse change initiatives in the United Kingdom's National Health Service between 1997 and 2004. These programs ranged from an effort to reduce the number of days that stroke patients were hospitalized to one that transferred authority for discharging patients from doctors to nurses. The odds of a successful implementation were high when change agents already had close relationships with influential leaders in a hospital, clinic, or administrative unit *and* those leaders supported the initiative. But when change agents had close relationships with leaders who strongly opposed the change ("resisters"), not only did they fail to convince them to implement the program, there were signs that such influence attempts backfired: the leaders' resistance stiffened further. Battilana and Casciaro did find, however, that when change agents had close ties to "fence-sitters"—leaders who were ambivalent about the change—they were often able to convince these reluctant friends and close colleagues with their logic and charm and to persuade them to implement it.

The upshot? When it comes to one-on-one influence, focus on supporters and fence-sitters. Try to pair the "persuaders" on your scaling team with powerful people who already trust and admire them. Beware of pairing up with resisters. Even if they are good friends and those resisters otherwise admire your skills and judgment, your efforts may provoke them to harden their positions and may damage your relationship.

5. From the Few to the Many

This is the classic scaling strategy: a group of determined people bands together and labors to slowly spread their mindset, and associated actions and skills, throughout an organization or other network. The Tiger Team that Louise Liang led at Kaiser Permanente (KP) is a good example. Recall from chapter 2 how they developed a new mindset to guide the design and rollout of KP HealthConnect. The centerpiece was "Home as Hub," which the Tiger Team believed was "a 180-degree shift in how health care is seen throughout the world" because homes and other nontraditional settings would become the primary places where patients received health care rather than hospitals and clinics. And such care would be provided by nurses and a host of other professionals "beyond the physician." The Tiger Team had only about thirty core members but—by helping, converting, and recruiting hundreds of KP employees, and hiring a small army of consultants to help with IT chores—they were able to spread an electronic health record system to some 170,000 employees and 9 million patients. As they worked with health care providers throughout KP, and providers and their patients started using KP HealthConnect, this mindset shift to "Home as Hub" started taking hold. And it is still happening at KP and, now, in most other large U.S. health care systems.

When we talked to Louise Liang, she emphasized that the Tiger Team believed that both the operation of the system and KP's long-term success depended on this shift—it was needed to cut skyrocketing health care costs, while providing patients with better and more flexible care. Liang called the technology a "Trojan Horse" that helped the Tiger Team smuggle in a new mindset. Another of our scaling heroes, Claudia Kotchka, used the same phrase to describe how her team infiltrated Procter & Gamble.

One aspect of Kotchka's strategy, and "perhaps the most effective part," entailed "hiring and putting experienced designers in each business unit." She called this the "Trojan Horse effect" because, once they got a "seat at the table" and worked with a business's leadership team, these experienced innovators did what came naturally to them—using design thinking to solve problems. The connect-and-cascade process kicked in: as they helped colleagues in other disciplines solve problems, not only did these colleagues come to value the innovators' knowledge and skills, but many learned and began applying the methods themselves. Kotchka discovered a related lesson about implanting "Trojan Horses": putting just one designer in a business didn't work. They felt lonely and didn't have like-minded coworkers to bounce ideas off and serve as allies. So Kotchka insisted on placing at least two experienced innovators in a business or none at all.

The key, as experiences at both Kaiser Permanente and P&G show, is that successful scaling depends on never forgetting that you are fighting a ground war rather than an air war. The few must use their grit and skill to teach and convert others, who, in turn, start the domino chain of goodness in motion. One participant in a Stanford executive program, after he heard Kotchka's P&G story, summed up this lesson: "What you're telling us, Claudia, is that it is cool to have a great little design thinking group for a little while, but if you are in a big company, pretty soon, it becomes a matter of 'infect others or die.'" She didn't disagree.

6. Brokers: Bridging Disconnected Islands

Brokering is an especially powerful version of the "one to many" and "few to the many" tools. As we've seen, disconnection in an organization is the enemy of scaling. Recall how Master Sergeant Chad Walker's unit didn't learn about the "IED defeat handbook" developed by the Center for Army Lessons Learned (CALL) until their last month in combat. When a pocket of people have got something good, but no path connects them and their knowledge to others who need it, excellence can't spread.

Research by sociologist Ronald Burt shows that many organizations are divided into disconnected silos, camps, geographical settings, departments, teams, and roles. When Burt and his colleagues document how different units or employees interact, they often find "nodes" that have no direct or indirect connections— just as there were no links between Walker's combat unit and CALL. Burt calls these "structural holes"—they are the white space between disconnected "nodes" in a network. This is where people and groups called "brokers" or "knowledge brokers" come in—they become bridges between otherwise disconnected people, groups, or organizations. Brokers "fill" these holes and transfer information, expertise, ideas, and influence between those who have it and those who need it. For example, a few years after his disturbing experience with CALL's disconnection from his combat unit, Master Sergeant Walker became CALL's senior enlisted adviser. Essentially, Walker became a broker. He used his connections to combat leaders and units in Iraq and Afghanistan to spread the word about CALL—many didn't know it existed before Walker reached out to them. And he encouraged them to connect with CALL's staff and one another—for example, through one of CALL's thirty-five online forums, such as NCO Net, which is open only to noncommissioned officers.

Many other scaling teams we've talked about also bridged disconnected nodes. Recall how Heather Vilhauer's team spread and refined the Thrive program for the Girl Scouts. They linked the Thrive Foundation (and their knowledge) to participating girls and adult volunteers. Other brokers we've encountered build bridges in big bureaucracies. The "Alpha Team," those twenty-four managers in Singapore's Ministry of Manpower who learned design thinking, became a conduit to colleagues in their own ministry and other government agencies. Louise Liang's Tiger Team filled many structural holes (as Burt would put it), connecting historically siloed Kaiser Permanente regions—which enabled lessons from regions that implemented KP HealthConnect to travel to sister units and regions.

David Kelley, the primary founder of IDEO and the Stanford d.school, is the most effective broker whom we know well. The ways he thinks and acts are instructive to any bridge builder bent on scaling up excellence. In 2002, the d.school existed only as an elaborate fantasy in Kelley's mind. But Kelley kept telling everyone he knew that he was determined to build a gathering place for students and faculty at Stanford—and for inventive and caring people from every part of the world. Kelley wanted a place that blended and connected people who didn't usually work together or talk to one another but would benefit if they did. And he wanted a place that taught design thinking, used it to tackle tough problems, and was packed with people who had diverse talents and connections—people who would improve design thinking and expand its reach.

A glance at the more than fifty classes that the d.school offered in 2012 and 2013 shows that Kelley's dream has come true. To give you a taste, these classes included "Disruptive Solutions for

Poverty in America," "d Media: Designing Media That Matters," "Sex and Design," "Design for Science," "From Play to Innovation," "LaunchPad: Design and Launch Your Product or Service," and "Rebooting Government with Design Thinking." The d.school is part of the Stanford School of Engineering, but it brings together students and faculty from all corners of the campus: business, education, medicine, law, sociology, psychology, philosophy, and art, as well as engineering. Some classes are taught by full-time faculty, but many are taught by people with "real" jobs outside Stanford. For example, Maryanna Rogers, who teaches "d.science," is the director of innovation at the Tech Museum of Innovation. Brendan Boyle, who teaches "From Play to Innovation," is a partner at IDEO. In addition to these fifty classes, the d.school has hosted an endless parade of projects, executive programs, community outreach efforts, workshops, tours, alumni reunions, and parties over the past decade.

While many people deserve credit for the d.school's success, none of this would have happened without Kelley's masterful brokering. We've boiled down his efforts to five key elements:

1. *He is curious about strangers and their ideas.* Kelley has such a broad network, in large part, because he is relentlessly interested in and eager to meet people who know things that he doesn't—and to have detailed conversations with them. This penchant for collecting diverse people has led him to meet, talk, and work with faculty and students from every corner of Stanford. This breadth is bolstered by Kelley's network beyond Stanford. He hangs out with everyone from car geeks, to architects, to rock musicians, to cooks, to actors, to the owner of the oldest distillery in Utah—as well as lots of engineers, entrepreneurs, and executives. His diverse network spills into the d.school. It isn't unusual to meet, say, a biologist, a sociologist, a physician, an M.B.A. student, the

CEO of a nonprofit, a high school teacher, a filmmaker, and a sculptor during a ten-minute stroll through the place.

2. *He lives and breathes the mindset but isn't obnoxious about it.* Kelley balances this breadth of contacts, experience, and ideas with a strong point of view. Somehow, in the course of a conversation with almost anyone on anything, he manages to gently interject his view of life and design thinking. Whether he talks to a nineteen-year-old undergrad about her major or the comedian Robin Williams, he somehow teaches them an intriguing bit of design thinking and helps them apply it to some personal challenge or problem—often right on the spot.

3. *He has strong opinions, weakly held.* Kelley has and expresses strong views about design thinking and the d.school. But he does not cling to them irrationally. He routinely changes course (often radically) when he decides doing so is best for the project he is working on, the d.school, IDEO, or other groups or people whom he influences.

4. *He listens and learns.* It is difficult to learn from others when you are "all transmission and no reception." In contrast, Kelley asks more questions and makes fewer statements than any senior executive we've ever met. He gives advice only after hearing what you need. And Kelley is adept at using what he gleans from all that listening for his own benefit. For the d.school, this means using others' stories and ideas to improve design thinking and how the place operates.

5. *He convenes, introduces, and connects.* Kelley is constantly connecting people who can help the d.school teach more compelling classes and serve its students and faculty better. As one of his friends puts it, Kelley is a "convener" of people who ought to know each other but don't know that yet—through everything from throwing parties, to planned

"matchmaking," to bringing in visitors to tour the d.school. Whether David is giving a tour to the CEO of a big company or a student who is thinking about taking a class, he connects them to others in his charming way—introducing his guest to almost everyone who walks by and then explaining why they really need to know each other.

David Kelley is skilled and relentless in his efforts to link people, teams, and organizations that need each other—but hadn't known that before. But he isn't unique. These five hallmarks reflect the ways that many other successful brokers whom we've known, studied ourselves, and read about in scholarly articles approach life and spend their time.

7. Create Crossroads Where People Connect

Bazaars are largely self-organizing and sometimes rather chaotic "marketplaces" that bring together "sellers" and "buyers." The word *bazaar* comes from the Persian word for "market." It conjures up images of ancient people gathered in the town square to sell and buy wares, as well as modern variants such as flea markets, farmers' markets, and street fairs. When it comes to scaling excellence in and across organizations, bazaarlike settings enable people to build new connections and strengthen old ones—largely through one-on-one interactions. Additional examples include trade shows; job fairs; "poster sessions," where scientists from the R&D organization display and discuss their findings; and a meeting of the Vermont Oxford Network (which focuses on improving care for newborn infants) that Sutton attended, where staff from several dozen neonatal intensive care units (NICUs) gathered together for a couple hours in a convention hall: staff manned tables displaying their unit's infant mortality rate and provided information about steps they were taking to improve the care they gave.

Regardless of the exact form they take, bazaars set the stage for the informal exchange of ideas, emotions, plans, goods, and money that help individuals and teams and, in doing so, strengthen a larger network.

For example, StartX is a small nonprofit broker that links Stanford students, postdocs, professors, and alumni who have ideas for starting companies to a network of mentors and funders. Since StartX was founded in 2010, over 2,400 people from one thousand young companies have applied to this "start-up accelerator;" ninety companies have been accepted. "Demo Day" is one place that StartX companies make connections. Demo Day used to be as much "broadcast" as "bazaar": ten or so start-ups each did a five-minute pitch to a couple hundred potential mentors, funders, customers, and employees that attended. In 2013, Demo Day shifted to "very brief pitches on stage, without any of the typical slide shows," so they could "get right to the good part": talking with those mentors, funders, and purveyors of other rocket fuel that a new company needs to get off the ground.

Recall Chris Fry and Steve Greene, who grew Salesforce's development organization from forty to six hundred people. They ran a different kind of bazaar, an internal job fair, to create connections and increase accountability among team leaders and developers. As we saw in chapter 4, developers were free to move to new teams without getting permission from bosses—and could do so every four months. Fry and Greene's goal was to make it as easy to change jobs within Salesforce as it was to move to a new company. An active internal job market emerged as team leaders wooed skilled developers from other teams—and worked to keep their own top performers from jumping ship. Fry added that another advantage of the internal market was that it exposed weak team leaders—who couldn't keep good people—to senior management.

This market was stoked by a job fair held every four months, just before developers had the chance to switch teams. Fry told us that, typically, about fifty teams participated and that it "worked like poster sessions at a conference; each team had boards that described their work and staffed a booth." They served drinks to create a light and friendly atmosphere. Developers wandered around and had informal conversations with the leaders and other members of teams they wanted to learn more about and possibly join. Greene added that, although team leaders and potential new members did size one another up, the main focus was "on a developer meeting the other team members, talking about the cool work they were doing and seeing if they all liked each other and the work." Every now and then, a leader made an offer to a developer and he or she accepted: about 20 percent of Salesforce's developers choose to change teams each year.

Create a Common Heartbeat

Recent studies show that when people share rhythms with others they develop stronger emotional bonds and are more likely to pitch in for the common good. One study showed that even when a pair of strangers had never met before and didn't talk, they still liked each other more if both simply walked in the same direction together, rather than in different directions. Another study found that married couples that commute in the same direction rather than different directions are more satisfied with their relationships. This finding held true whether they commuted alone or with others and whether or not the partners left for work at the same time. Another "rhythm" study used the Canadian national anthem, "O Canada." When people sang or danced together as they listened to "O Canada," rather than sitting with others and reading the words to themselves as they heard the song, they were more likely to donate money to a common pot as opposed to keeping it all for themselves.

Stanford's Chip Heath speculates that rhythmic marching, dancing, and singing have an evolutionary basis: groups where members are "in synch" with each other have stronger emotional connections and are more adept at the coordination and cooperation required to gather and grow food and defend themselves—and thus have members who are more likely to survive and breed. Individual members who are unable, or too selfish, to synchronize their actions with others in their tribe or group are exposed, shunned, and thus less likely to breed.

When people share the same daily, weekly, monthly, and seasonal rhythms, connections among them form faster and stay stronger. The people trust each other more deeply, and coordination becomes easier because they see and experience the world in the same way. After all, they are frequently in the same place, doing the same things, and working on the same problems together. In this vein, we've encountered several organizations that use regular stand-up meetings to maintain strong bonds, keep fresh information flowing, and reinforce a shared mindset. A few years back, Sutton talked with David Darragh, the CEO of New Orleans–based Reily Foods, about the fifteen-minute stand-up meeting he has with his top management team every weekday (except Mondays, when they have a longer sit-down meeting). Darragh explained, "The rhythm that frequency generates allows relationships to develop, personal tics to be understood, stressors to be identified, personal strengths and weaknesses to be put out in the light of day, etc. All of this not only helps the members of the team understand their individual roles but to also understand how they can get the best out of one another."

Not only do these daily meetings strengthen connections in the team, they also mean that members have a constant supply of fresh information about the challenges that Reily faces and solutions that are and are not working. This information then cascades through the company. Darragh added that news about pressing problems often emerges during the daily meetings: a member of the team is assigned as a "steward" on the spot and then quickly assembles a team to tackle it. Darragh said he prefers the word *steward* rather than *leader* because he doesn't want to let the rest of the team off the hook—all should feel accountable and be ready to jump in and help as needed.

A stand-up meeting called "the daily scrum" is a key element of most "agile" software development methods. Agile approaches are relatively rapidly paced, collaborative, improvisational, and unstructured methods for developing software, as compared to more traditional top-down, plan-driven, "waterfall" approaches. Under most agile methods, the work—writing a new piece of software or fixing bugs—is synchronized with and divided into two- to six-week chunks called "sprints." During daily scrums, each team member answers three questions: (1) What did you do yesterday? (2) What will you do today? and (3) Are there any impediments in your way? Then, much as happens at Reily Foods, fellow team members jump in to give advice and make plans to help team members overcome challenges.

Chris Fry and Steve Greene implemented agile methods at Salesforce to bond people within and across teams, focus them on shared goals, and encourage cooperative and fast-paced work throughout the development organization. Fry described these as intertwined "iteration rhythms" in a "time-boxed environment" where teams worked in two- to four-week "sprints" to produce prototypes. Every team in the development organization "had demos or sprint reviews once a month" where they showed their work to executives and other teams. This meant, as Fry explained, that "we had a monthly rhythm of getting visibility into every single team across the organization." Finally, "There was a release rhythm, which was every four months, three times a year. And they were always the same distance apart"—where finished software products were released and made available to clients. In short, four intertwined rhythms—daily scrums, sprints every two to four weeks, monthly demos, and releases every four months—bound together everyone in each team and throughout the organization even as everyone worked on different (but interconnected) tasks. By the time Fry and Greene left Salesforce to move to Twitter, the development organization "had delivered roughly forty major releases with thousands of people working on them, all on time, down to the day." Fry concluded that, "It is not the meetings that matter; it is the rhythm that matters."

Leaders as Connectors: Three Litmus Tests

As we've emphasized in this chapter, scaling requires leaders to find or develop pockets of excellence, connect people and teams, and ensure that excellence continues to flow through those ties. We've seen that such leadership can come from people or teams at the top, the middle, or the bottom of organizations. And we've shown that there are many ways to skin this cat—from the rental of a campaign bus by Joe McCannon's team for the 100,000 Lives Campaign, to Claudia Kotchka's success at installing those "Trojan Horse" design thinkers in P&G businesses, to surgeons who learned world-class skills from working alongside Dr. William Halsted at Johns Hopkins.

The key lesson is that scaling is propelled by leaders who think and act like "connectors." A big part of this role involves exposing or creating links that ought to be made for the greater good. Many scaling veterans are adept at asking questions that reveal missing or weak links, which sets the stage for building stronger networks. For example, during the decades that HP founders Bill

Hewlett and David Packard led the company, they routinely had in-depth, and often tough, conversations with the general managers and teams that ran key HP businesses: pressing them to prove that they were making great products and had even better ones on the drawing board, and insisting that they meet and learn from people elsewhere in HP who could help their businesses—or who needed their help. And while being a high-ranking and powerful connector like Bill or David helps get people's attention and spurs them to act, it isn't essential. As we saw with Joe McCannon and Master Sergeant Chad Walker, some of the most savvy connectors are skilled at asking and acting on questions that uncover weak or missing links—but wield little formal authority and don't have powerful carrots and sticks at their disposal.

There are also more subtle ways to expose weak or missing connections. We propose two litmus tests that emerged from Rao's conversations with a group of fifty CFOs at a Stanford executive program. Rao suggested the first litmus test to the CFOs on the basis of our conversations with other senior executives. You ask diverse members of the team, department, or organization about key aspects of their strategy, operations, policies, philosophy, and pressing problems they face. If they give you inconsistent and clashing answers to your queries, it is a sign of trouble—especially if they seem to have no knowledge or interest in the other answers that their colleagues give you. The CFOs agreed that such inconsistencies suggest that people aren't talking to each other enough and don't know enough about one another's skills, contributions, opinions, or views on how the team or organization ought to operate—that the bonds among them are too weak and that they aren't operating on the basis of a shared mindset. These are symptoms that you are dealing with an organization—or part of one—where, as writer and poet Gertrude Stein once said (about Oakland, California), "There is no there there."

The CFOs suggested a second litmus test, a diagnostic question: Is there more direct evidence that people are having a lot of one-on-one interactions, or conversely, that there is little if any interaction? The CFOs suggested watching what people do: if they talk informally, look at each other, and go to lunch together. In a healthy business, you will see subtle but frequent exchanges such as smiles, winks, and quick conversations that suggest strong human bonds and a constant flow of information. In unhealthy businesses, interactions will be infrequent and strained, and if you hang around for a while you will notice that people behave as if their colleagues were invisible. One CFO suggested that weak connections can also be gleaned from the e-mails that people send and don't send: there may be occasional blasts to the group as a whole but little evidence of one-on-one exchanges or that people are reaching out to create or strengthen ties with coworkers. Such workplaces feel a bit like a group dental practice, hair salon, or real estate office where there is a shared receptionist but each dentist, stylist, or agent has his or her own book of business and thinks and acts like a free agent. One especially bad sign (which we've seen in too many universities we've visited) is when people have been members of the same group or department for years but don't know where each other's offices are located.

The upshot is, when a leader hears inconsistent and clashing answers from people who ought to be talking and exchanging information (litmus test #1) and observes silence, shallow and infrequent interactions, and related signs that people are "alone together" (litmus test #2), these are symptoms that people are not living a shared mindset and that smart ideas and effective practices are not flowing through a network. When that happens, a leader's job is to use tools and tactics like those described in this chapter to start connecting people and cascading excellence.

Another part of a connector's role is to snip or weaken links that create tunnel vision or distorted and dangerous views of reality. When people are too closely connected they can lose the ability to imagine, hear, or remember—let alone act on—information that clashes with their beliefs and ingrained behaviors. Consider a study by Rao and his colleagues on why it took so long for researchers at the Centers for Disease Control to correctly identify the West Nile virus—they mistook it for Saint Louis encephalitis. These researchers focused on diseases in human populations and were members of a fairly tight-knit and prestigious network—which led them to ignore twenty-seven thoughtful questions and suggestions from less prestigious researchers who specialized in how diseases spread among animals. As a result, the Centers for Disease Control misdiagnosed the disease.

Those researchers were much like many other powerful teams that try to do good work but fail. They were imprisoned in a web of connections of their own making that filtered out crucial opposing views and new information. And they intimidated and chased away people and groups that tried to give them disconfirming advice. Ultimately, their tunnel vision condemned them to waste time, reach a flawed conclusion, and embarrass themselves.

There is a similar danger within organizations and projects that are led by very tight-knit and powerful scaling teams. Leaders and other members of such teams can delude themselves about the wisdom and impact of their actions. They may suffer from what psychologists call "confirmation bias," the tendency to trust, remember, and act only on information that supports what you already believe. Confirmation bias is fueled when they reward subordinates and peers who flatter them, skew the data to confirm their views, screen out messengers and messages that deliver news they don't want to hear—and ridicule and punish people who present them with uncomfortable truths they don't want to accept.

This challenge raises a third and final litmus test for leaders and powerful scaling teams: Have you done everything possible to make sure that the ties that bind you don't also blind you?

CHAPTER 7

BAD IS STRONGER THAN GOOD

Clearing the Way for Excellence

Disneyland is advertised as "the Happiest Place on Earth." That may sound hokey. And you might not be a fan of Disney parks. But it's hard to argue with the company's commitment to bringing that mindset to life. Disney's managers, frontline employees, researchers, engineers, and "imagineers" who design the parks fret and sweat over the smallest details. They experiment with and study virtually every aspect of their "guests'" experience: the logistics of dealing with large crowds; the nuances of how their buildings, landscaping, and seating shape what guests think and feel; the tiny details of each "attraction" (i.e., rides and shows), the uniforms, sounds, smells; and how cast members ought to interact with guests.

As Disney executive Karin Kricorian discussed in chapter 1, the cast is taught to be especially vigilant about spotting and eliminating "dissonant details" that can undermine guests' good cheer. This vigilance is reflected in hundreds of ingrained actions and decisions. Take the efforts to keep the parks squeaky clean. As

Forbes contributor and communication specialist Carmine Gallo writes, "While most Disneyland guests look up at the rides, I look down at the ground. Disneyland is notable for what you don't see—wrappers, gum, or spilled popcorn. I'm always amazed that thousands of people can walk down Disneyland's Main Street and yet it remains spotless."

This attention to dissonant details is especially impressive when it comes to the rare guest who gets angry or upset. Every cast member—from street sweepers, to ride operators, to food servers, to executives who are working in the park for a day or two (which happens often)—is schooled to move in quickly when a guest is visibly upset, sobbing, or otherwise coming unglued. The company uses lectures, role playing, and constant coaching and feedback to teach the cast to be calm and supportive, to listen and empathize, and—when warranted—to apologize and make amends on the park's behalf. They are taught to gently guide particularly distraught guests to private, or at least less crowded, locations. Cast members are also trained to be attuned to more subtle signs of unhappiness, such as a child who looks sad or bored, or a dad who looks irritated or frustrated. They are adept at creating "magical moments" that lift such guests' spirits. Of course, children, and a surprising number of adults, are cheered by encounters with characters in Mickey Mouse or Goofy costumes. But cast members from street sweepers to executives working the front line use smiles, friendly jokes, and kind words to lift the spirits of guests who strike them as a bit down or upset—consciously following their Disney training to be "aggressively friendly."

Disney has its own special brand of excellence. As in other cases of successful scaling, Disney cast members act as if eliminating the negative is at least as important as amplifying the positive. And that's the message of this chapter. Destructive behaviors of just about every stripe—selfishness, nastiness, anxiety, laziness, dishonesty, for example—pack a bigger wallop than constructive

behaviors. That may seem unfair. But leaders and teams in organizations that scale effectively realize that, to clear the way for
spreading and sustaining something good, they've got to take out
the bad and keep it out.

Indeed, "Bad is stronger than good" is the conclusion that Florida State psychologist Roy Baumeister and his colleagues reached
after examining more than two hundred studies. They found that
a little bit of bad undermined a whole lot of good everywhere they
looked, that "bad emotions, bad parents, and bad feedback have
more impact than good ones, and bad information is processed
more thoroughly than good." They discovered that bad events have
a stronger, more lasting impact than good ones and that negative
actions and feelings are more contagious than positive—regardless
of whether they occur during interactions with strangers or loved
ones, and whether they occur during fleeting moments, such as
when people are shown pictures of happy versus angry people,
or during major life events such as getting married or divorced.
Research on dating and marriage is especially revealing—and
instructive for anyone who wants their relationship to endure.
Studies of married couples show that the absence of negative interactions is far more important to their relationships than the presence of positive interactions—and predict if couples stay married
or get divorced. Such findings led psychologist John Gottman to
propose the five-to-one rule: "for a relationship to succeed, positive and good interactions must outnumber the negative and bad
ones by at least five to one."

There is sound evidence that "bad is stronger than good" in
organizational life too. A variation of the five-to-one rule was uncovered when the moods of forty-one employees were measured
at random intervals throughout the workday. Employees used a
handheld device to complete a short checklist, where they indicated if they were feeling "blue," "contented," "happy," and so on.
The researchers discovered that negative interactions with bosses

and coworkers had a five times greater impact on their moods than positive interactions. Or consider how "bad apples" shape work group effectiveness. Will Felps and his colleagues at the University of Washington contrasted the impact of the worst team members with the best and average team members. They found that bad apples (according to measures such as follow-through, enthusiasm, and emotional stability) had a disproportionately negative impact on group dynamics—fueling conflict and weakening social bonds. Bad apples also undermined performance. Felps found that if just one deadbeat or asshole joins a small group, performance drops by 30 percent to 40 percent. Destructive members appear to pack such a punch because bad emotions and actions are so much more contagious than good. Teammates also spend so much time thinking about and dealing with the bad apple that precious time and emotional energy are diverted from the work at hand.

Research on cheating college students shows how bad behavior can spread like a plague through social networks. Sociologist Rick Grannis surveyed and tracked some two thousand UCLA undergraduates over three years. Students reported how often they cheated in their classes during an academic term, if other students encouraged them to cheat, and if they had encouraged fellow students to cheat. This study is unusually rigorous. For example, Grannis verified reports from students about their own cheating by checking with students who encouraged them to cheat and with students whom they encouraged to cheat (there was over 90 percent agreement about such reports). He found that students cheated primarily because they were encouraged to do so by fellow students and that they, in turn, encouraged others to cheat as well. When a student was encouraged to cheat by just one fellow student, the odds that he or she would then encourage others to cheat went up thirty-two times! When a student was surrounded by classmates, students in a dormitory, or fraternity brothers or sorority sisters who encouraged them to cheat, cheating was nearly certain to take place.

Grannis concluded, "If five people encourage you to cheat, welcome to the club, you are a cheater." This is the ugly side of the connect-and-cascade process described in chapter 6—domino chains of bad behavior.

First we'll consider two causes of bad behavior that are toxic to the accountability so essential for scaling up excellence, and how to head off such behavior. Next we'll explore eight solutions that leaders and teams can use to prevent and eliminate destructive beliefs and behaviors.

It's Not My Problem

On June 19, 2008, forty-nine-year-old Esmin Green had already spent twenty-four hours in a waiting room at Kings County Hospital when she slumped over, slid on the floor, and "convulsed for more than a half hour and then became still." Even though numerous patients and several employees noticed her distress, no one stepped in to assist her or call for help. A nurse eventually found her dead. The memo that President Alan Aviles sent to the staff of this psychiatric hospital described the scene:

> A surveillance tape of the waiting area revealed that she had tumbled out of her chair onto the floor a full hour earlier. She lay there, her head under a waiting room chair. During that one-hour period, two of the hospital's security officers and an attending psychiatrist saw her on the floor. None of these individuals went to her aid or examined her condition. A nurse entered the waiting area after the patient had been on the floor for nearly an hour, approached the patient and nudged the patient's leg with her foot,

as if she thought the patient might be asleep. When the patient did not respond, that nurse failed to examine the patient and left the area to summon another nurse. The second nurse examined the patient and ultimately called a team to attempt resuscitation.

Kings County fired several employees, apologized to Green's family, and paid them a $2 million settlement. Unfortunately, incidents like this are not new. When people like those security guards, the attending psychiatrist, and Green's fellow patients see themselves as bystanders, they shirk accountability and fail to act even when they know the right thing to do and have the means to do it.

In 1964, newspaper reports emerged that twenty-eight-year-old "Kitty" Genovese had been brutally stabbed to death in New York City and that even though thirty-eight witnesses heard or saw the event, none called the police or intervened. The resulting public outcry provoked Columbia University psychologists John Darley and Bibb Latané to conduct a series of now classic studies on "bystander effects." In one of their first experiments, they put research subjects into a room and asked them to complete a questionnaire. After a minute or so, thick black smoke began pouring in from under the door. When subjects sat alone, 75 percent reported the smoke to researchers before the six-minute experiment ended. In another condition, subjects sat in the room with two "confederates" who pretended to be completing the questionnaire and then had no reaction even as the smoke got so thick that it obscured everyone's vision, irritated their eyes, and caused some to cough. When surrounded by two "bystanders" who did nothing, subjects followed suit and did nothing too—only 10 percent reported the smoke before the experiment ended.

In the subsequent fifty years, more than 105 studies explored why bystanders often don't take corrective action. Several factors help explain why people who witness bad behavior in organizations and elsewhere don't move to stop it—and shed light on how to encourage them to intervene. Ambiguity is the first reason. Subsequent studies show that, even in situations that may seem dangerous or destructive to casual observers, witnesses are often unsure whether events are bad enough to warrant intervention. Several witnesses to the "Kitty" Genovese murder said they didn't call the police because they believed it was a loud lovers' quarrel; others thought that it was an argument that had spilled out of a local bar onto the street. In addition, as the *New York Times* reported in a 2004 retrospective, "The great majority of the 38 so-called witnesses did not see any part of the actual killing; and . . . what most of them did see, or hear, was fleeting and vague." The lesson is, to stop destructive behavior in organizations, you've got to remove any doubt among witnesses that the words and deeds in question are, indeed, very bad.

The second factor is what Darley and Latané called "diffusion of responsibility"—even though bystanders may recognize a situation as bad, with so many others around, surely someone else will do the right thing (or has done so already). But the problem is that everyone thinks that way, so no one acts. These forces help explain Esmin Green's death: idle employees and patients assumed that someone else had helped or would help her. Disney shows how an organization can counter such assumptions that "it's not my job" or "someone else will do it." When you are a Disney employee and are working in one of their parks, no matter what your job title is, when a guest appears to need help, it is *always* your job to jump in and assist them. When there is trash on the ground, you always pick it up.

The third factor is that, because no one else is helping, people may worry that other witnesses will disapprove if they jump in and do what they believe is right. Research on schoolyard bullies shows that these creeps are emboldened to act when fellow students who witness their taunting and violence don't report them to teachers or step in to stop their cruelty. As a Finnish study by

Christina Salmivalli and her colleagues shows, students who witness bullying often privately disapprove of it and feel guilty about not trying to stop it. But they don't act because they fear being ostracized by peers. Ambiguity also plays a role. Their schoolmates' inaction causes witnesses to question their own judgment, to wonder if bullying is just normal schoolyard behavior that some kids must endure.

In short, three kinds of moves can reverse bystander inaction in organizations, and elsewhere. First, make sure that each person feels personally obligated to reverse or repair problems, no matter what others around him or her do or don't do. Second, make sure that everyone knows and agrees on what bad behavior looks like. Err on the side of being explicit, loud, and repetitive. Don't assume that what *you think* is bad is the same as what *they think* is bad. Third, make sure that bad behavior doesn't become "normalized," collectively seen as a necessary evil, inevitable and unstoppable, expected and accepted, or even good naughty fun.

Good People, Perverse Incentives, and Bad Behavior

Destructive mindsets often emerge when organizations use incentives meant to fuel *good* behavior—but when the easiest way (and sometimes the only way) to get those goodies is to do something *bad.* After a while, bad behavior doesn't seem so wrong because everyone around you does it, they seem to encourage (or demand) that you do it, and you press others to sin along with you.

Consider the teachers and administrators led by Atlanta public school superintendent Dr. Beverly Hall from 1999 to 2010. Hall was determined to raise students' scores on annual achievement tests and used powerful carrots and sticks to make it happen. Hall didn't just link financial incentives for teachers and principals to students' test scores; she linked their job security and prestige to constant improvements. The *New York Times* reported, "Principals were told that if state test scores did not go up enough, they would be fired—and 90 percent of them were removed in the decade of Dr. Hall's reign." Hall also used pride (and humiliation) to crank up the pressure. She held rallies at a big stadium where "Dr. Hall permitted principals with the highest test scores to sit up front near her, while sticking those with the lowest scores off to the side, in the bleachers." It seemed to be working. The fifty-two thousand children in Atlanta schools started outperforming those in every urban area in Georgia and, although many were from poor families, they "often outperformed wealthier suburban districts on state tests." These results led the American Association of School Administrators to name Hall as the superintendent of the year in 2009. And Hall earned over $500,000 in performance bonuses during her years in Atlanta.

Hall's house of cards began to collapse in 2009 when the *Atlanta Journal-Constitution* uncovered extraordinary swings in test scores at nineteen Atlanta schools. For example, West Manor School fifth graders went from being among the state's worst performers to being among the the best; the odds of this improvement were about one in a billion. At Gideon Elementary, an average of twenty-seven out of seventy answers on each math test were erased and changed from wrong to right—massively higher than the statewide erasure rate.

A two-year probe by Georgia officials involved 2,100 interviews and reviews of over eight hundred thousand documents. Investigators concluded that the Atlanta public school system was deeply dysfunctional and corrupt. They found that cheating had occurred at forty-four out of fifty-six Atlanta schools examined; thirty-eight principals and 178 teachers were implicated in organized efforts to cheat. At the Venetian Hills School, for example, a group of teachers and administrators who called themselves "the chosen ones" met regularly to alter answers on students' tests. At Gideon El-ementary School, teachers held a "changing party" at a teacher's home to alter tests. One Atlanta teacher admitted that cheating had gone on so long that "we considered it part of our jobs." In March of 2013, Dr. Hall was one of thirty-five Atlanta educators indicted by a grand jury for conspiring to "cheat, conceal cheating or retaliate against whistle-blowers in an effort to bolster C.R.C.T. scores for the benefit of financial rewards associated with high test scores."

This appalling story has two hallmarks of other cases where re-wards and punishments produce bad behavior. The first hallmark is that incentives are vivid enough and strong enough that, even-tually, just about everyone's behavior flips to the bad side. When you look around at your colleagues, everyone is bad, so it seems like a normal and sensible way to act. To paraphrase journalist Walter Lippmann, the sick situation evolves to the point where everyone thinks alike, so no one thinks very much. Similarly, in 2010, routine and expected bad behavior was revealed after leaky gas pipes maintained by the Pacific Gas & Electric Company (PG&E) exploded in San Bruno, California—killing eight people and destroying thirty-eight homes. Investigators discovered that, until 2008, the fewer leaks a supervisor's crew discovered, and the lower the repair costs, the bigger his or her bonus. As a result, few leaks were reported, so PG&E made big cuts in crews that found and fixed leaks. A PG&E employee who stepped forward to blow the whistle explained: "Everybody is reporting that we have this great, leak-proof system. They are not finding leaks, so you don't have to fix them. Since you don't have to fix them, you don't need the employees." After a few brave workers confronted senior exec-utives and told them, "I'm really amazed that more houses haven't blown up," they realized that the incentive system was causing safety problems.

When PG&E abolished the misguided incentives, the number

of leaks discovered began to skyrocket. The *San Francisco Chronicle* reported, "In Fresno, PG&E found 41 leaks in 2006, but a two-year-long intensive resurvey starting in 2008 turned up 7,628." PG&E started scrambling to fix the plague of unrepaired leaks created by these twisted incentives. But those efforts came too late for the victims who died or lost their homes in San Bruno in 2010.

The second hallmark is that misguided incentives encourage people to take the easy way out rather than to do the right thing—they fixate on the most efficient shenanigans for running the right numbers up (or down) and shun the hard work required to achieve true excellence. In Atlanta, this meant that teachers devoted so much effort to cheating and gaming the system (for example, by transferring low-performing students out of their classes) that it distracted them from teaching students to read and write. At PG&E, the incentives meant that employees didn't bother to look very hard for leaks. And when they did stumble on a gas leak, these rewards (and pressure from supervisors) often led them to downgrade it to "minor" when it was really a "major" leak that ought to be fixed within eighteen months. If a flaw in a gas pipe is suspected, federal rules require workers to test the pipe by filling it with high-pressure water or running an automated device through it. But the perverse incentives meant that "PG&E rarely used those methods before the San Bruno blast" because they were "inconvenient and expensive."

A bright side of the Atlanta and PG&E stories is that the shameful practices were ultimately exposed by people with the courage to do the right thing. In Atlanta, Jackie Parks was the brave teacher who broke the silence at Venetian Hills Elementary School and admitted that she was among "the chosen ones" who altered tests. Parks then agreed to wear a hidden listening device to record discussions about the cheating schemes with fellow teachers. At PG&E, gas crew foreman Michael Scafani complained relentlessly to superiors about the incentives and resulting dangerous leaks. Finally, after the persistent Scafani was able to get a meeting with CEO Peter Darbee in 2007, things began to change at PG&E. There was a management shake-up, supervisors in charge of gas safety were dismissed, and the incentives were gone by 2008. Once again, scaling—in these cases, banishing bad behavior to make way for good—came down to individuals with the will and skill to do the right thing.

Breaking Bad

The upshot of these cases and studies is that the *outcome* of spreading excellence depends on a *process* that enables people to prevent and eliminate destructive attitudes, beliefs, and behaviors. We now turn to eight methods that leaders and scaling teams can use for "breaking bad."

1. Nip It in the Bud

In 1982, criminologist George Kelling and political scientist James Q. Wilson advanced a simple idea: that "the sense of mutual regard and the obligations of civility are lowered by actions that seem to signal that 'no one cares.'" They called it the "broken windows" problem: in neighborhoods where one window is broken and left unrepaired, the remaining windows will soon be broken too. The broken windows theory suggests that allowing even a little bit of bad to occur or persist is a mistake because it signals that no one is watching, no one cares, and no one will stop people from doing even worse things. The theory soon started having a big impact on crime policies. Most famously, William Bratton embraced it as head of the New York City Transit Police. He implemented zero-tolerance policies for fare dodging on subways and buses and installed procedures that made it quicker and easier to arrest petty criminals. When Rudy Giuliani became New York City's mayor in 1994, he hired Bratton as police chief. Bratton used programs under banners such as "quality of life" and "zero tolerance" to crack down on petty crimes including subway fare evasion, public drinking, urination, graffiti, and intimidation by "squeegee men" who wiped the windshields of stopped cars and demanded payment. Soon, although these policies weren't the only factor, crime of all kinds began to plummet throughout New York.

A host of studies confirm that it is best to nip bad behavior in the bud. For example, in the 1990s Dr. Robert Cialdini and his colleagues ran a series of experiments where they somehow got a piece of unwanted litter in people's hands (e.g., by putting big flyers under the windshields of parked cars that were so big that they blocked visibility). Then the researchers observed if each person threw the litter on the ground or put it in the trash can. When there was no garbage on the ground, or just one or two pieces, people rarely littered. But when they saw a lot of litter, they usually tossed their piece on the ground rather than making the short trek to the trash can. Although everyone knows that littering is bad, when everyone else seems to be doing it, people conclude that it is an accepted norm—much like those cheating UCLA students, the students who didn't prevent bullying in Finnish schools, the cheating Atlanta school teachers, and the PG&E supervisors who discouraged their charges from finding leaky gas pipes.

The experiences in New York and studies such as Cialdini's imply that clearing the way for excellence in organizations depends on being a stickler about stamping out destructive behavior. If you look the other way or decide that some small violation isn't worth dealing with, things can quickly degenerate. The power of this "no broken windows" mindset is seen in Charles O'Reilly's and Barton Weitz's study of 141 supervisors in a large retail chain. O'Reilly and Weitz focused on how these supervisors handled salespeople with problematic behaviors such as "not punctual," "doesn't assist in stocking," "doesn't cooperate with fellow workers," "not courteous to customers," and "low sales productivity." Supervisors of the most productive units (where sales were higher and costs lower) confronted problems more directly and quickly, issued more verbal and written warnings, used formal punishments more often, and promptly fired employees when warnings failed. These supervisors believed in taking quick action against bad apples because they undermined their colleagues' performance. They also preferred to take personal responsibility for dismissing weak employees rather than handing this dirty work off to other managers.

This isn't an argument for treating people with disrespect or striking fear in their hearts. As research on preventing errors in workplaces from hospitals to manufacturing plants shows, when people live in fear of being humiliated, demoted, punished, or otherwise disgraced and shunned, they don't admit mistakes and don't help others avert problems. When failure happens, it is treated as an occasion for blame rather than for learning. Venture capitalist and d.school professor Michael Dearing teaches the entrepreneurs he funds and mentors that growing a company sometimes requires taking actions that can upset and even harm the people you lead. For example, at times you've got to give employees negative feedback and you may need to fire or lay people off—but "there is a difference between what you do and how you do it."

The best bosses nip bad behavior in the bud but treat people with dignity in the process. We asked CEO Mauria Finley how she struck this balance as her start-up, Citrus Lane, grew from four to twenty people (her company sends monthly care packages of baby goods to moms and raised $5.1 million in 2012). Finley explained that her years as a manager and executive at Netscape, eBay, and elsewhere taught her to never withhold bad news and to never hesitate to tell employees when and why their work isn't up to snuff—but to deliver such messages with as much empathy as she can muster. One of Finley's direct reports described her as a "compassionate hardass," which is exactly what she aims to be.

2. Get Rid of the Bad Apples

Most people aren't born bad. Many employees who are prone to selfishness, nastiness, incompetence, laziness, and cheating change their ways after receiving feedback and coaching—or moving to a workplace where management or peers don't tolerate such behavior. So we advise against assuming that bad behavior is incurable and firing or transferring destructive people at the first hint of trouble. That said, as the O'Reilly and Weitz study suggests, the best leaders and teams act quickly and decisively to remove destructive characters when lesser measures fail. And one of the most reliable ways to eradicate a destructive mindset is to remove the bad apples.

Before we turn to human organizations, consider what happened to a baboon troop after its nastiest members left the scene. Biologist Robert Sapolsky and his colleagues have tracked a wild baboon troop in Kenya for over thirty years. When the research first began in 1978, some troop members routinely pilfered food from a garbage dump at a nearby tourist lodge. Not every troop member dined at the dump. Only the largest, strongest, and most aggressive males earned the privilege. To get to the food, they battled for dominance with males from another troop that also ate there—snarling, swiping their claws at them, chasing them, and making threatening gestures such as baring their teeth. Then, between 1983 and 1986, infected meat from the dump killed 46 percent of the troop's adult males: the most dominant, biggest, and meanest ones. As in other baboon troops studied by biologists, these alpha males constantly bit, pummeled, glared at, bullied, and chased males of similar rank in their own troop, as well as lower-ranking males and occasionally the females too.

After the deaths, the surviving and once lower-status males

became the troop's alpha males. Sapolsky and colleague Lisa Share observed that aggression by the new alphas and other troop members soon plummeted. Unlike the old alphas, the new ones directed their aggression almost entirely toward fellow dominant males. They rarely directed it at lower-status males and never at females. Troop members also spent a larger percentage of their time grooming and sat closer together, and hormone levels indicated that the lowest-status males suffered less emotional distress than their counterparts in other baboon troops—apparently because they didn't have to endure constant threats and an occasional scratch or bite from a big mean male. This cultural shift persisted at least through the late 1990s, well after all the original kinder and gentler alpha males had died off. This meant that the "pacific culture," as Sapolsky and Share called it, was passed on to new generations. In addition, as Sapolsky explained, when young males from other troops joined this "pacific" troop, they quickly learned not to be "jerky new guys" because "We don't do things like that around here."

The baboons' experience dovetails with research on repairing broken organizations, including an evaluation of turnaround efforts in thirty-six low-performing Chicago public schools. The University of Chicago's Marisa de la Torre and her colleagues found that various solutions were tried in these schools, including bringing in turnaround specialists, "reconstituting" the staff, and closing the school and reopening it with all new staff. There was a common theme across all thirty-six turnarounds—leaders, principals, and assistant principals were replaced in every school. And at least 50 percent of the teachers were replaced in thirty-two of the thirty-six efforts. The results show that, compared to similar and equally low-performing schools, these efforts improved student performance on standardized tests in the twenty-two elementary schools—but not in the fourteen high schools studied (in Chicago, unlike Atlanta, there were no signs of cheating). The researchers caution, however, that school turnaround is a process, not an event. It took several years before the elementary schools began to improve, and high schools are larger and more complicated, and student behavior more ingrained, so change takes longer (indeed, there were signs that several of high schools were starting to improve as the study was ending).

The researchers warn that just changing leaders and staff isn't enough—as shown by a seven-year study comparing one hundred schools that had improved with one hundred others that had failed to do so. This study found that successful school turnarounds depend on five factors: effective leaders, collaborative teachers, strong family and community ties, ambitious instruction, and a safe and orderly learning climate. When a turnaround includes all five factors, "a school is 10 times more likely to improve and 30 times less likely to stagnate" than if it has only one or two factors. Once again, we see that, when it comes to scaling up excellence, the best path is rarely the easiest.

Finally, bad apples aren't just a problem that leaders and scaling teams need to tackle in the long run. Lazy, overbearing, mean-spirited, incompetent, and dour people can ruin teams and organizations that are responsible for short-term projects. As the research on teams shows, their negativity distracts and infects their colleagues. In such cases, skilled leaders move to blunt the bad apples' negative influence, sometimes extracting these destructive characters on the spot. For example, Stanford's Perry Klebahn is known for his mastery at coaching and turning around dysfunctional teams of executives that participate in hands-on d.school programs. Typically, these three- to six-day programs each serve sixty or so executives who are dispersed among ten or twelve five-person teams, each with its own coach. Past projects have focused, for instance, on improving customer experiences at BP gas stations and the local Tesla dealership, as well as improving donors' experiences at the Stanford Blood Bank. As each program unfolds, Klebahn wanders from team to team and watches each intently, does quick check-ins with coaches, and—when he spots a troublesome team member—often jumps in to provide one-on-one coaching, offer encouragement, and nudge him or her to participate in more constructive ways. As he does so, Klebahn assesses how "salvageable" the potential bad apple might be. Then, each night, Klebahn and d.school colleague Jeremy Utley (his partner in leading most programs) run a debriefing session where the dozen or so coaches discuss what is going well—and what needs repair—in individual teams and the program.

During several programs in recent years, Klebahn, Utley, and the coaches identified a number of bad apples who harmed their groups so much that, in their opinion, they ought to be removed. So Klebahn "puts all the bad apples in one barrel." He puts all these destructive characters together in one new team, moves them to a corner where they won't infect others, and recruits a no-nonsense coach to guide them. This technique works. Klebahn tells us that the dynamics and quality of prototypes improved markedly in teams that have have bad apples removed, and although a couple of teams packed with bad apples have done poor work, a couple of others have produced "shockingly good prototypes."

When Klebahn read this description of the "all in one barrel" method, he said that the surprising improvement reminded him of a lesson from his past leadership roles—which include being founder and CEO of Atlas Snowshoes, senior vice president at Patagonia, and CEO of Timbuk2: employees who are bad apples in one setting are sometimes good apples in another. In particular, he said, at the d.school, when a "bad apple team" is filled with "big personalities," especially "alpha types," and has a coach who can handle them, constructive dynamics can emerge. This seems to happen because, although those big personalities may have trampled over less aggressive teammates, there is a "balance of power" when you put them all together. These "alpha types,"

Klebahn observed, usually have lot of energy; the trick is getting them to channel it toward the design challenge rather than toward pushing around other teammates.

3. Plumbing Before Poetry

The broken windows theory has direct implications for James March's distinction between leaders as "poets" and as "plumbers," those equally crucial and complementary roles that we discussed at the close of chapter 3. The theory suggests that getting people to focus on the small, mundane, and sometimes gritty details of organizational life is an effective path for eliminating the negative. In March's lingo, you'd better fix the plumbing before you start spouting out the poetry. Consider the incredible mess that the Alameda Health System (AHS) in Oakland, California, was in a decade ago, and the steps that its new leaders took to clean it up. AHS is a public health care system that serves mostly poor and indigent patients with 475 hospital beds and 500 physicians in six major facilities. In 2012, AHS employees performed over 5,000 surgeries and provided nearly 300,000 outpatient visits.

The system, especially its flagship Highland Hospital in Oakland, was "a poster child for public-hospital dysfunction." By 2005, AHS had churned through ten CEOs in eleven years. The hospital was losing $1 million a month and had accumulated deficits of over $50 million, in part because employees did such a poor job of collecting payments from Medicare and MediCal (the government agencies that reimburse health care expenses for older patients and those without insurance).

Working conditions were horrendous. A doctor was beaten and strangled by a patient—and left on the floor for half an hour before a janitor found him. HIV-infected blood was routinely mixed in with regular trash. Nurses often openly defied doctors and supervisors. Employees' cars filled the parking garage, forcing patients to circle around and around to find parking spots. AHS consumed millions of dollars of public funds and was under fire for paying $3.2 million to a consulting firm—which recommended that three hundred workers be fired and patient services slashed.

New CEO Wright Lassiter and new COO Bill Manns decided that so many things were broken at AHS that talking about values and strategy, giving speeches, making lofty calls for change, or any other form of poetry, would backfire. There was no reason for employees to believe that they could fix the place when a parade of administrations before them had failed. So they focused just on fixing the plumbing: on repairing one broken part at a time. They started by launching a sixteen-week "grassroots money hunt," which they now describe as "the foundation of our success." They put eighty-five top managers into twelve "odd-couple teams" that each included doctors, nurses, managers, and technicians. The teams were asked to find $21 million by cutting costs and increasing revenue. Lassiter told them, "It's up to you. We barely know where the restrooms are, so we're not going to solve this problem. You're going to solve it." The teams pored over contracts and costs and came up with one good idea after another. For example, they replaced a $96.50 tool used to test the umbilical cord blood of newborns with a 29-cent solution that worked just as well—saving $322,000 a year. They found new sources of revenue, as well, especially in diabetes care, where they implemented a referral system that drove hundreds of new patients from community clinics to AHS.

Then Lassiter and Manns laid off eighty AHS employees (not the three hundred recommended by the consultants) but found new jobs for many of these displaced workers elsewhere in AHS. Between the money hunt and layoffs, they dug up $23 million. Next, they tackled an especially tough problem: working with the union to get rid of terrible nurses. As a veteran physician told *Fast Company,* "I'd say, 'Nurse, draw this man's blood,' and she'd say,

'Why don't you do it yourself?' And I would. This kind of thing happened every day before [Lassiter] got here." This doctor went on to say that most nurses at AHS were highly professional and that "even they wanted those nurses gone."

Dozens of these toxic nurses were fired. Lassiter and Manns refused to deal with these nurses via layoffs. They wanted the union and fellow staff members to understand that such destructive behavior wouldn't be tolerated—and to work with rather than against management to expel these bad apples. Lassiter and Mann also worked with unions to free up those parking spots. Not only was the time that patients were spending looking for spots infuriating to them, it was costing AHS a lot of money. Appointments were delayed, wait times ballooned, and revenue suffered. The unions agreed to offsite parking with a shuttle service for employees. This change not only opened up spaces. It also created a gateway experience where employees lived a mindset that Lassiter and Mann hoped to spread—putting patients' needs first.

AHS still faces vexing obstacles as health care costs skyrocket and funding sources remain uncertain. But since Lassiter and Mann arrived, the emphasis on plumbing rather than poetry has generated positive financial margins for AHS each year (except 2011). External evaluators report that the quality of patient care at AHS is on a steady upswing, and a new $668 million hospital building is under construction. Lassiter remains cautious about offering poetry, but when prodded, he admitted, "I want to make this place as good or better than the private hospitals."

4. Adequacy Before Excellence

A related implication of the AHS story, as well as the "bad is stronger than good" research and the broken windows theory, is that— before we labor to spread something marvelous—the first order of business should be to drive out bad behavior. This may seem like obvious advice. But as our friend and colleague Jeffrey Pfeffer loves to say, great leaders and teams are masters of the obvious—and it is a rare talent.

We applaud organizations that spread services intended to delight customers. As we discussed in chapters 4 and 6, we're impressed with Intuit's Design for Delight, or D4D, program. But we don't recommend starting such an effort until you've cleared out the negative elements of customer experiences—something that Intuit did long before launching the D4D effort. Unfortunately, research by Corporate Executive Board (CEB), a consulting firm, found that many companies don't follow this seemingly obvious path. When they surveyed one hundred customer service heads, eighty-nine reported that "their main strategy is to exceed expectations." But CEB's surveys of over seventy-five thousand customers revealed that most aren't looking for over-the-top service; they enjoy it when it happens, but what drives them away—and really hurts companies—is bad service: "They exact revenge on airlines that lose their bags, cable providers whose technicians keep them waiting, cellular companies whose reps put them on permanent hold, and dry cleaners who don't understand what 'rush order' means."

CEB's research shows that customer loyalty has more to do with how well companies keep their "basic, even plain vanilla promises" than with how well they dazzle customers. CEB researcher Matthew Dixon and his colleagues report that 25 percent of customers are likely to say something positive about a customer service experience, but 65 percent are likely to say something negative. Similarly, they discovered that 23 percent of customers who received good service told ten or more people; 48 percent who had bad service experiences told ten or more people. This research shows that making things easy is especially crucial for maintaining customer loyalty and heading off or reversing dissatisfaction. Smart companies, for example, find ways to ensure that customers don't have to call them back a second time to make a purchase, set an appointment, complete a transaction, or resolve a problem. One CEB client, an Australian telecommunications company, eliminated productivity metrics for reps who work the phones in their call centers. The company now evaluates their performance on the basis of "interviews with customers, asking them if the service they received met their needs." As a result, although calls now take slightly longer, the percentage of repeat calls has fallen by 58 percent.

5. Use the Cool Kids (and Adults) to Define and Squelch Bad Behavior

As we saw in chapter 6, the kinds of people that you recruit for a scaling effort, and when you recruit them, have a big impact on its success. Many of the lessons from chapter 6 apply to eliminating bad behavior as well, including recruiting guilt-prone leaders, energizers, and a diverse scaling team. For example, Princeton researchers Elizabeth Paluck and Hana Shepherd evaluated and helped implement an intervention designed to reduce bullying in a Connecticut high school. Along with other methods, the intervention involved recruiting eleven leaders from diverse cliques to help stop taunting, teasing, fighting, cruel rumors, and other kinds of "drama" among the school's 290 students.

The main focus of the intervention was to identify the cool kids in the school and convince them to help fellow students understand what bullying looks like, how it feels to be bullied, and what they can and should do to stop it. The intervention team used social network analysis to identify two kinds of cool kids, or "social referents," which Paluck and Shepherd define as "highly connected and chronically salient actors." The first were "widely known" students who had connections to many students in the school and were described as having high status by many students.

The second were "clique leaders," who each led a tightly interconnected group but were not necessarily widely known.

The researchers identified eighty-three cool kids with this method, randomly selected twenty-four (thirteen "widely known" and eleven "clique leaders"), and recruited them to lead the intervention. At the start of the year, the selected cool kids received antibullying training by facilitators from the Anti-Defamation League. They were taught to identify roles in harassment episodes, including ally, bystander, perpetrator, and victim. Each student also wrote an essay about his or her experiences playing those roles. Five students were selected by facilitators and teachers to read their essays at a schoolwide assembly that October. The remaining students "performed a skit illustrating common types of harassment at the school and ways to speak out against it." The assembly started with that skit, which was about a girl rumored to be a "slut." It showed the damage she suffered and concluded with another girl standing up for the victim. Then the five selected cool kids read their essays. For example, one girl described how she had been teased so much that she had to switch schools. And a boy described how he had gotten into a physical fight that created a vicious cycle of fighting and insults.

The cool kids then invited other students to share their own experiences. All the students were then divided into small groups to discuss what they had learned from the assembly and how they could help stop the "drama." There were follow-up events throughout the year. During school assemblies, the selected cool kids read announcements about stopping harassments, created a series of posters with pictures of them wearing T-shirts about the program, and often wore the T-shirts around school. They also sold wristbands for a dollar with the slogan "Don't stand by, be an ally."

The researchers found that, especially for students with ties to the cool kids who led the intervention, there were constructive changes in school norms. Fewer students believed it was normal to start "drama" or other conflicts, or normal to mind your own business during drama, or acceptable to step back from conflict and not defend your friends. There were also encouraging changes in behavior. Teachers reported that students with ties to the leaders of the intervention were more prone to defend fellow students from harassment and less likely to "contribute to a negative school environment."

For better and for worse, most workplaces are similar to high school in many ways. As in the above study, the cool people have a disproportionate impact on what others construe as bad (and good) behavior—and whether or not their less cool colleagues will take individual responsibility for stopping it when it rears its ugly head. Thus an effective way to eliminate the negative is to recruit the most admired and connected people in your organization, teach them what "bad" looks like, and encourage them to stop being perpetrators.

A senior executive from a large retail chain in South America told Sutton how he became fed up with members of his senior team who kept staring at and tapping away at their smart phones during meetings. They did so even though he repeatedly asked them to put away their phones before meetings began. There had been several occasions when their obsession with "those damn little screens," in his words, caused members to miss important facts and fail to weigh in when their wisdom was needed. So the executive pulled aside two of the most respected and admired members of his team (who were also two of the worst offenders) and asked them to keep their phones off and in their pockets during meetings and to help him encourage fellow team members to do the same. It worked. The two role models whom he targeted didn't look at their phones during the next meeting and began aggressively pressing teammates to stop doing so. Now, when a team meeting starts, the ritual is that everyone—more or less simultaneously—powers off their phones and puts them in a pocket or purse. The executive didn't have much luck changing the norm as the lone advocate. But once he recruited those two influential members—the local cool kids—to stop themselves and others from being bad, the team's norms changed rapidly.

6. Kill the Thrill

As Mark Twain said, "There is a charm about the forbidden that makes it unspeakably desirable." Indeed, a common and often vexing obstacle to spreading excellence is that being bad sometimes feels so good. As George Kelling and James Q. Wilson pointed out, one reason that it is hard to stop people from breaking windows once they start is "It has always been fun."

One of our favorite examples of the thrill of bad behavior— and how to squelch it—comes from an intervention that the University of Toronto's Gary Latham helped invent, implement, and study at a large sawmill (which employed about one thousand hourly workers and two hundred managers). Latham was brought in by management because hourly employees were stealing about a million dollars' worth of equipment per year and management couldn't figure out how to stop them. Part of the problem was that the union was so strong that punishing the thieves was impossible. Latham described a worker who was stopped by a supervisor because his toolboxes looked very heavy. The union responded by flooding the HR department with so many grievances that HR staffers begged the supervisor to back off; so supervisors adopted a "hear no evil, see no evil" approach to employee thievery. Another part of the problem was that in the sawmill, much as in schools with rampant bullying, although many workers disapproved of stealing and did not do it themselves (e.g., so "I can live with myself" and "I am setting an example for my kids"), there was strong peer pressure against reporting thieves. One worker told Latham, "If you want to get along here, you better play the game."

Latham's interviews also revealed an interesting twist: workers didn't need most of what they stole. They stole because it was challenging and a source of prestige among peers. They bragged to Latham, "We are so good we could steal a head-rig from a sawmill" (a head-rig weighs more than a ton). They even tried to involve Latham in their antics; one worker asked, "Doc, tell us what you want, and we will get it out within 45 days." When the company's senior managers learned about Latham's findings, they recommended installing surveillance cameras to catch the thieves. Latham responded that several hourly workers had asked him to make exactly that suggestion to management because stealing the equipment would be such a thrill! Management quickly abandoned the idea.

Latham also learned some intriguing details about the incentives and disincentives for the thefts. The workers did not fear being punished by management. The worst part of stealing all this stuff was that, because they never sold it, the thieves often had heated arguments about whose turn it was to store the stuff. Although workers weren't afraid of management, they did fear "the wrath of their spouses," who complained that the loot was "clogging up their garages, basements, and attics."

Latham spent hours discussing and debating potential solutions with management. They considered and rejected financial incentives that might put "the thrill" into job performance rather than theft—senior managers were concerned that workers would see this as a reward for their stealing. Eventually, with Latham's help, they decided to "remove the outcome expected from stealing: namely, the thrill." They created a library system where employees could check out the equipment for personal use anytime they wished—they just had to sign a form releasing the company from liability.

The result? The theft rate immediately dropped to virtually zero. After all, it was no fun to steal anymore, and bragging about stealing something that was free did not earn you prestige among peers. Stealing remained virtually absent for years after the library system was implemented, even though the workers almost never actually checked out any equipment. Nor was there an upswing in other kinds of bad behavior such as vandalism, graffiti, or absenteeism.

Management also created an amnesty day. This idea was also inspired by libraries, which often have a few days a year where people can return long-overdue books without being fined. Similarly, one spring day, employees were invited to return missing equipment without fear of punishment. No questions were asked. Management told employees they assumed that anything returned was brought back as a favor to a friend and that the employee had not stolen it. On the first amnesty day, workers arrived with so many truckloads of stuff that management extended the event: truckload after truckload arrived for several more days. Apparently, as Latham's interviews suggested, many workers (mostly men) had been getting grief from their wives for years because the stolen stuff was taking up so much space in garages, storage sheds, and so on. So they jumped at the chance to get rid of it.

Latham's experience is chock full of lessons about the causes of bad behavior and how to squelch it. First, as many studies of theft demonstrate, what people steal and how much they steal is often driven by peer pressure, not by what management does. Stealing and other forms of bad behavior are often ways to garner prestige from colleagues. Second, although financial incentives can cause—or stifle—bad behavior, they are often unnecessary. If you can identify other powerful incentives and disincentives (such as those annoyed spouses), you can sometimes stop bad behavior without spending a penny. Third, in addition to pride and prestige, there are often intrinsic joys to engaging in bad behavior: for many employees, stealing was one of the most challenging parts of working at the sawmill. Finding ways to reduce such thrills, and replace them with more constructive ones, is a tough but rewarding challenge.

7. Time Shifting: From Current to Future Selves

You can sometimes break bad by getting people to think about the person they hope to be, not just the person they are now. New York University's Hal Hershfield and his colleagues found that when individuals are preoccupied with their present selves (rather than focusing on the link between who they are now and who they will and want to be in the future) they are more prone to lie and behave unethically—for example, when playing a negotiation game with someone else. People who focus only on their present selves don't think very much about how the choices they make now may prove costly to them later. They disagree with statements such as "I consider how things might be in the future, and try to influence those things with my day-to-day behavior."

In another Hershfield study, undergraduates were brought into a virtual reality room and asked to look at computer-generated avatars of themselves in the mirror: students in one group saw avatars of their current selves; students in the other group saw aged avatar versions of themselves as sixty-eight-year-old men or women. When they exited the room, the researchers asked the students, among other questions, what they would do if someone gave them $1,000. Those who had seen sixty-eight-year-old avatars of themselves allocated twice as much money to retirement accounts as those who had seen avatars of their current selves.

Amanda Shantz and Gary Latham saw a related effect in a series of three experiments with 145 employees who worked at a call center to raise money for a university. They randomly assigned employees to one of two groups. One group was given written directions about how to convince people to donate funds.

Employees in the other group got the same directions, but they were printed on a backdrop with a photograph of a woman winning a race. Those employees exposed to the photograph raised substantially more funds—apparently because this simple cue focused their attention on their future selves, especially on the links between the small things that they did during each call and the goals that they hoped to achieve.

Leaders can sometimes help employees shift to their future selves by making ambitious goals more vivid and emotionally compelling. For example, former Xerox CEO Ann Mulcahy led an impressive turnaround of the troubled Xerox Corporation after she became CEO in 2001. A few months into her tenure, instead of writing a traditional vision statement, she and her senior team wrote an imaginary *Wall Street Journal* article about Xerox that would appear in 2005: "We outlined the things we hoped to accomplish as though we had already achieved them. We included performance metrics—even quotes from Wall Street analysts. It was really our vision of what we wanted the company to become."

Time shifting does not always require a big hairy goal, as management guru Jim Collins would put it, to convince people to eliminate the negative and accentuate the positive. Sometimes it just requires finding ways to make the impact of employees' negative actions more vivid to them, so they will work harder to link short-term actions to long-term consequences. Executives from British Gas told Rao about how they had tackled such a problem in India. In some cities, the company is the only supplier of energy. This allowed them to act—as comedian Lily Tomlin used to joke when AT&T had a monopoly in the U.S. telephone industry—as if "We don't care, we don't have to." British Gas employees were often dismissive and downright contemptuous of customers. Managers hit upon an ingenious solution. They recruited consumers to behave like frontline British Gas employees and asked employees to take the role of consumers. The consumers gave the employees a stiff dose of their own medicine: they ignored them when they came into the office to pay bills, forced them to wait as they tended to personal matters, and treated them with disdain—glaring at them and insulting them about everything from their personal appearance to their ignorance of company procedures. When employees realized that this was exactly how they treated customers who came in to pay bills—the very basis of their salaries—their eyes opened and accountability began to take hold.

8. Focus on the Best Times, the Worst Times, and the End

In 2008, Sutton and Stanford colleague Debra Dunn invited Disney's Karin Kricorian to give a talk to their class—which was working with Bonny Simi and other managers at JetBlue Airlines to improve customer experiences. Kricorian, who has a Stanford PhD in marketing, reminded the students not to forget Nobel Prize winner Daniel Kahneman's "peak-end rule": no matter how good or bad an experience is, or how long it lasts, judgments about it are shaped disproportionally by the best and worst moments and if it ended well or badly. At about that time, three students, Annie Adams, Whitfield Fowler, and Simone Marticke, had been following JetBlue passengers through their travel journeys in and out of the airport. Kricorian's comments hit home because their interviews revealed that, for many passengers, the worst part of the experience was at the baggage claim carousel. Passengers reported that the baggage area and the carousel itself were confusing and that they were tired from their trips, anxious about when (and if) their baggage would arrive, and surrounded with similarly tense people. In other words, the baggage carousel experience was a double-whammy: the peak—the worst part—and the end were wrapped together into a single unpleasant package.

Kricorian's advice and their own observations inspired the team to test a prototype called "Blue Cares." They made blue

T-shirts with a logo on the front that blended JetBlue and Stanford d.school themes. On the back, the shirt said, "Don't tell anyone, but you're our favorite customer." They went to the airport, hung out in the baggage claim area, and offered to help customers. Following another lesson that they had gleaned from Kricorian and Disney, the trio focused on helping passengers who looked most anxious or confused—both because these people needed help and because, if their anxieties were calmed, their negative emotions would not infect others. Adams, Fowler, and Marticke (each with a cell phone in hand) answered all kinds of questions from grateful passengers, ranging from "I have these expensive snowboards coming out, what carousel is it?" to "Where do I go to get a wheelchair for my mother?"

The passengers found the prototype useful and appreciated the effort to add some humanity to one of the worst parts of the airline travel experience. When Bonny Simi told a large group of JetBlue managers and executives about the prototype, they were impressed with it and with the positive responses it generated from customers and JetBlue employees. Even though adding this new role to the JetBlue cast wasn't economically feasible given the competitive pressures in the airline industry, Simi said the team's prototype was quite useful because it reminded company leaders to redouble their efforts with current crew members to make the baggage claim experience flow as smoothly for passengers as possible.

More broadly, the Blue Cares prototype is a reminder that, although scaling excellence involves removing and reducing as many bad experiences as possible, not all junctures are created equal. This insight doesn't just apply to customer experiences; it also applies, for example, to employees' careers. The peak-end rule suggests that going out of your way to create better experiences is especially wise as an employee leaves an organization or team. This holds whether the departure is involuntary or voluntary. Our familiar friend, venture capitalist Ben Horowitz, told our scaling class about the best advice he ever got about handling layoffs: be there to say goodbye to people, help them carry their boxes out, shake their hand or give them a hug, and say thank you. The person losing a job will feel a little better (or at least less bad), everyone who isn't losing a job will feel better about staying with the company, and you'll feel a little better as well. And in the future, if things brighten up at your current company, or if you ever try to recruit that same person (or someone he or she knows) to join you in some future company, your odds of success will be far greater than if you had hid in your office and had been afraid to look that person in the eye.

Warning Signs: Five Dangerous Feelings

This chapter demonstrates that relentless vigilance is essential for reducing and eradicating destructive beliefs and behaviors—and provides tools and tactics for "breaking bad." We wrap up by taking a different vantage point on this challenge, one that the leaders and teams we learn from, teach, and coach about scaling find especially helpful. We home in on five feelings that, when pervasive, signal that bad behavior already exists—or soon will. These feelings are symptoms of the sorts of bad behaviors that infect a team or organization. Each provides clues about the root causes of such destructive deeds and guidance about which cures will clear the way for scaling up excellence.

The first dangerous feeling is *fear of taking responsibility,* especially the sense that it is safer to do nothing, or something bad, than the right thing. We saw how fear kept teachers in Atlanta from standing up to Dr. Hall, kept New Yorkers from intervening to save "Kitty" Genovese in the 1960s, and kept doctors and nurses in the Alameda Health System from standing up to incompetent and surly colleagues. Silence is one of the most reliable signs that people are afraid to take personal responsibility and that the learning and self-criticism that fuel excellence aren't happening. In her study of drug treatment errors in eight hospital nursing units, Harvard's Amy Edmondson demonstrated the stifling effects of such fear. At first, Edmondson was bewildered when her findings revealed that nurses in units with the best managers and best coworker relationships reported making as many as ten times more mistakes than nurses in the worst units! At the outset, her theory had been that when people worked in trusting and caring settings, and focused on finding and fixing mistakes, they would make fewer errors—so these findings were the exact opposite of what she had predicted.

Edmondson decided to recruit a researcher who had no knowledge of these surprising findings to spend two months doing interviews and observing the eight units. The researcher's findings, along with her own observations, led Edmondson to realize that nurses in the worst units were reporting fewer mistakes because they were afraid to talk about, let alone admit, mistakes. They were treated like naughty children and belittled when they admitted to—or got caught—making errors. Their silence was not golden: they didn't admit mistakes, didn't tattle on others, and didn't talk with their supervisors or fellow nurses about how to stop such errors down the line. In the best units, nurses and their managers held the opposite view. Stopping mistakes was viewed as so crucial that everyone was expected to admit and report mistakes immediately and discuss the root causes with colleagues. And when nurses learned how to avoid a mistake, they felt accountable for passing the lesson along to their colleagues. As Edmondson emphasized in this and subsequent writings, the best leaders, teams, and organizations drive out fear by creating "psychological safety" and encouraging people to be noisy and mindful error makers.

A similar lesson emerges from a study of "error management cultures" in sixty-five Dutch companies. In companies that had superior financial performance, the prevailing beliefs were that errors provided useful information about improving performance. Errors were seen as a normal part of the learning process, occasions for analysis and discussion, and something that should be shared with colleagues "so they don't make the same mistake." This research, along with more fine-grained experiments, indicates that when, instead, people play a game of "gotcha" and focus on pointing the finger of blame (especially on blaming their mistakes on others) accountability evaporates, fear runs rampant, and little is learned. As Edmondson's work shows, leaders and other influencers need to own up to their mistakes and, whether or not they are responsible for making a particular error, to focus on what can be learned rather than on who ought to be humiliated and stigmatized. Yes, as we've seen, leaders must sometimes remove the bad apples who make the same mistakes over and over or infect their peers with destructive emotions and actions. As Citrus Lane CEO Mauria Finley contended, however, such hard decisions should be implemented with as much empathy and compassion as you can muster.

The second bad feeling is the *fear of being ostracized,* or socially excluded. This particular brand of fear fuels bullying in many schoolyards and prevented those sawmill workers who were morally opposed to stealing, and never did it themselves, from expressing disapproval to their thieving coworkers. As we saw at that Connecticut high school, one trick for overcoming this destructive feeling is to turn the social pressures upside down, so that people who do the wrong thing, rather than the right thing, are pressured by peers to desist and, if they don't, are embarrassed and shunned. Similarly, when the clever and unconventional Ben Horowitz spoke to our scaling class, he lamented that Silicon Valley venture capitalists are notorious for their rudeness to entrepreneurs, which includes keeping them waiting and waiting and waiting for scheduled meetings. Horowitz said that he battles this bad behavior by charging his partners and associates ten dollars per minute when they are late for a meeting with an entrepreneur. He imposes the fine, in cash, on the spot and explains to the entrepreneur why he is collecting the money. As Horowitz pointed out, the embarrassment provides a far stronger incentive to be on time than the lost money.

In general, embarrassment and exclusion are best applied in small doses and with proper precautions. As we saw in the Atlanta schools, in the wrong hands, such pressures can fuel a climate where people feel compelled to do anything (including lying and cheating) to avoid public humiliation. Embarrassment is most effective when it steers people toward a viable (and ethical) path to pride and inclusion. For example, when that executive from the South American retail chain recruited the "cool" members of his team to change norms about using cell phones in meetings, they did embarrass colleagues a bit to remind them that the ban was no longer hollow talk. But their main emphasis was on making the simple act of shutting off your phone and putting it away necessary for claiming full inclusion.

The third dangerous feeling is *anonymity*. That feeling that no one is watching you very closely, so you can do whatever you want—be selfish, dishonest, unpleasant, free-riding, or a bit careless about your work. Subtle cues that create feelings of anonymity can provoke bad behavior. Recent evidence shows that darkness instills "a psychological feeling of illusory anonymity, just as children playing 'hide and seek' will close their eyes and believe that others cannot see them." Apparently, darkness and dim lighting trigger "the belief that we are warded from others' attention and inspections." The University of Toronto's Chen-Bo Zhong and his colleagues compared how participants behaved in a room that was brightly lit versus a room that was dimly lit (but bright enough so their actions were visible). Participants received both a brown envelope with $10 inside and an empty white envelope. They were instructed to solve math problems for five minutes, score their own work, and reward themselves with fifty cents for each correct answer—and return any unearned money to the white envelope. Participants in the two rooms performed the same. But those in the darker room cheated more, taking significantly more money than they earned compared to their counterparts in the well-lit room. These researchers also randomly assigned people to wear dark sunglasses or clear glasses. Each person was given $6 and was asked to keep some money for him- or herself and to give some to a stranger. Those wearing dark glasses kept more and gave less to strangers.

Michael Dearing, the venture capitalist and d.school colleague we've mentioned before, explained to us that executives who run large retail stores have long used bright lights and other tactics to make employees and customers feel less anonymous. In the 1990s, Dearing managed a large retail store in Boston called Filene's Basement. His mentors taught him that when employees of all ranks worked in brightly lit, open spaces, "shortage" or "shrink" (i.e., lost, damaged, or stolen merchandise) went down and labor efficiency went up. Dearing asserted that open doors, glass partitions, bright lighting, and frequent "drive-bys" by senior leaders kept the iconic 130,000-square-foot store "healthy" and protected merchandise from accidental or intentional loss. In a store that generated more than $100 million in annual sales, small improvements in shortage and labor productivity made big differences. The studies by Zhong and his colleagues suggest that Dearing's mentors had taught him evidence-based practices, not just ones based on arbitrary industry traditions and superstitions.

There is another way that the feeling of anonymity can be dangerous: accountability is difficult to sustain when employees perceive the people they serve as nameless and faceless, as mere objects or numbers to be processed, rather than as living breathing human beings who deserve their full attention and talents.

Making such humanity more vivid to employees increases accountability. For example, when radiologists review X-rays, they devote closer attention to their work after seeing pictures of patients' faces. In a study by Emory University's Srini Tridandapani and his colleagues, ten licensed radiologists were first asked to examine twenty pairs of chest X-rays (a total of 200 reviews); each pair was supposed to be for the same patient at two different junctures in his or her life—and most were. But some of the pairs in each set (between two and four) were intentionally mismatched, so that the radiologists, rather than examining two pictures of the same patient, were actually reviewing pictures of two different patients. When the radiologists reviewed these first two hundred images, they detected 12.5 percent (three of twenty-four) of the mismatches. The same ten radiologists were then each asked to review another batch of ten pairs of chest X-rays from different patients; as before, there were mismatches in each set. This time, however, the patient's picture was attached to each pair of X-rays. The radiologists then detected 64 percent (sixteen of twenty-five) of the mismatches. In other words, when patients were anonymous, radiologists were far less attentive than when they were reminded of the patient's humanity. Similarly, another study of fifteen radiologists who examined over one thousand images found that seeing a patient's pictures increased their feelings of empathy and resulted in more meticulous work.

The fourth warning sign is *feelings of injustice*. Numerous studies show that when people feel as if they are getting a raw deal from their boss or employer they give less in return; bad behavior runs rampant; and effort, efficiency, quality, civility, and other excellence metrics plummet. Indeed, although the workers at that sawmill stole because it was fun, the main reason that most workers steal is to get even for perceived injustices ranging from unfair pay cuts, to pay disparities, to disrespectful and emotionally distant bosses. The fundamental lesson from this research was summarized by Michael Dearing earlier in this chapter: "There is a difference between what you do and how you do it." Whether you are doing something bad like giving people pay cuts or demotions, or something good like giving them raises and promotions, employees will work harder, go out of their way to do extra work, stay later, and be more loyal to you if you take the time to explain why your actions were necessary, talk to them about how these changes will unfold, and treat them with dignity along the way. Recall Ben Horowitz's advice about being visible and compassionate during layoffs—if you do symbolic things like that and avoid objective injustices whenever possible, people will return the favor. But once they catch a whiff of injustice (especially if you've been coldhearted and mean-spirited), they won't lift a finger to do extra work and, if they can get away with it, will start arriving late, leaving early, doing sloppy work, and stealing more money, merchandise, or office supplies to even the score.

The fifth dangerous feeling is *helplessness*. When people believe that they are powerless to stop bad forces and events, they shirk responsibility, fail to act, lay low, and hide. After all, as psychologist Martin Seligman's classic research on learned helplessness demonstrates, even when people can easily escape from a bad situation, or change a situation to make it better for others, if they believe there is nothing that they can do to improve their lot in life, then they will do nothing but sulk and suffer. When learned helplessness sets in, people feel like the emotionally defeated dogs that Seligman studied early in his career. These unfortunate dogs had been subjected to one random electric shock after another that they could not escape; later, when these same dogs were put in a situation where they could easily escape a shock by jumping over a low wall, they didn't even try to move. They just crouched and whimpered as each shock hit.

The key to curing helplessness in both animals and humans is to convince them that, despite what happened in the past, there are steps they can take now to make things better. Employees at the Alameda Health System were a lot like Seligman's dogs before CEO Wright Lassiter and COO Bill Mann arrived. They had been in a downward spiral for so long that they felt it was impossible to improve the system's finances, patients' experiences, or their own work lives. Why try? It had never worked before. That is why Lassiter and Mann were smart to skip the poetry and just get people started on that money hunt right away. These diverse and influential employees not only dug up over $20 million; in doing so, they demonstrated to themselves and to their colleagues that they weren't helpless—that they had the power to eliminate the negative and accentuate the positive in the Alameda Health System.

Finally, we close with an overarching lesson about eliminating the worst and bringing out the best in an organization. It pops up throughout this chapter and is implied at numerous junctures in *Scaling Up Excellence*. When someone can find some way to direct a team's or an organization's attention toward the people affected by what it does (and away from members' own needs and wants), they will take greater responsibility for doing the right thing. This was certainly true for those radiologists who detected more errors in X-rays when the patient's picture was staring back at them. It was also evident when CEO Wright Lassiter at the Alameda Health System convinced union leaders that their patients—and ultimately the workers they represented—would be better off if their members took a shuttle to and from an employee parking lot rather than to compete with patients for parking spots.

A similar shift also seems to be unfolding in the Atlanta schools. After Dr. Beverly Hall was dismissed in 2011, Erroll B. Davis Jr. was brought in to clean up the mess. Davis was sixty-seven years old at the time and was supposed to be retiring as chancellor of the Georgia University System to spend time with his wife of forty-three years. She tried to talk him out of taking the job, and so did Michael Bowers, one of the directors of the state investigation that had uncovered the cheating. Bowers advised Davis, "You're crazy as a bedbug to take that job at your age." Davis didn't need the money and had nothing to prove. But he couldn't resist because he felt obligated to do the right thing and believed that he was the right person to do it—much like those effective but guilt-prone leaders that we learned about in chapter 5. As Bowers put it, "You know why he did it? He is a genuine public servant."

Davis has taken many big steps to make things better in Atlanta—especially to make it safe for teachers and administrators to engage in good behavior but unsafe for them to engage in bad behavior. Davis fired nearly two hundred cheating teachers and administrators who were exposed by the state's investigation. He then implemented a zero-tolerance policy for cheating. After one teacher had allegedly given her students answers to a standardized test, Davis investigated and immediately removed her from the classroom. He explained, "I do not want people who cheat teaching children. Can I do that? We'll find out. If I lose, so be it, sue me."

But we are most impressed by the little things that Davis has done—such as the ways he has treated teachers with basic dignity and respect that never existed during Dr. Hall's reign. One day, Davis walked from class to class at Slater Elementary and said to every teacher, "I want to thank you for what you do; I couldn't do your job." We were especially struck with a simple change when he moved into his new office—it reminded us of those studies with the radiologists. When the office was occupied by Dr. Hall, she covered a wall with bar graphs of test scores for all one hundred Atlanta schools. Davis took down the graphs and replaced them with big color photographs of the schoolchildren that he serves.

III

PARTING POINTS

CHAPTER 8

DID THIS, NOT THAT

Imagine You've Already Succeeded (or Failed)

We learned a lot about the Problem of More during the last seven years. Much of it was humbling. We didn't find any quick, easy, or sure-fire solutions for building and multiplying pockets of exemplary performance. Even the best scaling efforts that we studied were plagued with stretches when everything seemed to go wrong, people felt discouraged, and the path forward was mysterious and maddening. Yet we believe our journey led to useful and often encouraging lessons about how to create, spread, and sustain excellence in organizations.

Chapter 1 opened with the most important lesson that we learned: scaling ought to be treated as a ground war, not just an air war. Next, we introduced seven scaling mantras, starting with "Spread a mindset, not just a footprint" and ending with "Slow down to scale faster—and better—down the road." Chapter 2 examined key scaling choices, especially the trade-offs and tensions between "Buddhist" and "Catholic" strategies. The next five chapters dissected key scaling principles: "Hot causes, cool solutions,"

"Cut cognitive load, but deal with necessary complexity," "Build organizations where 'I own the place and the place owns me,'" "Connect people and cascade excellence," and "Bad is stronger than good." We also considered several overarching lessons under various guises, especially that the best leaders and teams treat scaling as a marathon rather than a sprint, are dedicated to gaining insights from every accomplishment and setback, and are driven by the nagging feeling that things are never quite good enough—by the "relentless restlessness" that Pixar's Brad Bird pegged as a hallmark of organizations where, little by little, people keep getting better at what they do.

Look Back from the Future

This final chapter focuses on how to turn such knowledge, and everything else you know about scaling, into action. We've discussed implementation mindsets and methods throughout this book. After all, knowing the right thing to do provides no advantage unless you actually do it. We close with an additional twist, a mind trick that goads and guides people to act on what they know and, in turn, amplifies their odds of success. We build on Nobel winner Daniel Kahneman's favorite approach for making better decisions. This may sound weird, but it's a form of imaginary time travel. It is called "the premortem." Kahneman credits psychologist Gary Klein with inventing the premortem technique and applying it to help many project teams avert real failures and the ugly postmortems that often follow.

A scaling premortem works something like this: when your team is on the verge of making and implementing a big decision, call a meeting and ask each member to imagine that it is, say, a year later. Split them into two groups. Have one group imagine that the effort was an unmitigated disaster. Have the other pretend it was a roaring success. Ask each member to work independently and generate reasons, or better yet, write a story, about why the success or failure occurred. Instruct them to be as detailed as possible and, as Klein emphasizes, to identify causes that they wouldn't usually mention "for fear of being impolitic." Next, have each person in the "failure" group read his or her list or story aloud, and record and collate the reasons. Repeat this process with the "success" group. Finally, use the reasons from both groups to strengthen your scaling plan. If you uncover overwhelming and impassable roadblocks, then go back to the drawing board.

More broadly, premortems spur participants to use "prospective hindsight," or, in grammatical terms, to think and talk in "future perfect tense." For example, instead of thinking "We will devote the next six months to spreading patient-centered care," travel to the future and think "We will have devoted six months to spreading patient-centered care." Now comes the critical element: you imagine that a concrete success or failure has occurred and look "back from the future" to tell a story about the causes. We saw an example of such imaginary time travel in the last chapter: recall that, in 2001, Xerox CEO Anne Mulcahy and her team wrote a make-believe 2005 *Wall Street Journal* article about the company's resounding success. This mock article listed performance metrics and quotes from experts about the specific steps that Xerox had taken to achieve a stunning turnaround during the prior four years.

Pretending that a success or failure has already occurred—and looking back and inventing the details of why it happened—seems almost absurdly simple. Yet renowned scholars including Kahneman, Klein, and Karl Weick supply compelling logic and evidence that this approach generates better decisions, predictions, and plans. Their work suggests several reasons why the premortem approach helps inoculate organizations against the scaling "clusterfugs" that we discussed in chapter 1—where illusion, impatience, and incompetence taint a scaling team, in turn making life hell for everyone involved.

For starters, looking "back from the future" helps people overcome blind spots. As we saw in chapter 1 and chapter 7, as upcoming events become more distant, people develop more grandiose and vague plans and overlook the nitty-gritty daily details required to achieve their long-term goals. Looking back from the future helps people bridge short-term and long-term thinking—a hallmark of successful scaling. Weick argues that this shift is effective, in part, because it is far easier to imagine the detailed causes of a single outcome than to imagine multiple outcomes and try to explain why each may have occurred. Beyond that, analyzing a single event as if it *has* already occurred rather than pretending it *might* occur makes it seem more concrete and likely to actually happen, which motivates people to devote more attention to explaining it. Weick uses studies of a professor's itinerary for a trip to Europe, Super Bowl predictions, and an imaginary traffic accident to demonstrate that people conjure up much richer histories when they look backward from the future rather than forward to the same hypothetical events. A similar effect is seen in experiments by Wharton Business School's Deborah Mitchell and her colleagues, which show that prospective hindsight, or imagining that an event has already occurred, "increases the ability to correctly identify reasons for future outcomes by 30%."

Looking back from the future also dampens excessive optimism, especially if the imagined outcome is a failure, is mediocre, or falls just short of being as wonderful as expected. As Kahneman and other researchers show, most people overestimate the chances that good things will happen to them and underestimate the odds that they will face failures, delays, and setbacks. Kahneman adds that "in general, organizations really don't like pessimists" and that when naysayers raise risks and drawbacks, they are viewed as "almost disloyal." Recall that, in chapter 1, the Stanford

IT team moved forward with a "big bang" implementation of the unfinished and unproven financial system. The scaling team charged ahead and forced four thousand people to use the system even though they knew that data would be missing and transactions would be slow and difficult. They did not postpone the launch or roll it out (as originally planned) to one group at a time to limit damage and maximize learning along the way; instead, irrational optimism prevailed. Somehow the team convinced themselves that things really wouldn't be that bad. Their impatience, illusion, and incompetence are symptoms of a classic clusterfug, which, in this case, rendered thousands of competent Stanford employees unable to perform their jobs properly for many months.

The decision might have been different if, before pulling the trigger, leaders had asked the team, "Imagine it is September of 2004 and Oracle Financials proved to be a terrible disaster. What happened? Be as detailed as possible." As Klein explains, premortems undercut the "damn-the-torpedoes attitude often assumed by people who are overinvested in a project." Those Stanford leaders might also have asked another question: "If you were advising another university in the same situation as us, what would you suggest?"

Harvard's Max Bazerman demonstrates that people are less prone to irrational optimism when they predict the fate of others' projects or businesses rather than their own. Bazerman observes that, when it comes to home construction or renovation projects, most people estimate that their friends' projects will run 25 percent to 50 percent late and over budget. But those same people estimate their own projects will be "completed on time and near the projected costs." The world needs dreamers and their dreams. Without them, there would be no new and wonderful inventions and no inspired new ideas to spread far and wide. But dreams of what is possible are best balanced with hard facts and realistic projections about what is probable. Engaging in prospective hindsight can increase the odds that the dreams we select to pursue do, in fact, come true.

A premortem can also shatter illusions that everyone on a scaling team concurs with a decision that is about to be made or that everyone believes an effort is going well and will continue to do so. Powerful and overconfident leaders often reward people who agree with them and punish those who are brave enough (or perhaps dumb enough) to disagree with their delusions. The resulting corrosive conformity is evident when people don't raise private doubts, known risks, and inconvenient facts. In contrast, as Klein explains, a premortem can create a competition where members feel accountable for raising obstacles that others haven't: "The whole dynamic changes from trying to avoid anything that might disrupt harmony to trying to surface potential problems." Klein describes a premortem with a Fortune 50 company where a senior executive imagined that a billion-dollar environmental project had failed because the CEO who championed it had retired— and the new CEO wasn't committed to the project's success. In a proper premortem, voicing such impolitic bad news and risks is safe, expected, and encouraged.

Was Scaling a Good Idea?

New isn't always improved. More sometimes turns out to be less. Growth doesn't necessarily lead to progress. Waiting is sometimes more effective than charging ahead. And at times, "you can't get there from here"—it is impossible to spread goodness from where it flourishes to where you want it to sprout next. The "imagine you have succeeded (or failed)" approach is especially useful for "go, no-go" decisions; for deciding if a scaling effort is worth launching at all, should be implemented as quickly or early as planned, or ought to continue.

Several kinds of premortem questions are instructive to mull · over. Start with feasibility. Was it actually scalable? Were you able to spread a pocket of goodness in ways that maintained quality and were economically viable? For example, about thirty years ago, Hank Jotz, who makes racing sails for small boats, had grown his San Francisco shop from a solo act to a six-person operation. Despite the expansion, Jotz wasn't making any more money. He ran the numbers and discovered that only one factor determined how much money he made each year: the number of hours he spent sewing. As Jotz told Sutton, "I realized that I was just running a hippie support system." So he closed his booming but not very profitable shop and went back to being Jotz Sails' sole employee— and has been happier ever since.

Feasibility questions also focus on if it was wise to scale as fast and as far as you did. As chapter 5 implies, teams that launch start-ups should look back from the future and ask, "Did we get too big too soon?" This concern is reinforced by "the Startup Genome Project," in which Max Marmer, Bjoern Herrmann, and colleagues surveyed 3,200 high-growth start-ups. They found that 74 percent of these young organizations suffered from premature scaling, which Marmer and Herrmann conclude is the main reason that so many start-ups grow too slowly or fail. Companies that stall or disband hire about 50 percent more employees in early growth stages compared to their more successful counterparts— which don't add employees until needed. Hiring too many people too soon burns through cash, creates unnecessary administrative burdens, undermines innovation, and causes companies to focus on landing customers before they have anything worthwhile to sell them. As venture capitalist Michael A. Jackson put it, "Getting venture money can be like putting a rocket engine on the back of a car. Scaling comes down to making sure the machine is ready to handle the speed before hitting the accelerator."

Other premortem questions ought to focus on the toll that

scaling took on people's lives. Even if you did ultimately succeed at spreading something wonderful far and wide, was it worth the cost? We aren't talking about money; we are talking about the burnout, fatigue, and even physical damage sometimes inflicted by prolonged and intense scaling efforts. Much like those climbers who reach the Everest summit, only to die on the descent, the victims might not have started the trek if they knew the ultimate price. The Oracle Financials fiasco falls into this category. The system works fine now. But we suspect that Stanford's chief information officer Chris Handley, who apparently left because of his starring role in this clusterfug, wouldn't enlist again if he could turn back time.

In other cases, you might enlist again, but only if you could reduce the distress and exhaustion. Ed Catmull, Pixar's cofounder and president, described a stretch when employees worked "brutal" hours for eight months to complete *Toy Story II*. Several employees suffered repetitive stress injuries and one had to leave the field permanently. One warm June day, a father was supposed to drop his baby off at day care, but he forgot the baby was in the backseat, drove straight to work, and left him trapped in the car in Pixar's parking lot. A few hours later, his wife, who also worked at Pixar, asked him about the baby. The distressed couple ran to the car and found him unconscious. The baby was revived with cold water and was fine. But Catmull's team decided that, although *Toy Story II* was finished on time and was a huge hit, they would never again travel down that harrowing path. So they made major changes, including limiting the hours that people worked, bringing in repetitive stress experts, and hosting physical fitness activities and classes. Catmull explained they learned to act—and not just talk—as if "we are in it for the long haul."

Finally, we suggest asking questions about the destination you will have reached if your dreams do come true. Sometimes success isn't all it's cracked up to be. Imagine you have built a large and respected company or nonprofit. Or you have spread quality tools, lean practices, or design thinking far and wide. Ask your team, "Are we happy living in the world we've built?" As we saw in chapter 4, as an organization grows, whether you like it or not, it will require more hierarchical layers, managers, rules, and (often) annoying administrative processes. It will also become increasingly difficult to maintain personal relationships with all your colleagues (let alone learn their names). Even if scaling up has made you rich, you may be uncomfortable within the walls of your own creation.

About fifteen years ago, Sutton had striking conversations with Mitch Kapor and his wife Freada Klein about their experiences at the Lotus Development Corporation. Lotus began as a small firm that Kapor started with a few friends in 1982. Lotus 1-2-3, the company's spreadsheet, quickly became the hottest-selling program for the (then new) IBM personal computer: sales hit $50 million in 1983 and jumped to over $150 million by 1984. Kapor didn't have the desire or temperament to run a big company, so he remained chairman and promoted ex-McKinsey consultant Jim Manzi to CEO. Manzi grew Lotus to over one thousand people by 1985 and stocked it with many "sales types" and "process types" from traditional corporations such as Procter & Gamble, Coca-Cola, and IBM. Kapor and other early Lotus employees enjoyed their new wealth, but many were counterculture types who chafed at the corporate attitudes and trappings: "The thrill of the start-up had turned into the drill of a major corporation," as author Robert X. Cringely put it.

In 1985, Freada Klein (then head of organizational development) did an experiment that confirmed that Lotus had become a place where its founders were misfits. With Kapor's permission, Klein pulled together the résumés of the first forty Lotus employees. On most résumés, Klein only altered the employees' names, but she changed Kapor's more extensively because his past as a transcendental meditation teacher and disk jockey was known throughout Lotus. Klein explained that most of these early employees had skills the growing company still needed, but many had done "risky and wacko things" such as being community organizers, being clinical psychologists, living at an ashram, or like Kapor, teaching transcendental meditation. Then Klein did something sneaky. She submitted all forty résumés to the Lotus human resources department. Not one of the forty applicants, including Kapor, was invited for a job interview.

The founders had built a world that rejected people like them. Kapor stepped down as Lotus's chairman in 1986 because "it wasn't my ambition to run a big company. I wanted to do this great product and make a big business out of it. But I didn't find the positive parts of running this big show to be very gratifying. . . . I like to be left alone to do my own thing. But instead, I was a prisoner of the spreadsheet." Lotus was eventually bought by IBM for $3.5 billion. Since leaving Lotus, Kapor has spent his time working with small companies and nonprofits, where he feels more at home.

Did This, Not That

When *Scaling Up Excellence* was nearly completed, we stopped to reflect on the Preface and the first seven chapters. After a few weeks of fretting and debating, we converged on seven lessons that are essential for scaling up without screwing up. We've added new twists to each lesson, including framing each from a "back to the future" perspective. The premortem isn't just a technique for one or two meetings before scaling commences or key decision points. Leaders and teams who weave prospective hindsight into such efforts gain a different and (the evidence suggests) superior vantage point. This means that instead of asking, "What will we do tomorrow?" you ask, "If we do have a successful day tomorrow, what will we have done?" and framing the next week, month, year, and so on in a similar fashion. In this spirit, we describe each lesson as if you already "did this, not that" rather than that "do this, not that."

1. We Started Where We Were, Not Where We Hoped to Arrive

The Preface ends with advice that scaling star Claudia Kotchka gives to people who ask where to begin an innovation effort: "Start with yourself, where you are right now, and with what you have and can get right now." We first heard Kotchka offer this advice to executives right after they heard a manager describe how she was fomenting design thinking in her big company. (Sorry, we can't use real names—let's call her Emma.) Emma started by redecorating her cubicle with design thinking materials, such as guidelines for developing empathy and Post-it notes with ideas from brainstorming sessions. She also cut her hair and dyed it a new color to signal to colleagues (and remind herself) that she was doing something different. During visits to the company's retail stores, Emma asked customers to try various prototypes intended to engage them as they waited for service. She also recruited salespeople to develop and test new phrases to say to customers. Emma didn't talk about design thinking, she just lived it. Emma also ran training sessions to teach colleagues about topics including "beginner's mind," "extreme users," and "Wizard of Oz" prototypes (with fake functionality for testing ideas with users). Because her company was secretive and competitive, when Emma invited colleagues to sessions she was vague about the topic, limited enrollment so participants felt like "the chosen ones," and asked them to keep the content hush-hush for a while. These tactics attracted considerable attention. In response, several jealous colleagues even organized secretive workshops on similarly vague topics.

Emma started with no budget, staff, or colleagues who practiced design thinking. Now several dozen colleagues have joined her. Emma, like everyone who succeeds at scaling, started her journey where she was and made the best of what she had. The same goes for teams with lots of money and people at their disposal. Dr. Louise Liang from Kaiser Permanente had a multi-billion-dollar budget to scale KP HealthConnect. But her Tiger Team still faced tough obstacles, especially skepticism generated by a decade of failed IT implementations and resistance to a somewhat standardized system from regions that had always operated as silos. Liang's team also succeeded because they started where they were and with what they had. The first rollout was in Hawaii because leaders there were willing to take risks. It was among the smallest regions, so implementation was less difficult than in a big region. Liang also had spent several years working in Hawaii at a health care system that collaborated with KP earlier in her career. So she had friends and allies who would go the extra mile to support the project, and she understood the local quirks, strengths, and landmines. Hawaii was a prime location to create that first pocket of excellence, which was then cascaded throughout Kaiser Permanente.

2. We Did Scaling, Not Just Swarming

Some leaders enjoy presiding over exciting kick-off events but lack the grit required for a prolonged ground war. As one executive lamented to us about her CEO's zest for inaugurating new initiatives, launching new products, and announcing and celebrating mergers, "She loves planning and hosting the party but has little interest in cleaning up the mess." Her boss loved the thrill of swarming together to discuss bold ideas and big plans but was allergic to the daily grind required for effective scaling. Although creating enthusiasm and spreading awareness about new beliefs, behaviors, and initiatives are useful first steps for mobilizing a mindset, they aren't enough. People have to live it or it won't stick.

Training was central to many of the scaling efforts that we've highlighted, including Facebook's Bootcamp and Bridge International Academies' training camp. Training was also a key element of the intervention that streamlined Wyeth's manufacturing processes—which cut costs by 25 percent and increased quality. Members of each "minitransformation" team were taught skills such as how to engage in difficult conversations with colleagues, provide coaching and feedback, practice lean manufacturing, and run a team huddle. In each case, although training helped set the stage for people to live a new mindset, it wasn't seen as sufficient. At Wyeth, teams were coached by managers and consultants as they harnessed these new skills to implement big changes in their own work flow and practices. Then they helped transfer what they had learned to other Wyeth teams.

Unfortunately, training sometimes creates little more than a brief swarm of activity. Much like corporate kick-offs where follow-up is lame or nonexistent, training has little effect when new behaviors and beliefs are taught but no steps are taken to enable people and teams to live those lessons. A few years back, the U.S. Transportation Security Administration (TSA) developed compelling metaphors to capture and communicate a new employee mindset for guiding the airport security experience. One metaphor was that a shark is easier to spot in calm rather than rough seas (i.e., a nervous terrorist is easier to notice when the screening setting is relaxed and quiet than tense and loud). Another was that a TSA officer should act more like a vigilant and helpful English pointer dog and less like an intimidating and insensitive Doberman pinscher. These metaphors highlight the security value of creating a calm and courteous screening experience with officers who are alert to passengers' moods and actions. The metaphors were used as a starting point for developing training to help TSA officers project calmness and competence, become more aware of passengers, and apply their own judgment and critical thinking as they screened passengers.

Stephanie Rowe, the former TSA executive who led this effort, described to us how these materials were rolled out during two-day sessions for the 1,100 TSA employees who conducted this training (a group that was scaled rapidly from 4, to 12, to 80, to 480, to 1,100). Rowe's videos of these meetings where "trainers were trained" show that the attendees were enthusiastic about spreading the new ideas and skills—they clapped, shouted slogans, and beamed with pride. In turn, these 1,100 trainers taught the materials to some fifty-four thousand TSA officers during four-hour sessions at more than 450 airports. Much effort was devoted to making this training engaging and influential. Most trainers believed that if officers lived the mindset and actions they taught, the TSA screening experience would become more humane for officers and passengers and the odds of catching people with bad intentions would increase.

Alas, as frequent flyers, we've seen little evidence that this single exposure has had much impact on how most TSA officers think and act as they screen passengers. Rowe believes there have been enduring effects at some airports that have visionary leaders and among those trainers who were especially energized by these ideas. But she admits that making fifty-four thousand officers aware of the new mindset and teaching them some new ways to do their jobs was only a start. Although a potentially valuable first step, changes in senior leadership and TSA budget priorities meant that few follow-up efforts were made to support or empower officers to ensure that their actions on the job reflected what they were taught. In short, this training triggered enthusiastic swarming for a few months among TSA employees. It had a big footprint because fifty-four thousand officers each received a few hours of training; but there is little evidence that it spread an enduring mindset because few serious steps were taken to enable and encourage the officers to live it.

3. We Used Our Mindset as a Guide, Not as the Answer to Every Question and Problem

The TSA experience demonstrates how crucial it is to spread (and live) a mindset, not just run up the numbers and plaster some logo or banner on as many people and places as possible. Yet, like all deep rooted human beliefs, mindsets are double-edged swords. You need them, but you should never stop asking whether the time is ripe to cast them aside. Karl Weick again offers an intriguing vantage point. After reading Norman Maclean's *Young Men and Fire,* Weick became fascinated with people and teams that battle forest fires. Maclean devoted the last fourteen years of his life to this analysis of why thirteen of sixteen smoke jumpers perished while battling the Mann Gulch fire in Montana in 1949. Weick discovered that similar reasons explained why the thirteen fire fighters died at Mann Gulch and why fourteen more were killed while battling a blaze at South Canyon, Colorado, almost fifty years later: "In both cases, these 23 men and four women were overrun by exploding fires when their retreat was slowed because they failed to drop the heavy tools they were carrying. . . . All 27 perished within sight of safe areas."

Weick views this reluctance to drop once—and usually—helpful tools as analogous to many decisions in organizational life. We saw how the inability to modify an ingrained mindset doomed Home Depot's efforts to expand to China; they failed because executives couldn't abandon the "do it yourself" approach that had proven so profitable in other markets. Scaling up in new places, with new people, and over time requires constant vigilance. You must be ready to drop your old tools, no matter how skilled you and your colleagues are at using them, how good they've been to you in the past, or how comforting it feels to hold them. If your old tools don't seem to be working at the moment, it might help to recall high-wire artist Karl Wallenda. After surviving on the wire for over sixty years, Wallenda fell to his death at the age of seventy-three, "still clutching his balance pole, when his hands could have grabbed the wire below him."

4. We Used Constraints That Channeled, Rather Than Derailed, Ingenuity and Effort

Chapter 2 is devoted largely to navigating the Buddhism-Catholicism continuum. We unpacked three diagnostic questions to help scaling teams decide how much to encourage adaptation to local needs and tastes as opposed to requiring conformity to existing templates or procedures. A key lesson about this spectrum warrants further emphasis and explanation: scaling flows more quickly and easily when people operate under a small number of ironclad constraints that they can rarely, if ever, crash through.

Research on creativity and innovation provides an enlightening perspective on constraints. On first blush, it may seem that imagination will flourish when "anything goes." Yet virtually all creative feats are accomplished by people, teams, and organizations that face challenging and immovable constraints. Much of the famous art created during the Renaissance in Europe, for example, was commissioned by benefactors—usually the church and governments—that bound artists to contracts that stipulated many details, including materials, colors, and sizes. You've probably seen pictures of Michelangelo's famous statue of David, and perhaps you've visited it at the Accademia Gallery in Florence. The statue was started, but never finished, by Agostino di Duccio in

1463. Michelangelo was hired in 1501 to complete it. The contract mandated that he finish it within two years. It also specified how the statue should look and be positioned. Within those guidelines (and the limits imposed by a hunk of marble that had been partially sculpted almost forty years earlier), Michelangelo was able to sculpt many nuances as he saw fit—and ignore many critics, including a government official who pestered him to make David's nose smaller. The result was the Renaissance's most famous sculpture—renowned for its great size and the striking contrast between David's intense facial expression and his relaxed, almost nonchalant, pose.

Celebrated architect and furniture designer Charles Eames asserted that "design depends largely on constraints"; that an innovator's "willingness and enthusiasm" to work within and around unchangeable elements determines success or failure. It isn't a question of whether there will be constraints; it is a question of whether people have the will and skill to find ways around the constraints and transform them into virtues. Research on creativity and constraint demonstrates that, when options are limited, people generate more, rather than less, varied solutions—apparently because their attention is less scattered. For example, a study of college students who played a computer game found that they produced more solutions, and more imaginative solutions, when there were fewer allowable exits in the mazelike game.

When it comes to scaling, certain parameters are always impossible (or very difficult) to change, including budgets, schedules, technologies, weather, and geography. And, no matter where an effort lands on the Buddhism-Catholicism continuum, effective scaling depends on building a few key barriers that steer people away from doing things that will produce needless confusion, generate unnecessary risks, and squander time and money. Even when careful repetition and replication are required, smart scaling teams keep the list of constraints short to ease cognitive load and direct attention to the most pressing challenges. The guardrail strategy used by Louise Liang's Tiger Team when deploying KP HealthConnect demonstrates that even in a fairly Buddhist organization it is wise to enforce a few crucial "non-negotiables." The right constraints helped Kaiser Permanente employees focus on what mattered most (serving patients), increase economic efficiency (by limiting the number of software programs they purchased and maintained), improve the speed and consistency of customer service (by pressing health care providers in all regions to respond to patients' e-mails within twenty-four hours), and reduce customer confusion and cognitive load (by demanding that all customer interfaces look and work the same).

Several months after learning of the Tiger Team's guardrail strategy, Sutton attended a World Economic Forum workshop in Palo Alto for forty or so leaders of growing companies. During the session on scaling up culture, Sutton mentioned the tensions between "Catholic" and "Buddhist" approaches. A few minutes later, Scott Wyatt, managing partner of NBBJ, a renowned international architecture and design firm, commented that they were a quite Buddhist organization. But he added that the firm's leaders had discovered they needed "guardrails" (his word) to constrain NBBJ's ten offices and seven hundred employees. Wyatt later explained to us that, when he had first become managing partner seventeen years earlier, NBBJ's "anything goes" culture was causing many efficiency and branding problems. The firm was using so many different computer-aided design (CAD) systems that people often had trouble collaborating on projects. There was little consistency in how people answered the phone, offices and services were branded in wildly varied ways, and individualism was so rampant that each architect used his or her own personal symbol to indicate "North" on drawings. Wyatt's team set out to create "one firm," rather than a place akin to "a house full of stray cats with the windows open, where all you could do was provide food so they would keep coming back, but otherwise they could do whatever they wanted."

NBBJ has since installed a few key guardrails. For example, CAD systems and marketing materials are now standardized. These and other constraints have helped enormously. Now people at NBBJ can collaborate more easily and clients aren't confused by inconsistent branding and marketing messages. Wyatt reports that instilling a "persona, shared ways of doing and being that are emblematic of what it is like to work at NBBJ and to work with us," was especially challenging. One guardrail was essential for making this happen: a commitment to doing only "value-based" rather than "commodity-based" work. Maintaining such discipline is easy when clients are clamoring for a firm's services. But when a major downturn hits (such as the 2009 meltdown), it is tempting to resort to "commodity-based" work in order to pay the bills. Wyatt explained that, in the end, doing so is always a mistake because it damages a firm's brand and undermines its ability to land value-based work down the road.

NBBJ uses a practice that helps its partners live this mindset. When a partner lands a potential piece of work, it is reviewed by one or two other partners who won't be involved in the project. The firm will not commit to the project unless both (or all three) partners support a "go decision." Particular attention is devoted to accepting only value-based business. Wyatt added something that dovetails with Daniel Kahneman's warnings about human overconfidence: this practice is necessary because "architects are so naturally confident that they believe they can do anything." Ending bad projects before they begin doesn't just save money and protect the brand; it saves people from living through a "horrible five to ten years," the typical duration of an NBBJ project.

5. Our Hierarchy Squelched Unnecessary Friction, Rather Than Creating and Spreading It

In chapter 4, we quote an intriguing exaggeration from Chris Fry, Twitter's head of engineering: "The job of the hierarchy is to defeat the hierarchy." Fry and fellow executive Steve Greene don't believe that the hierarchy should be used to unleash anarchy. They mean it should be used, in Greene's words, to "build a better organizational operating system"—a lesson that they gleaned from scaling up Salesforce.com's development organization. Fry and Greene emphasize that, although more roles and processes are needed as organizations and projects expand, skilled leaders wield their power to eliminate needless friction and complexity—not burden employees with "rules, tools, and fools" that make it tougher to do their jobs and waste money and talent.

In April 2013, Sutton attended a gathering at Intuit where CEO Brad Smith and Chairman Bill Campbell ("the Coach" whom we introduced in chapter 1) had a rollicking discussion about "creating awesome products." The pair echoed Fry and Greene's advice, emphasizing that they were bent on reducing friction for engineers, on doing everything possible so that the people who build Intuit's products don't feel as if "they are walking through muck." Smith and Campbell also emphasized to the large audience (mostly Intuit employees) that people in staff positions need to think and act the same way. We followed up with Intuit to learn more about how the company's leaders lived this belief. We were especially struck by the changes they've made to speed and smooth the decision-making process. After an internal task force examined how product teams decide what goes into a new software release, they found that too many managers were too involved in such decisions. The process was inefficient, unclear, and sometimes demoralizing for team members. After a detailed analysis, the task force rolled out a new decision process. It grants far more decision authority to small scrum teams that use agile software development methods. Management's role in each decision is limited to (at most) a pair of approvers: one sponsor to remove roadblocks and one coach to provide vision. The rest of the decision is left to the scrum team that knows the product and the target customers best.

This Intuit story demonstrates how a hierarchy ought to function during scaling: the best organizations perform constant subtraction, not just addition and multiplication. The story also reinforces a basic insight about scaling: "Many hands make light the work" is a dangerous half truth. We've shown how adding more people to an organization, a project, or a team creates costly side effects. As more people come aboard, members do (and should) devote more time and effort to communication, coordination, and the maintenance of warm and trusting bonds. Despite such efforts, coordination and relationships are still prone to degenerate as more members join. Recall Hackman's rule: "No work team should have membership in the double digits. . . . The number of performance problems a team encounters increases exponentially as team size increases."

A useful corollary is: if a team has leadership and performance problems, don't start by blaming the leader or hunting for bad apples to reform or remove. Consider its size first. Follow what founders Akshay Kothari and Ankit Gupta did at Pulse News when communication problems started cropping up: if a team has more than six or seven members, break it into two or three subgroups.

Melissa Valentine and Amy Edmondson's "pod" study in chapter 4 confirms the virtues of keeping teams small as organizations grow. When the emergency department's disorganized mass of twenty-five or so doctors and nurses were divided into multiple five- or six-person pods, there was a marked improvement in communication, satisfaction, trust, and accountability.

And patients spent an average of three hours less during a visit to the emergency department—"throughput time" plummeted about 40 percent, from eight hours (8.34) to five hours (5.29) per patient.

6. We Worked with People We Respected, Not Necessarily Our Friends

Chapter 6 shows that, although most people prefer to be around others who are similar to them, new mindsets, skills, and practices travel faster and farther when team members have varied backgrounds, skills, and viewpoints. When a scaling effort is launched by a broad group that is representative of an organization's people and positions (rather than a narrow subset), members will have professional, social, and emotional ties to colleagues throughout the organization. As we saw with the first team assembled by Bonny Simi at JetBlue to tackle "irregular operations" problems, a diverse team can use its extensive (and often nonoverlapping) relationships as pathways to spread excellence to many corners of a network.

In addition, as Linda Abraham, cofounder and executive vice president for global development at comScore, puts it, "There is a strong tendency to hire people like you, who agree with you; but that is the worst thing for building out a team." Abraham reports that this was a hard-won lesson from cofounding two companies—that it helped comScore survive and keep getting stronger despite some tough times since it was formed in 1999 (including the 2001 dot-com bust and the 2009 financial meltdown). The company, which measures and draws insights about what people do online, now has 1,100 employees working in thirty-two offices and twenty-three countries and has annual sales of about $280 million. Abraham attributes comScore's success, in part, to "people that aren't necessarily the ones you want to have dinner or socialize with, who not only have different skills for rounding out the team, but who see the world differently than you do, who think in a different mode." Abraham added that the goal should be to hire people whom you respect and who bring new thinking to the organization; whether you like them should be secondary. Teams need to work together regardless of whether they are "friends." Diversity of style, thought, and culture can sometimes generate friction. But if it is productive friction, and if your team frames it that way, it can help build resilience "almost like allergy shots for your organization." Abraham emphasizes that this approach works best if "you are not too proud to empower them to try out ideas that are different from yours, or to change your mind when they prove you wrong."

Abraham's advice is bolstered by research that shows teams are more adept at problem solving and creativity when members argue in an atmosphere of mutual respect—when each member feels compelled to "fight as if you are right, and listen as if you are wrong." Abraham's advice, and the supporting research, remind us of a story we heard from Ivan Ernest, who led Google's HR efforts in engineering as the company grew from 1,200 engineers in 2005 to 12,000 in 2010. Ernest explained that constructive arguments are crucial to Google's culture—it's a place where evidence and logic, rather than one's position and past accomplishments, are expected to prevail. Ernest was once at a meeting led by Google cofounders Sergey Brin and Larry Page where he got into a heated argument with an "exceptionally strong-willed" head of engineering. Ernest began to worry that he was pushing this more senior colleague too hard and doing so in front of Google's founders to boot. Then, suddenly, his opponent stopped in midsentence and said, "I now strongly disagree with myself. You are right." That's how life looks in the healthy organizations that Linda Abraham is talking about.

7. Accountability Prevailed, Free Riding and Other Bad Behaviors Failed

We've emphasized how organizations that are filled with employees who feel as if "I own the place and it owns me" squelch free riding and create social pressures to step up and do the right thing. We saw such accountability at Netflix, at Tamago-Ya, and, most dramatically, at the Taj Hotel during that terrorist attack. The Taj story that closed chapter 5 focused on the hotel staff's extreme bravery and self-sacrifice. The same accountability that Taj employees demonstrated that awful day is evident in the ordinary things they do (and have done for years) to put "guests front and center." This mindset was revealed when John Thomas (now a vice president at Rambus) and his family stayed at the Taj in 2005. After the long flight from the United States to India, they were greeted at the airport by a driver from the Taj. Their three-year-old daughter, Aaria, was tired and hungry, and despite her parents' best efforts she cried throughout the drive. When they arrived at the hotel, a staff member immediately greeted them with a key and informed them that there was no need to stand in the check-in line or deal with their bags. It was all taken care of, and the family could go straight to their room to tend to their cranky child. When they walked into the room, a warm glass of milk and cookies were waiting. Much to her parents' relief, Aaria gobbled down the milk and cookies at once and was smiling and giggling within minutes. When the astonished John Thomas called reception to thank them, he asked how they had known about Aaria's unhappy state. The Taj staffer reported that the driver had called en route to inform reception about the family's predicament, and they had taken care of the rest.

As we mulled over Aaria's story, and reviewed cases, press reports, and the stories that other Taj guests told us, we realized that accountability pervades the place because, while the hotel has a clear hierarchy and specialized roles, every employee—regardless of rank—is selected, trained, rewarded, and coached to take pride in advocating for guests, learning about each guest's particular needs, and gently pressing and teaching his or her Taj colleagues to do the same. This mindset explains the feeling of ownership that, rather than becoming weaker with each handoff, persisted and shaped many small actions, such as passing a message about the Thomas family's cranky daughter from the driver to the front desk and on to other Taj staffers. In contrast, recall Annie and Perry Klebahn's United Airlines experience that opens chapter 5. The absence of ownership led a contractor to lose track of their daughter Phoebe. It meant that no employee would allow Phoebe to call her worried parents or camp employees to inform them that United had fumbled but she was fine. And this lack of accountability made it acceptable (and perhaps routine) for numerous United employees to decline to help the distraught parents until Perry reminded one that she too was a parent—not just a United employee.

Lack of ownership and weak pressures to do the right thing aren't evident just when employees shirk from providing adequate customer service (or elect not to do so because doing nothing is safer than trying to do the right thing). It also happens when the game of work encourages every employee to look out for him- or herself and no one else; when pay and promotion are linked to selfish acts such as ignoring or even undermining colleagues, people learn that their success and security hinges on thinking first, last, and always of "me" rather than "we or us." When that happens, ownership and feelings of mutual obligation evaporate, and unfortunate assumptions frame and fuel nearly everything that people do. A newly hired executive at a big financial services firm told Rao that he began to realize that free riding ran rampant in the company when a colleague remarked, "I am assigned to this team for 20 percent of my time, and so I am only accountable for 20 percent of the team's goals!"

In contrast, excellence spreads and persists when accountability pressures permeate a workplace—when that feeling of ownership for problems and solutions pervades each handoff, each meeting, and each interaction with the people whom an organization serves. A compelling illustration comes from case studies by the Organ Donation Breakthrough Collaborative, a consortium formed among forty-five U.S. hospitals in 2003 to increase the rate of organ donation. Thousands of people die each year in the United States because they need a new heart, lung, liver, or kidney but none is available. In the typical U.S. hospital, organs are "harvested" from about 50 percent of patients who die, have agreed to be donors, and have viable organs. But approximately 15 percent of U.S. hospitals have a "conversion" rate over 75 percent. The Collaborative's case studies uncovered the mindsets and practices that permeate such places. At every stage, staff members involved with potential donors and their families aggressively (but tactfully) pursue every potential opportunity. All the staff—not just doctors and nurses but receptionists, administrators, and clergy too—work to ensure that donations happen.

The "team huddle" is a key practice that such hospitals use to fuel accountability and communication when a viable donor is near death. Teams have a series of brief stand-up meetings to discuss the family's understanding of the patient's condition, as well as the family's emotional state and experience at the hospital. These steps are essential for gaining the family's trust, determining the best manner and time to raise the issue of organ donation, and deciding which team members will take which actions.

"All teach, all learn" is the motto that guides these huddles, as well as many other actions in hospitals with the highest donation rates. When everyone feels obligated to do the right thing, each person feels compelled to be both a teacher and a student—to share everything he or she knows with colleagues and to learn as much as possible from others as well. When that happens, accountability spirals upward—not destructive expectations that "it's not my job," or worse still, the belief that "if I do the right thing, something bad will happen to me."

The Satisfactions of Scaling

We've detailed many of the difficulties of spreading excellence from the few to the many. We started by calling scaling "the Problem of More" and describing it as a "vexing" challenge that "nagged and gnawed" at leaders and teams. We documented many obstacles and showed that there are no easy paths to scaling success. Yet an upbeat theme runs throughout *Scaling Up Excellence,* one that infused nearly every conversation that we had with people about their scaling projects: an unmistakable, irrepressible, and contagious sense of pride. We don't mean false, conceited, arrogant, or selfish pride—the kind that undermines accountability and creates clusterfugs. Rather, we mean authentic pride, the feeling that "we did something good together," and the faith that, although it won't be easy, if we continue to invest the effort, to act as if "I own the place and the place owns me," and stick together, then good things will keep happening.

Think of that first meeting at JetBlue when most of Bonny Simi's colleagues believed that her "irregular operations" project was doomed to fail. Simi was undaunted and asked the skeptical group to humor her for just that one day—to map out the steps required to shut down and then reopen JetBlue's Kennedy Airport operations when bad weather hit. Simi allowed herself to feel proud for just a moment when she saw how much progress the group made that first day, that they were willing to stick with the project a bit longer and to help recruit other (equally skeptical) colleagues to give it a try. Then, little by little, the team worked together to identify—with those pink Post-it notes—parts of the system that needed to be changed. Team members felt proud as they started fixing one flawed element after another and spreading the changes across the company. Now, when Simi and the hundreds of JetBlue employees who ultimately joined the "Irregular Operations Integrity Team" look back on their ingenuity and hard work, they feel proud because "we did something good together." As reservation agent Annette Hill put it, being on the IROP team made her feel, "This is our company—it's not theirs—it's ours."

These are the kinds of satisfactions that propel effective scaling efforts day after day, that scaling veterans remember with well-deserved pride, and that entice them to join the next effort, even though the last one was so much darn work.

TEACH US MORE, LEARN MORE

Dear Reader,

The publication of *Scaling Up Excellence* is a major milestone on our learning journey, but not the end. We invite you to join us as we continue to learn about the challenges of spreading constructive beliefs and behavior in organizations. Please visit our website at scalingupexcellence.com to read about what we've learned and been fretting over lately, see comments and stories from readers, and add your own ideas. Given the interactive process that we used to learn about spreading excellence, we would especially appreciate if you e-mailed us your scaling stories and questions to mystory@scalingupexcellence.com. Please note that by sending us your story, comment, or observation, you are giving us permission to use it in the things we write and say. But we promise not to use your name unless you give us explicit permission.

You can follow Sutton (@work_matters) and Rao (@huggyrao) on Twitter. And we encourage you to connect with each of us on LinkedIn.

Thanks so much, and we look forward to hearing from you.

Robert I. Sutton
Huggy Rao
Stanford University

ACKNOWLEDGMENTS

Many people helped us during the long journey that created this book; as the Appendix explains, *Scaling Up Excellence* was, in large part, the result of seven years of conversation between us and a large and diverse band of smart scaling veterans, students, colleagues, and others. We thank each of you and apologize to anyone we have forgotten. We couldn't have finished this long strange trip without you.

For starters, we thank our Stanford colleagues. Jeff Pfeffer was—as always—magnificently supportive, insightful, critical, and cynical. We appreciate Jeff's encouragement to be the best Bob Sutton and the best Huggy Rao we can be, rather than mediocre imitations of someone else. Chip Heath challenged our ideas, coached us on the book publishing world, encouraged us to stand up for our convictions, and—one day—created a prototype cover for the book (we didn't use it, but it amazed his brother Dan). Now that's a full-service colleague! Other supportive Stanford colleagues include Steve Barley, Tom Byers, Chuck Eesley, Pamela Hinds, Maggie Neale, Charles O'Reilly III, Bernie Roth, Amin Saberi, Tina Seelig, Baba Shiv, Jeremy Utley, and Melissa Valentine. Rao thanks Madhav Rajan, senior associate dean at the Stanford Business School, for his encouragement and support. Sutton thanks Peter Glynn (chair of the Department of Management Science and Engineering) and Jim Plummer (dean of the Stanford Engineering School) for their encouragement and tolerance of his quirks and flaws. David Hoyt of the Graduate School of Business did the writing and research for many of the cases that we've drawn on in this book—Dave is a master of this craft and a delight to work with.

Ariadne Scott, Stanford's Bicycle Program coordinator, went to heroic lengths to help with the bicycle helmet project in our scaling class, as did Debra Dunn from the Stanford d.school. A host of former and current Stanford students supported us in diverse ways, including Betsy Bradford, Lei Liu, Joachim Lyon, Govind Manian, Daniela Retelny, Bobbi Thomason, Dan Tuttle, and Gonzalo Valdés. We are grateful to Rebecca Hinds for her inspired writing and editorial skills and to Liz Gerber (now a faculty member at Northwestern University) for her sharp eye and design skills. We thank Isaac Waisberg (now at Tel Aviv University) for his work on the Wyeth case. There are several Stanford staff members who helped us enormously in dozens of ways. Sutton appreciates the support from his assistant Roz Morf and information technology guru Tim Keely. Rao especially appreciates Tina Bernard and Jeannine Williams, both role models of excellence. We both appreciate the remarkable support—and perseverance—of Ronie Shilo from the Stanford Center for Professional Development.

A number of colleagues outside of Stanford shaped our ideas in crucial ways. Karl Weick of Michigan inspired us not just through his remarkable work and ideas but also by being the very model of a great scholar and for asking Rao some remarkably difficult questions. We also thank Teresa Amabile and Amy Edmondson (both at the Harvard Business School), Kim Elsbach (University of California at Davis), Adam Grant (Wharton Business School), Joe Porac (Stern Business School, New York University), and Barry Staw (University of California at Berkeley) for sharing their papers and ideas, and for their encouragement. Rao appreciates stimulating conversations with Robert Dewar, Rad Wilson, Mohan Reddy, and Mike Sokoloff on rejuvenating large organizations. Sutton offers special thanks to the late J. Richard Hackman for his warmth and teasing, for caring so much about the little things, and for teaching him so much about how groups function and how to study them.

As we emphasize in the Appendix, we worked with many scaling veterans to gather stories and develop our ideas. We thank Linda Abraham (comScore), Brad Bird (Pixar), Shona Brown (former Google executive), Tim Brown (IDEO), Denis Bugrov (Sberbank), Ed Catmull (Pixar), Sarah Chou (former Stanford student and a member of "the Watermelon Offensive"), Chip Conley (Joie de Vivre hotels), Delos Cosgrove (Cleveland Clinic), Chris Cox (Facebook), David Darragh (Reily Foods), Cassie Devine (Intuit), Doug Dietz (General Electric), Ivan Ernest (Google),

Tony Fadell (Nest), Barry Feld (Cost Plus), Joe Felter (Stanford researcher and retired U.S. Army colonel), Mauria Finley (Citrus Lane), Chris Flink (IDEO), Chris Fry (Twitter), Nick Gottuso (retired Hillsboro, California, police captain), Steve Greene (Twitter), Ankit Gupta (Pulse News), Kaaren Hanson (Intuit), Maia Hansen (McKinsey), Marc Hershon (creative human being at large), Ben Horowitz (Andreessen Horowitz), Drew Houston (Dropbox), Michael Kamarck (former Wyeth executive), Elyse Kidman (Pixar), Dr. Uma Kotagal (Cincinnati Children's Hospital), Akshay Kothari (Pulse News), Karin Kricorian (Disney), Dr. Louise Liang (retired, Kaiser Permanente), John Lilly (Greylock), Kali Lindsay (the Stanford student who told her bike accident story to our class), Shannon May (Bridge International Academies), Joe McCannon (formerly of the Institute for Health Improvement), Lenny Mendonca (McKinsey and Half Moon Bay Brewing Company), Yusuke Miyashita (IDEO), Donna Morris (Adobe), Whitney Mortimer (IDEO), Shantanu Narayen (Adobe), Colonel Peter Newell (former leader of the Rapid Equipping Force, retired, U.S. Army), Holly Parker-Coney (Adobe), Susan Peters (General Electric), Dan Portillo (Greylock), Diego Rodriguez (IDEO), Mike Schroepfer or "Schrep" (Facebook), Prasad Setty (Google), John Thomas (Rambus), Heather Vilhauer (Girl Scouts of Northern California), John Walker (Pixar), Xiao Wang (former New York City schools administrator), and Karen Weiss (Intuit).

Several people were unusually helpful and tolerant of our relentless requests. Bonny Simi from JetBlue helped us at every turn: she's invited hundreds of Stanford students and visiting executives to design solutions for JetBlue over the years, done numerous presentations to students and executives, invited us to write a case about JetBlue, allowed us to interview her many times, and always taken the time to correct and add facts to our descriptions. The persistent and enthusiastic Claudia Kotchka (a retired Procter & Gamble executive), another of our scaling heroes, taught many Stanford classes, allowed us to interview her many times, and provided us with precise and helpful ideas about what effective scaling looks like and feels like. We met Dr. Louise Liang (now retired from Kaiser Permanente) just a few months before this book was finished, but she was remarkably helpful in telling us her story in detail and for reviewing (and making key edits) in our description of the Tiger Team's rollout of KP HealthConnect. John Lilly, now a venture capitalist at Greylock, reviewed and critiqued our ideas, invited us in to do a case study when he was CEO of Mozilla, has been a class guest multiple times and, when we sent him an e-mail about anything, always replied with wise and often surprising words. Michael Dearing, who teaches at the Stanford d.school and is a venture capitalist at Harrison Metal, contributed multiple ideas to this book, especially the Buddhism-Catholicism continuum. We are grateful to Annie and Perry Klebahn for letting us use the United Airlines story that begins chapter 5; Perry also contributed several other scaling stories to this book—as usual, largely through his actions rather than his words. We are deeply thankful to David Kelley, the primary founder of both IDEO and the Stanford d.school. David has helped us in so many ways that it is impossible to name them all: by letting Sutton hang out for years at IDEO, allowing Sutton to join the group that started the d.school, allowing Rao and Sutton to start the first d.school executive program, giving us so much of his weird and wise advice, and most of all, showing us how scaling is accomplished by a skilled and compassionate leader. We are also grateful to Tom Neilssen and Les Tuerk from BrightSight for working with us to arrange workshops and speeches, which helped us develop our scaling ideas and in many other ways.

This book would not have survived the journey from half-baked idea, to proposal, to finished manuscript without our relentless and practical literary agent—Christy Fletcher—who has served as guide, friend, and shield. We are also appreciate the support provided by her colleagues at Fletcher & Company, especially Kevin Cotter, Melissa Chinchillo, and Sylvie Greenberg. Don Lamm (who has been in the book business for over fifty years) offered his wisdom and wry wit during early conversations about this project. Roger Scholl, our editor at Crown, was an insightful reader, pressing us gently but firmly to refine our arguments and language, and especially to get out of the weeds and remember the big picture. Our partners at Crown Books, including Tina Constable, Mauro DiPreta, Tara Gilbride, Ayelet Gruenspecht, Jessica Morphew, Michael Nagin, and Derek Reed, have been equally supportive and responsive. Justin Gammon displayed remarkable imagination, design skill, and persistence during the process of designing the book cover. Many people gave us thoughtful feedback on the numerous prototypes that were developed, especially Claire Dolan, Deb Stern, Hunter Wimmer, Whitney Mortimer, and Arianna Tamaddon.

Sutton gives his love to his three children, Tyler, Claire, and Eve, for putting up with their father's obsession with another book—and offering so much encouragement, even though he is a strange man who, in their view, serves long stretches of solitary confinement in the garage. Sutton offers particular thanks to his youngest, Eve, who, in her final years before going off to college, has again—through our shared wall—endured the tap tap tap (or as she puts it the "bang, bang, bang") of her dad's clumsy two-finger typing technique as he worked away on yet another book project.

Finally, this book would not have been possible without our loving wives, Marina and Sadhna. They were our not-very-silent partners in this long project—wellsprings of patience and beacons of light who gave us nourishing affection and encouragement, shielded us from demands, and offered wisdom about scaling and everything else in life. We owe a deep debt of gratitude to these two remarkable women.

THE SEVEN-YEAR CONVERSATION: HOW WE DEVELOPED THESE IDEAS

We have over fifty years of combined experience on projects that generate knowledge about organizations, notably efforts to write peer-reviewed academic papers for outlets such as the *Administrative Science Quarterly* and the *American Journal of Sociology*, articles for managerial audiences in publications including the *Harvard Business Review* and *McKinsey Quarterly*, and books such as this one that address practical challenges. Yet neither of us had ever experienced anything quite like the path that ultimately led to *Scaling Up Excellence*. This Appendix describes key details of the philosophy, learning strategy, and methods that we used during this long, unpredictable, sometimes frustrating, and endlessly fascinating seven-year effort. Although the journey is now punctuated by the completion and publication of this book, it will continue for years to come.

RIGOR AND RELEVANCE

Our guiding philosophy was inspired by "Repairs on the Road to Rigor and Relevance," a 1995 article by Barry Staw of the University of California at Berkeley. As our Preface explains, "Regardless of what we did during any given week, we wove together two goals: uncovering the most *rigorous* evidence and theory we could find and generating observations and advice that were *relevant* to people who were determined to scale up excellence." This meant bouncing back and forth between "the clean, careful, and orderly world of theory and research—that rigor we love so much as academics—and the messy problems, crazy constraints, and daily twists and turns that are relevant to real people as they strive and struggle to spread excellence to those who need it."

As the project unfolded, several twists on this philosophy emerged. We are strong advocates for evidence-based management. We believe that leaders and teams make better decisions about scaling (and other vexing management challenges) when they draw on quantitative and qualitative data about their own organizations, patterns in other organizations, and research on human and group behavior. This perspective is woven in throughout *Scaling Up Excellence*. Even when we tell a story or offer a management tip but don't mention a specific theory or piece of research, in all likelihood some academic paper or book lurks behind the scenes (but we omit it because describing it would be overkill). Yet, while writing this book, we became increasingly aware of the limits of evidence-based management. The massive pile of theory and data that we reviewed is not sufficiently developed, integrated, or consistent to allow members of a scaling team to simply look up the right answers and apply them. The behavioral sciences haven't advanced to this point and probably never will. In the case of scaling, there are so many different aspects of the challenge, and the right answers vary so much across teams, organizations, and industries (and even across challenges faced by a single team or organization), that it is impossible to develop a useful "paint by numbers" approach. Regardless of how many cases, studies, and books (including this one) you read, success at scaling will always depend on making constantly shifting, complex, and not easily codified judgments.

Scaling is akin to flying a plane or performing surgery. Much like the best pilots and surgeons, leaders and teams charged with scaling will practice their craft with greater skill—and screw up less—if they know and apply the best evidence. But that isn't enough. You wouldn't want to be operated on by a surgeon who had memorized every study on, say, how to do appendectomies, yet had never actually performed the procedure. Similarly, scaling, like other complex leadership challenges, is a craft that requires years of hands-on experience to master. That's why we draw so heavily on cases and stories about leaders, teams, and organizations that have been in the thick of scaling; our academic theory and research are valuable only when they ring true to people who wrestle with such challenges, enable them to understand the obstacles they face, and guide them in practicing their craft.

SEVEN YEARS OF CONVERSATION

Nearly all of our past publications have resulted from more or less the same process—the same one used by many other academics and business writers. We first spend several months or years gathering ideas and evidence. Next, we analyze those facts and reach conclusions. Finally, we present "the truth" to people who read our articles and books and attend our classes and speeches. For the first year or two of this journey, we traveled down this familiar path. We did case studies, reviewed theory and research, and huddled to develop insights about scaling challenges and how to overcome them. Little by little, this process changed from a private conversation between the two of us to ongoing conversations about scaling with an array of smart people. We were at the center of this process: making decisions about which leads, stories, and evidence to pursue; choosing which to keep, discard, or save for later; and weaving them together into (we hope) a coherent form. Yet this book is best described as the product of years of give-and-take between us and many thoughtful people, not as an integrated perspective that we constructed in private and are now unveiling for the first time.

Hundreds of people played direct roles in helping us, and thousands more played indirect roles—even if they didn't realize it. We detail the forms these interactions took below in the overview of our seven core methods. Yet, from another vantage point, we did pretty much the same thing every day during the last five years of this project: we engaged with people who knew about scaling and used their ideas to try to make our ideas better. We still did many things alone or just with each other. When we read academic articles, cases, or media reports we didn't involve others; the two of us talked about our emerging ideas, and we wrote the text. Yet early on we realized that our usual "hide for a long time, discover the 'truth,' and then broadcast it" approach wouldn't allow us to boil down the ideas, advice, and stories we were collecting into a book that was—for our tastes—rigorous and integrated and, at the same time, useful and engaging to people who face real scaling challenges. As a result, we shifted to a less efficient but, in our view, more effective approach.

We began actively recruiting people to help us develop and evaluate our work, and we continued doing so until the book was completed. Sometimes, we e-mailed them questions about topics that we didn't understand very well, and—surprisingly often—they went to great lengths to provide insightful answers. For example, in chapter 5, we discuss venture capitalist John Lilly's experiences as a "coordinator" in the introductory computer science class at Stanford. The role was crucial to Lilly's development as a leader and entrepreneur as well as that of other high-tech leaders, including Yahoo! CEO Marissa Mayer. When we asked Lilly a one-sentence question about being a coordinator, he shot back a four-hundred-word e-mail that concluded, "Is that what you were looking for? Happy to talk more, it's one of my favorite topics." Later, Lilly reviewed a draft of the section to make sure that we had it right. We also presented our emerging principles to Lilly several times over the years; he was always thoughtful and never pulled punches when we had missed something. We used related approaches to gather stories and ideas from other scaling veterans, including Louise Liang on the KP HealthConnect rollout and Joe McCannon on the 100,000 Lives Campaign (Rao had already written a case on the campaign, but we wanted more details). We used similar methods to unearth shorter snippets, such as chapter 3's story about the coatrack ritual, which Omnicell's CEO Randall Lipps created to remind his team to check their egos at the door.

Well before we wrote a page of this book, we began presenting our "half-baked scaling ideas" to people who were (or had been) knee-deep in scaling challenges. The first time was at a presentation that Sutton gave to six people on Kaaren Hanson's "D4D" team at Intuit in early 2009. Our ideas evolved over the years in response to lessons from these presentations—right up to the weeklong scaling session that Rao taught to 158 senior executives (from more than thirty different industries and twenty-five countries) at Stanford in the summer of 2013. Our rough calculations reveal that we presented versions of these ideas to over six thousand people from one hundred diverse audiences. Sometimes these were big audiences, such as two thousand beer distributors or several hundred executives who ran large prisons. Sometimes our audience was just one person, as in our dinner with Oliver Chow, a senior executive and scaling veteran from MediaTek (a semiconductor firm). We asked for explicit feedback and received plenty of tough critiques. We also watched people's eyes, faces, and body language; we kept ideas and stories that they found engaging and discarded or revised those that induced yawns or sent them to their smart phones. For example, audiences always perked up when we talked about "Buddhism versus Catholicism" but tuned out when we dug too deeply into social network analysis.

Finally, whether we were in the mood for it or not, once people heard we were writing a scaling book, they often sought us out to hear our ideas, to tell us their stories, to ask for advice, and, just as in scheduled talks, to offer critiques and suggest new leads. For example, after one consultant we met at a cocktail party heard the word *accountability*, he cornered us for forty-five minutes to detail how the demise of such ownership and the "associated blame game" had ruined one of his client companies. Another time, Sutton was not really in the mood to talk about scaling with his wife, Marina Park, but realized he had best do so. Park and her colleagues were working on a proposal to fund a scaling effort: to spread the Girl Scouts' Thrive program (described in chapter 2) from Northern California to eight of the nine largest U.S. Girl Scout councils. The Thrive Foundation for Youth funded this two-year project, and the scaling efforts are now under way.

We used each of the seven methods below to discover, develop, and test what ultimately appeared in *Scaling Up Excellence*. But producing this book didn't feel as if it entailed slicing, dicing, and sorting our efforts into these clear-cut categories. The seven methods were mashed together in our minds as we moved from one conversation to another with the thoughtful and helpful people who joined us on this journey. We think of this book as a compact summary of the most important and engaging scaling lessons that we learned from this decidedly social process.

CORE METHODS

1. Combing Through Research from the Behavioral Sciences and Beyond

We drew on many academic studies to develop the ideas in *Scaling Up Excellence*. In addition to the one hundred or so peer-reviewed articles included in the notes, we considered at least another thousand that didn't make the cut. We focused on behavioral science research from psychology, sociology, and economics, along with more applied fields including organizational behavior, marketing, and strategy. We occasionally wandered into fields such as physics, computer science, and biology. And we drew on and modified several evidence-based themes that appeared in our earlier books, including Rao's *Market Rebels* and Sutton's *Good Boss, Bad Boss.*

This approach reflects our view that it is impossible to design and conduct a single study (or several studies) that begins to capture the key elements required to scale up excellence—or any other complex management challenge. We follow scholars in both the physical and the behavioral sciences who are trained to have limited faith in the results of any single study (even when something much simpler than scaling is examined); seasoned scholars only accept findings that have been replicated across many careful studies. The most robust conclusions about complex problems such as scaling are reached by standing on the shoulders of others, drawing on multiple studies, and weaving their findings together. Indeed, during the nearly daily talks between the two of us about this book, we focused most often on linking the stories and cases that we were gathering to rigorous theory and research in accurate, useful, and engaging ways.

2. Conducting and Gathering Detailed Case Studies

We worked with writers at Stanford (especially David Hoyt) to produce several teaching cases where scaling was a central theme, including cases on the 100,000 Lives Campaign, Wyeth Pharmaceuticals, JetBlue Airways, "Mutual Fun" at Rite-Solutions, and Mozilla. In chapter 5, we drew on a detailed post published on Sutton's *Work Matters* blog to describe Annie and Perry Klebahn's experiences when United Airlines lost their daughter Phoebe (as well as the various reactions to their story). We also used cases written by other colleagues on organizations including Tamago-Ya, Neiman Marcus, Ogilvy & Mather under Charlotte Beers, and the Taj Hotel in Mumbai under terrorist attack. We conducted diverse interviews or drew on published sources (or blended both methods) to describe Netflix, the KP HealthConnect rollout, Facebook's Bootcamp, Chuck Eesley and Amin Saberi's MOOC (massively open online course), and the Atlanta schools' cheating scandal. We also drew on book-length descriptions of organizations, including Adam Lashinsky's *Inside Apple* and Yum! CEO David Novak's *Taking People with You.*

3. Brief Examples from Diverse Media Sources

To uncover insights and stories, we scoured diverse media sources, including the *New York Times,* the *Wall Street Journal,* the *San Francisco Chronicle,* the *China Business Review,* the *Harvard Business Review,* *McKinsey Quarterly,* the *New Yorker,* the *Economist,* the *Atlantic,* and *Fortune.* We also drew on diverse websites including Mitchell Baker's *Lizard Wrangling,* Ben Horowitz's inspired *Ben's Blog, The Gamification of Work,* the British Psychological Society's *Research Digest,* and Sutton's *Work Matters* blog.

4. Targeted Interviews and Unplanned Conversations

During our many conversations with scaling veterans and other skilled people, we never stopped hunting for input to help us illustrate, develop, and test our emerging ideas. We conducted a blend of face-to-face, telephone, and e-mail interviews (including follow-up exchanges to verify facts and glean extra details) on a nearly daily basis. These interactions took many forms, and we engaged in too many to list here, let alone remember, each one. The Acknowledgments name and offer thanks to approximately one hundred people who joined us in these wide-ranging conversations.

5. Presenting Emerging Scaling Ideas to Diverse Audiences

We described above how the ideas and reactions from diverse audiences guided us as we wrote *Scaling Up Excellence.* Our strategy was to aim for a broad range of organizations and industry sectors—given that our goal was to develop a general perspective that most leaders and teams in most organizations would find helpful. These hundred or so audiences are also too long to list. To give you a sense of the breadth (with approximate attendance numbers), we presented our ideas to fifty health care executives and researchers at a scaling conference at the Cincinnati Children's Hospital; sixty judges and law school professors at a conference by the

Institute for the Advancement of the American Legal System in Colorado (on spreading judicial reform); four hundred partners at a law firm retreat in Arizona; twenty California high school principals and their senior teams; five hundred programmers, consultants, and executives at an agile development conference in Texas; fifty chief financial officers at Stanford; the top sixty executives of InBev (the world's largest beer company); twenty Google managers and executives in "Business Operations"; 250 members of the Stanford Human Resources Department; four hundred managers and executives from firms including McDonald's, Coca-Cola, and Pepsi at the Women's Foodservice Forum in Chicago; two hundred marketing researchers in Arizona; and four hundred project managers in Burlingame, California. Each group taught us something new, and we revised our scaling ideas and stories in response.

6. Teaching a "Scaling Up Excellence" Class to Stanford Graduate Students

We taught a "Scaling Up Excellence" class to fifty or so Stanford MBAs and School of Engineering master's students in both 2012 and 2013. Doing so helped us develop our ideas in three ways. First, it enabled us to discuss and refine them in response to 100 smart—and often critical—Stanford students. Second, our class guests included many of the book's scaling stars; some we met for the first time when they spoke to the class, others were old friends. They included Chip Conley from Joie de Vivre hotels, Chris Cox and Mike Schroepfer from Facebook, Barry Feld from Cost Plus, Chris Fry from Twitter, Karin Kricorian from Disney, Kaaren Hanson from Intuit, Ben Horowitz from Andreessen Horowitz, Ilya Prokopoff from IDEO, and Bonny Simi from JetBlue.

Third, and most important, we learned from hands-on projects where student teams worked to spread excellence. In 2012, teams worked with Ariadne Scott (coordinator of Stanford's bike programs) and Debra Dunn (d.school professor and former HP executive vice president) to increase bike helmet usage among Stanford students. Teams experienced many instructive failures and a few notable successes (including "the Watermelon Offensive" and a project that used graduate students' children to pressure their parents to don helmets) as they applied the scaling principles. In 2013, teams worked with Colonel Peter Newell, head of the U.S. Army's Rapid Equipment Force (REF), to speed the development and spread of technological solutions for soldiers on the front lines—especially by applying the "connect and cascade" principle. Several teams worked to help reduce "flash to bang time": the delay between when a problem is recognized (e.g., improvised explosive devices) and when soldiers develop or are given effective solutions. A big part of the challenge was linking soldiers' experiences and collective intelligence to REF engineers and other technologists who could generate prototype solutions. One team developed a system (akin to Amazon.com's product rating method) that soldiers used to rate potential solutions on a five-point scale. Another developed a Twitter-like system that used simple technologies and consumed minimal power so that soldiers could easily transmit suggestions and messages about challenges they faced to the REF team.

7. Participation in and Observation of Scaling at the Stanford d.school

We've been involved with the Stanford d.school since 2002, when it was a seemingly impossible dream that David Kelley shared with a few colleagues. Sutton was among the founding faculty and has cotaught more than a dozen d.school courses since 2005. He's been involved as the d.school has grown from four classes in a smelly and cramped double-wide trailer during the 2004–05 academic year, to a dozen or so classes in a larger but still cramped space in 2007–08, to more than fifty regular and short courses in a large, customized, and completely reconstructed building in 2012–13. Rao and Sutton also cofounded "Customer-Focused Innovation," the first d.school executive program (a partnership with the Graduate School of Business), first held in 2006 for twenty-seven executives and held for its seventh year in 2013 for sixty-five executives; it is now one of eight d.school programs that serve about five hundred executives per year. The d.school also teaches at least another one thousand participants each year via short workshops for groups ranging from elementary school teachers to physicians.

We've learned a bit about scaling from helping the d.school grow. More importantly, we've observed firsthand as David Kelley, the d.school's founder and inspiration, and other leaders, including Academic Director Bernie Roth and Managing Director Sarah Stein Greenberg, have confronted virtually every scaling challenge considered in this book. In addition, our leadership roles in the Customer-Focused Innovation program allow us to track executives who are spreading design thinking in their organizations, including our scaling heroes Doug Dietz from General Electric, Kaaren Hanson from Intuit, Bonny Simi from JetBlue, and executives from Capital One, Citrix, DIRECTV, Fidelity, Hyatt, Procter & Gamble, and SAP who give us frequent updates about their trials, tribulations, and triumphs.

NOTES

1. IT'S A GROUND WAR, NOT JUST AN AIR WAR

3   **"the black art of scaling a human organization":** Ben Horowitz, "Taking the Mystery Out of Scaling a Company," *Ben's Blog,* August 2, 2010, http://bhorowitz.com/2010/08/02/taking-the-mystery-out-of-scaling-a-company/.

3   **"only about 18 percent of U.S. bombs . . .":** Robert A. Pape, "The True Worth of Air Power," *Foreign Affairs,* March 1, 2004, www.foreignaffairs.com/articles/59714/robert-a-pape/the-true-worth-of-air-power.

4   **"In a major blunder . . .":** Benjamin S. Lambeth, *NATO's Air War for Kosovo: A Strategic and Operational Assessment* (Santa Monica, CA: RAND Corporation, 2001), 245, www.rand.org/pubs/monograph_reports/MR1365.

5   **"moving a thousand people forward a foot at a time . . .":** This and other information about Kotchka's experience is gleaned from various presentations we've heard Kotchka give to executives and students at Stanford, including a talk she gave to our "Scaling Up Excellence" class on January 10, 2013, and an interview she did with Rao on October 30, 2012.

5   **It has been a way of life for Shannon May:** The following information about Bridge International Academies is based on a telephone interview that Rao and Sutton did with Shannon May on February 25, 2013, and information on their website at www.bridgeinternationalacademies.com/; in addition, see Tina Rosenberg, "A by-the-E-Book Education, for $5 a Month," *New York Times,* May 22, 2013, http://opinionator.blogs.nytimes.com/2013/05/22/a-by-the-e-book-education-for-5-a-month/.

6   **Papa landed a job on a NASCAR racing team:** The information about Andy Papa's career that follows is based on a telephone interview that Robert Sutton conducted with Papa on December 8, 2008. In addition, Rao and Sutton have done at least ten "team-building" exercises with Papa over the years, where teams of students or executives enter a "tire-changing competition" and lessons about learning, leadership, and group dynamics are discussed. Papa often discusses his history and the rise of the "athletic mindset" at NASCAR during these sessions.

7   **grit "entails working strenuously . . .":** Angela L. Duckworth et al., "Grit: Perseverance and Passion for Long-Term Goals," *Journal of Personality and Social Psychology* 92 (2007): 1087–1101.

9   **Facebook demonstrates what it takes:** We witnessed Facebook's devotion to spreading a mindset—rather than just creating a big footprint—repeatedly over the years. We first heard of Zuckerberg's obsession with beliefs like "Move fast and break things" in 2005. Katie Geminder, then a Facebook executive, often visited our Stanford class "Creating Infectious Action" and told us how her twenty-two-year-old boss had very strong ideas about how *everyone* at Facebook ought to do things. In the ensuing years, we saw the power of this mindset during employee orientation sessions and all-hands meetings; our conversations about selection, training, and evaluation with Facebook executives; the class we taught where Stanford students were coached by Facebook engineers, marketers, and executives as they spread the site to new populations; interviews with executives and engineers for this book; and a presentation by Facebook vice presidents Chris Cox and Mike Schroepfer to our "Scaling Up Excellence" class on March 6, 2012.

12   **the one lesson "no Apple employee forgets":** Adam Lashinsky, *Inside Apple: How America's Most Admired—and Secretive—Company Really Works* (New York: Business Plus, 2012).

12   **John Lilly told us:** The quotes that follow are taken from an e-mail that John Lilly sent to Robert Sutton on June 26, 2012.

13   **an internal memo:** See Howard Schultz, memo to Jim Donald, February 14, 2007, posted on *Starbucks Gossip,* February 24, 2007, http://starbucksgossip .typepad.com/_/2007/02/starbucks_chair_2.html.

13   **his 2011 book,** ***Onward:*** Howard Schultz, *Onward: How Starbucks Fought for Its Soul Without Losing Its Life* (New York: Macmillan, 2011).

14   **Customers were affected by the music:** Adrian C. North, David J. Hargreaves, and Jennifer McKendrick, "In-Store Music Affects Product Choice," *Nature* 390 (1997): 132.

15   **they infused passenger cars with a citrus-scented cleaning product:** Summary by BPS Research Digest, "Passengers Litter Less on Carriages That Smell of Cleaning Product," March 27, 2012, http://bps-research-digest.blogspot .com/2012/03/passengers-litter-less-on-carriages.html.

15   **"more cleaning-related activities . . .":** M. de Lange, et al., "Making Less of a Mess: Scent Exposure as a Tool for Behavioral Change," *Social Influence* 7, no. 2 (2012): 90–97.

15   **used various "primes" to turn attention to money:** Kathleen D. Vohs, Nicole L. Mead, and Miranda R. Goode, "The Psychological Consequences of Money," *Science* 314, no. 5802 (2006): 1154–56.

16   **Psychologist Lawrence Williams described his sneaky study:** This quote is from a *Science* podcast for October 24, 2008, available at www.sciencemag .org/content/322/5901/608.2.full, that includes a segment on Williams's study and is based on his article: Lawrence E. Williams and John A. Bargh, "Experi-

encing Physical Warmth Promotes Interpersonal Warmth," *Science* 24 (October 2008): 606–07.

16   **Karin Kricorian, who leads Disney's efforts:** Karin's advice is taken from a telephone interview that Rao and Sutton conducted with her on October 12, 2012, and from a presentation that Kricorian gave to our Stanford "Scaling Up Excellence" class on February 19, 2013.

17   **Research by New York University's Yaacov Trope:** Yaacov Trope and Nira Liberman, "Temporal Construal," *Psychological Review* 110, no. 3 (2003): 403.

18   **Google's leaders tried to resist doing what was easiest now:** From a telephone interview that Robert Sutton did with Shona Brown on March 1, 2013.

20   **This mantra pops up under numerous guises:** This section is inspired by theory building and research on felt accountability, although we have broadened and revised this work in order to apply it to the challenges of scaling up excellence. In particular, we drew on D. D. Frink and R. J. Klimoski, "Toward a Theory of Accountability in Organizations and Human Resource Management," *Research in Personnel and Human Resource Management* 16 (1998): 1–51.

21   **"As a work space, it is something . . .":** Chris Smith, "Open City," *New York,* September 26, 2010, http://nymag.com/news/features/establishments/68511/.

21   **the technology platform called Venture Lab:** Rao and Sutton interviewed Chuck Eesley and Amin Saberi about developing and using this platform at Stanford, CA, on July 23, 2012. The URL for the "Technology Entrepreneurship" class taught by Eesley on the platform is http://venture-lab.org/venture.

24   **the definitions of that cussword in the *Urban Dictionary*:** See the definitions offered at www.urbandictionary.com/define.php?term=clusterfuck, accessed March 7, 2013.

26   **The first year of the Oracle Financials rollout was a nightmare:** Barbara Palmer, "Oracle System Woes Lower Campus Productivity, Morale," *Stanford Report,* February 25, 2004, http://news.stanford.edu/news/2004/february25/oracle-225.html.

27   **"slow progress in smoothing out the many problems":** "Chief Information Officer to Leave Post," *Stanford Report,* November 11, 2004, http://news.stanford.edu/news/2004/november10/handley-1111.html; Deborah Gage, "Campus Brawl: Oracle vs. PeopleSoft at Stanford," *Baseline,* June 8, 2004, http://depts.washington.edu/isfuture/docs/CampusBrawl.pdf.

27   **rap singer Dorrough's song "Get Big":** Horowitz, "Taking the Mystery Out."

28   **what "got us here but won't get us there":** Marshall Goldsmith, *What Got You Here Won't Get You There* (New York: Hyperion, 2007).

28   **Sutton saw this happen at the renowned innovation firm IDEO:** The observations of IDEO that follow are based on an eighteen-month ethnography of the company conducted by Robert Sutton and Andrew Hargadon during 1995 and 1996. Sutton and Hargadon spent an average of two days a week at the company during this stretch, attending many meetings and brainstorming sessions (including at least thirty Monday morning meetings) and having

informal conversations and semistructured interviews with most members of the company. Sutton has continued to track the company since 1997 in his role as an IDEO Fellow.

29   **Mr. Feld to speak to our scaling class:** From a presentation by Barry Feld to our "Scaling Up Excellence" class on February 21, 2012.

30   **"the automatic System 1":** Daniel Kahneman, *Thinking, Fast and Slow* (New York: Farrar, Straus and Giroux, 2011).

30   **A study by Clifford Holderness and Jeffrey Pontiff:** Clifford G. Holderness and Jeffrey Pontiff, "Hierarchies and the Survival of POWs during WWII," *Management Science,* forthcoming.

31   **"Don't just do something, stand there":** Jerome E. Groopman and Michael Prichard, *How Doctors Think* (Boston: Houghton Mifflin, 2007), 169.

31   **"You have to be like a race car driver . . .":** Carlos Ghosn, "Saving the Business Without Losing the Company," *Harvard Business Review,* January 2002, 9.

2. BUDDHISM VERSUS CATHOLICISM

36   **Intel's Copy Exactly! philosophy:** Chris J. McDonald, "Copy EXACTLY! A Paradigm Shift in Technology Transfer Method," in *1977 IEEE/SEMI Advanced Semiconductor Manufacturing Conference and Workshop* (New York: Institute of Electrical and Electronics Engineers, 1997), 414–17.

37   **"copying elements of the original template as precisely as possible":** Sidney G. Winter et al., "Reproducing Knowledge: Inaccurate Replication and Failure in Franchise Organizations," *Organization Science* 23, no. 3 (2012): 672–85.

37   **"replica trap":** Martha Stone Wiske and David Perkins, "Dewey Goes Digital," in *Scaling Up Success: Lessons Learned from Technology-Based Educational Innovation,* ed. C. Dede, J. Honan, and L. Peters (New York: Jossey-Bass, 2005), 27–47.

37   **Home Depot's DIY approach flopped:** Martha C. White, "Home Depot's Big Box Plans for China Lost in Translation," *NBC News.com,* September 18, 2012, www.nbcnews.com/business/home-depots-big-box-plans-china-lost-translation-1B5958257; Laurie Burkitt, "Home Depot Learns Chinese Prefer 'Do It for Me,'" *Wall Street Journal,* September 14, 2012, http://online.wsj.com/article/SB10000872396390444433504577651072911154602.html.

38   **Conley used a clever technique:** Based on presentation by Chip Conley to our "Scaling Up Excellence" class at Stanford University on January 31, 2012.

39   **making their luxury hotel chain a cultural chameleon:** The Four Seasons description that follows is from Roger Hallowell, Carin-Isabel Knoop, and David Bowen, "Four Seasons Goes to Paris: '53 Properties, 24 Countries, 1 Philosophy,'" 2003, Case No. 803069-PDF-ENG, Harvard Business School, Boston.

40   **Researchers, led by Stanford's Pamela Hinds,:** Personal communication, via e-mail, from Pamela Hinds to Robert Sutton, February 19, 2013.

40   **IKEA faced similar challenges:** Paula M. Miller, "IKEA with Chinese Characteristics," *China Business Review,* May 1, 2004, www.chinabusinessreview

.com/ikea-with-chinese-characteristics/; Anne VanderMey, "IKEA Takes on China," *Fortune,* November 30, 2011, http://features.blogs.fortune.cnn .com/2011/11/30/ikea-china-stores/.

42   **Gawande shows how delusions of uniqueness can amplify health care costs:** Atul Gawande, "Big Med," the *New Yorker,* August 13, 2012, www.newyorker .com/reporting/2012/08/13/120813fa_fact_gawande.

45   **"Rank Xerox violated one of the basic rules of replication . . .":** Claus Rerup, "Imperfection, Transfer Failure, and the Replication of Knowledge: An Interview with Gabriel Szulanski," *Journal of Management Inquiry* 13, no. 2 (2004): 141–50.

45   **That is exactly what the Girl Scouts of Northern California did:** This section is based on a telephone interview that Robert Sutton conducted with Heather Vilhauer on January 7, 2013, multiple conversations with Marina Park (CEO of the Girl Scouts of Northern California), and over a dozen e-mail exchanges with Shari Teresi (senior director, Volunteer Services, Girl Scouts of Northern California), Wendy Wheeler (interim director, Thrive Foundation), and Bonnie Scott (program officer, Thrive Foundation) between January and March of 2013. In the interest of full disclosure, note that Marina Park is Robert Sutton's wife. We also drew on the Girl Scouts Thrive webpage at www.girlscoutsnorcal .org/pages/events/thrive.html, accessed March 17, 2013.

47   **how Howard Schultz developed what eventually became the Starbucks coffee empire:** Gabriel Szulanski and Sidney Winter, "Getting It Right the Second Time," *Harvard Business Review* 80, no. 1 (2002): 62.

48   **"expansion of numbers" and maintaining "fidelity":** Cynthia E. Coburn, "Rethinking Scale: Moving Beyond Numbers to Deep and Lasting Change," *Educational Researcher* 32, no. 6 (2003): 3–12.

49   **"more motivated and creative":** Sarah A. McGraw et al., "Using Process Data to Explain Outcomes: An Illustration from the Child and Adolescent Trial for Cardiovascular Health (CATCH)," *Evaluation Review* 20, no. 3 (1996): 291–312.

50   **the UCSF researchers worked with teams of nurses:** Victoria Colliver, "Prescription for Success: Don't Bother Nurses," *San Francisco Chronicle,* Wednesday, October 28, 2009, www.sfgate.com/health/article/Prescription-for-success-Don-t-bother-nurses-3282968.php; Julie Kliger et al., "Empowering Frontline Nurses: A Structured Intervention Enables Nurses to Improve Medication Administration Accuracy," *Joint Commission Journal on Quality and Patient Safety* 35, no. 12 (2009): 604–12.

50   **McDonald's is an instructive case study:** John F. Love, *McDonald's: Behind the Golden Arches* (New York: Bantam, 1995), 294.

52   **In-N-Out Burger is among the most successful and admired fast-food chains:** For the information on In-N-Out Burger that follows, see Stacy Perman, *In-N-Out Burger: A Behind-the-Counter Look at the Fast-Food Chain That Breaks All the Rules* (New York: HarperBusiness, 2010), and the In-N-Out website, www.in-n-out.com/history.aspx, accessed March 17, 2013.

53   **they are zealots about creating and controlling everything in the films themselves:** Rao and Sutton interviewed Tom Porter at Pixar headquarters

in Emeryville, CA, on March 1, 2011. Other facts about Pixar here are from Ed Catmull's *Creativity, Inc.: Overcoming the Unseen Forces That Stand in the Way of True Inspiration* (New York: Random House, forthcoming).

53   **this giant firm needed to become more creative:** P. Sellers, "P&G: Teaching an Old Dog New Tricks," *Fortune,* May 15, 2004, http://money.cnn.com/ magazines/fortune/fortune_archive/2004/05/31/370714/index.htm.

54   **Liberty Ships:** On the learning curve for building Liberty Ships, see Linda Argote, *Organizational Learning* (New York: Springer, 2012); Peter Thompson, "How Much Did the Liberty Shipbuilders Learn? New Evidence for an Old Case Study," *Journal of Political Economy* 109, no. 1 (2001): 103–37.

54–5   **"I can't be in two places at once":** Jane Knoerle, "John Bentley Sells Woodside Restaurant," *Almanac News,* March 10, 2010, www.almanacnews.com/news/ show_story.php?id=6322.

55   **43 of the 181 babies that had received open-heart surgery at Bristol Hospital had died:** Michael Fitzpatrick, "After Bristol: The Humbling of the Medical Profession," *Spiked,* August 16, 2001, www.spiked-online.com/site/ article/11276/.

55   **Walmart ran up enormous losses:** Andreas Knorr and Andreas Arndt, *Why Did Wal-Mart Fail in Germany?* (Bremen: Institute for World Economics, University of Bremen, 2003), www.iwim.uni-bremen.de/publikationen/pdf/ w024.pdf.

57   **a massive electronic health record system called KP HealthConnect:** This section on KP HealthConnect is based on a presentation at Cincinnati Children's Hospital by Louise Liang (with help from Kaiser Permanente senior vice president Alide Chase) on March 21, 2013, at a "Getting to Scale" symposium; on a series of e-mails between Louise Liang and Robert Sutton in April and May of 2013; on a telephone interview by Robert Sutton with Louise Liang on May 10, 2013; on Donald M. Berwick's foreword to *Connected for Health: Using Electronic Health Records to Transform Care Delivery,* ed. Louise L. Liang (San Francisco: Jossey-Bass, 2010); and on e-mail exchanges with Kaiser researchers and administrators, including Terhilda Garrido and Samantha Quattrone, in May of 2013. Evidence that there has been a big drop in unnecessary tests is found at T. Garrido et al., "Effect of Electronic Health Records in Ambulatory Care: Retrospective, Serial, Cross Sectional Study," *British Medical Journal* 330, no. 7491 (2005): 581; and C. Chen et al., "The Kaiser Permanente Electronic Health Record: Transforming and Streamlining Modalities of Care," *Health Affairs* 28, no. 2 (2009): 323–33.

3. HOT CAUSES, COOL SOLUTIONS

67   **A helmet cuts the odds of a serious head injury:** Bicycle Helmet Safety Institute, "Helmet Related Statistics from Many Sources," n.d., www.helmets.org/ stats.htm, accessed March 27, 2013; Ariadne Delon Scott provided the statistics and other information about helmet use at Stanford.

69   **"The ancestor of every action is a thought":** Ralph Waldo Emerson, *Essays: First Series* (Stillwell, KS: Digireads, 2007), 53.

69 **"Thought is the child of action"**: Benjamin Disraeli, *Vivian Grey* (New York: Century, 1906), 195.

69 **to avoid seeing themselves—and being seen by others—as hypocrites:** Susan T. Fiske and Shelley E. Taylor, *Social Cognition,* 2nd ed. (New York: McGraw-Hill, 1991).

70 **Such feelings make people feel powerful:** D. Keltner, D. H. Gruenfeld, and C. A. Anderson, "Power, Approach, and Inhibition," *Psychological Review* 110 (2003): 265–84; L. Z. Tiedens, "Anger and Advancement Versus Sadness and Subjugation: The Effect of Negative Emotion Expressions on Social Status Conferral," *Journal of Personality and Social Psychology* 80 (2001): 86–94.

70 **"communities of feeling":** E. Hatfield, J. Cacioppo, and R. L. Rapson, *Emotional Contagion* (New York: Cambridge University Press, 1994).

73 **"The Valentine's Day Massacre":** This description of JetBlue's challenges is based on the 2010 case study "JetBlue Airways: A New Beginning" (Stanford Business School Case No. L-17), prepared by David Hoyt, Charles O'Reilly, Hayagreeva Rao, and Robert Sutton; a presentation given by Bonny Simi on January 29, 2012, to our "Scaling Up Excellence" class; and a series of e-mail exchanges between Bonny Simi and Robert Sutton in September and October of 2012 and in March of 2013 to clarify details and check facts.

79 **Institute for Health Improvement:** Hayagreeva Rao and David Hoyt, "Institute for Healthcare Improvement: The Campaign to Save 100,000 Lives," Graduate School of Business, Stanford University, Case No. L-13.

81 **"create one Ford":** Bryce C. Hoffman, *American Icon* (New York: Crown, 2011).

82 **"Pick a target, freeze it, personalize it, and polarize it":** Saul D. Alinsky, *Rules for Radicals* (New York: Random House, 1971), 130.

82 **"The only problem with Microsoft is they just have no taste":** The examples of Jobs's penchant for demonizing enemies are derived from Walter Isaacson, *Steve Jobs* (New York: Simon and Schuster, 2011). The quote about Microsoft is taken from the transcript of *Triumph of the Nerds,* which aired on PBS in June of 1996 and is available at www.pbs.org/nerds/part3.html.

82 **a report from John Lilly:** John Lilly, "Steve Jobs," *John's Blog,* October 9, 2011, http://john.jubjubs.net/2011/10/09/steve-jobs/.

83 **Irving Janis's classic research on groupthink:** Irving Janis, *Groupthink: Psychological Studies of Policy Decisions and Fiascoes* (Boston: Wadsworth, 1982).

84 **"BA could use this information to crush them …":** Martyn Gregory, "Battle of the Airlines: How the Dirty Tricks Campaign Was Run," *Independent,* January 12, 1993, www.independent.co.uk/news/uk/battle-of-the-airlines-how-the-dirty-tricks-campaign-was-run-martyn-gregory-reports-on-bas-dirty-tricks-campaign-which-he-uncovered-as-producer-director-of-thames-televisions-this-week-programme-1478010.html.

84 **riddled with HIV-infected needles:** Martyn Gregory, *Dirty Tricks: Inside Story of British Airways' Secret War Against Richard Branson's Virgin Atlantic* (London: Little, Brown, 1994).

85   **"Not one of the marchers . . .":** Brian Martin, *Justice Ignited: The Dynamics of Backfire* (Lanham, MD: Rowman and Littlefield, 2006), 38, based on a story by United Press reporter Webb Miller on May 21, 1930.

85   **"Whenever one takes a stand that is visible to others . . .":** Robert B. Cialdini, *Influence: The Psychology of Persuasion*, rev. ed. (New York: Morrow, 1993), 82.

86   **"breaching experiments":** Harold Garfinkel, *Studies in Ethnomethodology* (Malden, MA: Blackwell, 1984), 47.

86   **"aids to sluggish imagination":** Ibid., 38.

87   **"the most public person on the floor":** Bob Sutton, "IDEO CEO Tim Brown: 'I Found It Vaguely Embarrassing and Frustrating to Be in an Office,'" *Work Matters,* February 4, 2010, http://bobsutton.typepad.com/my_weblog/2010/02/ideo-ceo-tim-brown-i-found-it-vaguely-embarrassing-and-frustrating-to-be-in-an-office.html.

88   **"holding environments":** D. W. Winnicott, *The Child and the Outside World* (London: Tavistock, 1957).

90   **The gratitude they felt toward Marchionne:** Bill Sapirito, "Power Steering," *Time,* December 19, 2001, www.time.com/time/magazine/article/0,9171,2101857-1,00.html; "Sergio Marchionne: Resurrecting Chrysler," *60 Minutes,* originally aired on March 25, 2012, www.cbsnews.com/8301-18560_162-57403925/sergio-marchionne-resur; "Global Players: Sergio Marchionne, CEO, Fiat," *New Global,* March 9, 2010, www.thomaswhite.com/explore-the-world/global-players/sergio-marchionne.aspx.

90   **turn hope into reality:** Sergio Marchionne, "Acceptance Speech at Columbia Business School, Deming Cup Award Ceremony, New York," November 2, 2011, www7.gsb.columbia.edu/deming/sites/default/files/files/Sergio%20Marchionne%281%29.pdf.

90   **the little things Lipps had done to spark and spread excellence at Omnicell:** This story was first told by Randall Lipps to Rao in September of 2008 and was confirmed via an e-mail from Lipps to Rao on October 22, 2012.

91   **a potent recipe for changing hearts and minds:** Cialdini, *Influence.*

91   **He anointed people:** Based on Sergio Marchionne, "Fiat's Extreme Makeover," *Harvard Business Review,* December 2008, 45–48, and on Marchionne, "Acceptance Speech."

94   **The approach that Beers used to recreate and spread excellence:** Herminia Ibarra and Nicole Sackley, "Charlotte Beers at Ogilvy & Mather Worldwide (A)," Harvard Business School, Case No. 495031-PDF-ENG, 1995.

95   **both a "poet" and a "plumber":** James G. March and Mie Augier, "James March on Education, Leadership, and Don Quixote: Introduction and Interview," *Academy of Management Learning and Education* 3, no. 2 (2004): 169–77.

96   **encroaching on Apple's smart phone patents:** Nick Wingfield, "Jury Awards $1 Billion to Apple in Samsung Patent Case," *New York Times,* August 24, 2012, www.nytimes.com/2012/08/25/technology/jury-reaches-decision-in-apple-samsung-patent-trial.html.

97   **"101 Dumbest Moments in Business":** "Apple: One, Two, Three, Four, We'll Sue You If You Send Us More," CNNMoney.com, December 20, 2007, http://money.cnn.com/galleries/2007/fortune/0712/gallery.tech_flops.fortune/7.html.

4. CUT COGNITIVE LOAD

99   **gobble down the less healthy cake:** Baba Shiv and Alexander Fedorikhin, "Heart and Mind in Conflict: The Interplay of Affect and Cognition in Consumer Decision Making," *Journal of Consumer Research* 26, no. 3 (1999): 278–92.

99   **Miller's Law:** George Miller, "The Magical Number Seven, Plus or Minus Two: Some Limits on Our Capacity for Processing Information," *Psychological Review* 63 (1956): 81–97.

99–100   **they routinely ignored customers' questions and needs:** Kevin Peters, "How I Did It: Office Depot's President on How 'Mystery Shopping' Helped Spark a Turnaround," *Harvard Business Review,* November 14, 2011, 47.

100   **"They're suckers for irrelevancy . . .":** Eyal Ophir, Clifford Nass, and Anthony D. Wagner, "Cognitive Control in Media Multitaskers," *Proceedings of the National Academy of Sciences* 106, no. 37 (2009): 15583–87; also see Adam Gorlick, "Media Multitaskers Pay Mental Price, Stanford Study Shows," *Stanford Report,* August 24, 2009, http://news.stanford.edu/news/2009/august24/multitask-research-study-082409.html.

101   **higher death rates in NICUs with "shared governance":** I. M. Nembhard et al., "Learn How to Improve Collaboration and Performance," Harvard Business School Working Paper No. 08-002; a summary is at I. M. Nembhard et al., "Improving Patient Outcomes: The Impact of Front-line Staff Collaboration on Quality of Care," *Evidence-Based Management,* January 21, 2008, http://evidence-basedmanagement.com/2008/01/21/improving-patient-outcomes-the-impact-of-front-line-staff-collaboration-on-quality-of-care/. Anita Tucker conducted the additional analyses for 2003 and 2004 in September of 2012 and communicated them via e-mail to Robert Sutton on August 8, 2012.

102   **the bigger the team, the worse each member performed:** Bradley R. Staats, Katherine L. Milkman, and Craig R. Fox, "The Team Scaling Fallacy: Underestimating the Declining Efficiency of Larger Teams," *Organizational Behavior and Human Decision Processes* 118, no. 2 (2012): 132–42; Jennifer S. Mueller, "Why Individuals in Larger Teams Perform Worse," *Organizational Behavior and Human Decision Processes* 117, no. 1 (2012): 111–24.

102   **for most tasks, the best size is four to six:** J. Richard Hackman, "Leading Teams: Setting the Stage for Great Performances—The Five Keys to Successful Teams," interview by Mallory Stark, July 15, 2002, Harvard Business School Working Knowledge, http://hbswk.hbs.edu/archive/2996.html.

102   **"12 man mob":** James Webb, "Flexibility and the Fire Team," *Marine Corps Gazette,* April 1972, 25–28, www.jameswebb.com/articles/mcgazette-flexfireteam.html.

102   **the Two-Pizza Rule:** Richard L. Brandt, "Birth of a Salesman," *Wall Street*

Journal, October 15, 2011, http://online.wsj.com/article/SB100014240529702 0391430457662710299683 1200.html; Matthew May, *The Laws of Subtraction* (New York: McGraw-Hill, 2012), 59.

103   **When Pulse expanded to about twelve people:** Rao and Sutton interviewed Kothari and Gupta and spoke to its twelve employees about scaling on September 6, 2011.

103   **"If you belong to a group of five people . . .":** Malcolm Gladwell, *The Tipping Point* (New York: Little, Brown, 2000), 178–79.

104   **A 2012 analysis of 1.7 million Twitter users:** Bruno Goncalves, Nicola Perra, and Alessandro Vespignani, "Modeling Users' Activity on Twitter Networks: Validation of Dunbar's Number," *Bulletin of the American Physical Society* 57 (2012), www.plosone.org/article/info%3Adoi%2F10.1371%2Fjournal .pone.0022656.

104   **Administrators are often added at a faster rate:** There is some controversy and much nuanced argument among academics about whether "administrative bloat" is something that all organizations suffer from or whether, as organizations get larger and age, the proportion of administrators stays about the same or shrinks. For our purposes, it is enough to know that organizations do need to add more structure, people, and processes as they grow and that some organizations are more prone to bloat than others—such as universities, as the *Economist* shows. There is also reason to believe that, as organizations go through periods of growth and decline, they tend to keep adding increasing percentages of administrators year after year; at least that is the assertion in John R. Montanari and Philip J. Adelman's "The Administrative Component of Organizations and the Ratchet Effect: A Critique of Cross-Sectional Studies," *Journal of Management Studies* 24, no. 2 (1987): 113–23.

104   **Universities seem to be especially cursed:** "Declining by Degree: Will America's Universities Go the Way of Its Car Companies?" Economist .com, September 2, 2010, www.economist.com/node/16941775?story_id= 16941775&fsrc=rss.

105   **"non-faculty professionals":** "Higher Education: Not What It Used to Be," Economist.com, December 1, 2012, www.economist.com/news/united- states/21567373-american-universities-represent-declining-value-money- their-students-not-what-it.

105   **Northcote Parkinson observed a similar pattern decades earlier:** Cyril Northcote Parkinson, *Parkinson's Law, and Other Studies in Administration* (Boston: Houghton Mifflin, 1957).

105   **"Big Dumb Company" disease:** John Greathouse, "Infiltrating Big Dumb Companies: In Through the Out Door," *infoChachkie,* October 1, 2010, http:// infochachkie.com/infiltrating/.

106   **"Companies are killed by their need to keep on getting bigger":** Jonah Lehrer, "A Physicist [Solves] the City," *New York Times,* December 7, 2010, www .nytimes.com/2010/12/19/magazine/19Urban_West-t.html?pagewanted=1&_ r=2&ref=magazine.

106   **more than half had four or fewer employees:** U.S. Census Bureau, "Statistics

About Business Size (Including Small Business) from the U.S. Census Bureau," www.census.gov/econ/smallbus.html, downloaded June 13, 2013.

106   **just 25 percent had revenues over $100,000 and 4 percent exceeded $10 million:** Amy S. Blackwood, Katie L. Roeger, and Sarah L. Pettijohn, "The Nonprofit Sector in Brief: Public Charities, Giving, Volunteering: 2012," Urban Institute, 2012, www.urban.org/UploadedPDF/412674-The-Nonprofit-Sector-in-Brief.pdf.

106   **fast-growing newcomers:** P. Kim and J. Bradach, "Why More Nonprofits Are Getting Bigger," *Stanford Social Innovation Review* 10, no. 2 (2012): 14–16.

106   **the church has repeatedly risen to the challenges of spreading excellence:** Bill Keller, "2000 Years of Popes, Sacred and Profane," *New York Times,* July 7, 2011, www.nytimes.com/2011/07/10/books/review/book-review-absolute-monarchs-a-history-of-the-papacy-by-john-julius norwich.html?_r=0&adxnnl=1&pagewanted=all&adxnnlx=1365351022-95jSXe1N3OIt+dHgzOjFZA.

107   **economies of scale are evident in banks:** Simon Johnson, "Why Are The Big Banks Suddenly Afraid?" *New York Times,* August 30, 2012, http://economix.blogs.nytimes.com/2012/08/30/why-are-the-big-banks-suddenly-afraid/; Federal Reserve Bank of St. Louis, "Commercial Banks in the U.S.," May 17, 2013, http://research.stlouisfed.org/fred2/series/USNUM.

108   **controls, constraints, and building blocks:** John Cable, "For Industry to Flourish, 'Bureaucracy Must Die,'" *IndustryWeek,* May 25, 2012, www.industryweek.com/global-economy/innovation-flourish-your-organization-bureaucracy-must-die?page=1.

108   **people are especially ambivalent about hierarchies:** Deborah H. Gruenfeld and Larissa Z. Tiedens, "Organizational Preferences and Their Consequences," in *Handbook of Social Psychology,* 5th ed., ed. Susan T. Fiske, Daniel T. Gilbert, and Gardner Lindzey (Hoboken, NJ: John Wiley, 2010), 2:1252–87.

108   **middle managers are often a necessary complexity:** "How Google Grew into an Online Goliath," *Talk of the Nation,* September 16, 2011, National Public Radio, transcript at www.npr.org/2011/09/16/140537850/how-google-grew-into-an-online-goliath.

109   **"The job of the hierarchy is to defeat the hierarchy":** Based on an interview that Sutton and Rao did with Chris Fry and Steve Greene on December 6, 2012, at Stanford, CA, about scaling, and a presentation by Chris Fry in our "Scaling Up Excellence" class on March 7, 2013.

110   **"a built-in shock-proof shit detector":** Ernest Hemingway, "The Art of Fiction No. 21," interview by George Plimpton, 1963, *Paris Review,* Spring 1958, www.theparisreview.org/interviews/4825/the-art-of-fiction-no-21-ernest-hemingway.

111   **"In the rest of the corporate world . . .":** Adam Lashinsky, *Inside Apple* (New York: Business Plus, 2012), 68–89.

111   **Markovitz describes how his team was burdened:** Matthew May, *The Laws of Subtraction* (New York: McGraw-Hill, 2012), 64.

112   **Quality guru W. Edwards Deming blasted away:** William Edwards Deming, *Out of the Crisis* (Cambridge, MA: MIT Press, 2000), 102.

112   **UCLA's Sam Culbert called them bogus:** Samuel Culbert, *Get Rid of the Performance Review!* (New York: Business Plus, 2010).

113   **Adobe's leaders decided:** Based on a telephone interview that Rao and Sutton conducted with Adobe's Donna Morris and Holly Parker-Coney on December 10, 2012; a presentation that Morris gave on August 27, 2013, to Rao's "Managing Talent for Strategic Advantage" executive program; and multiple follow-up e-mails with Parker-Coney after the interview and presentations."

115   **"understanding evolves through three phases . . .":** Will Schutz, *Profound Simplicity* (San Diego, CA: Learning Concepts, 1982).

116   **one of these products, SnapTax, works "almost perfectly":** Jeffrey Battersby, "Review: Intuit TurboTax SnapTax," *Macworld*, February 28, 2013, www.macworld.com/article/2028957/review-intuit-turbotax-snaptax.html.

117   **slogging through some mighty messy complexity along the way:** Robert I. Sutton, *Good Boss, Bad Boss: How to Be the Best . . . and Learn from the Worst* (New York: Business Plus, 2010), 139.

117   **"liking for the stimulus will grow . . .":** R. B. Zajonc, "Mere Exposure: A Gateway to the Subliminal," *Current Directions in Psychological Science* 10, no. 6 (2001): 224–28.

117   **This "mere exposure effect" is evident before birth:** Barbara S. Kisilevsky et al., "Effects of Experience on Fetal Voice Recognition," *Psychological Science* 14, no. 3 (2003): 220–24.

117   **"prospect theory":** Daniel Kahneman and Amos Tversky, "Prospect Theory: An Analysis of Decision Under Risk," *Econometrica: Journal of the Econometric Society* 47, no. 2 (1979): 263–91.

118   **"It's always easier to kill someone else's darlings . . .":** Stephen King, *On Writing*, 10th anniversary ed. (New York: Simon and Schuster, 2010).

119   **Bird and Walker argue every day:** The warm and constructive conflict between Bird and Walker is well documented in the "extra material" in the two-disk "Collectors' Edition" of *The Incredibles*. Both Bird and Walker pointed to this footage when we spoke to them in 2008 about constructive conflict. The "baby Jack-Jack goo" story was described in an e-mail that John Walker sent to Sutton on May 15, 2013.

119   **Denis Bugrov, senior vice president at Sberbank:** Based on an interview that Robert Sutton conducted with Denis Bugrov on October 27, 2012, on the Stanford campus and a series of e-mail exchanges between Sutton and Bugrov in early November of 2012.

121   **the right load busters are especially crucial during taxing "handoffs":** K. E. Weick, "Puzzles in Organizational Learning: An Exercise in Disciplined Imagination," *British Journal of Management* 13 (2002): S7–S15.

122   **breaking organizations into smaller pieces can have striking benefits:** This section is based on a presentation by Melissa Valentine to Stanford's Department of Management Science and Engineering on January 6, 2013; on multiple e-mails between Valentine and Sutton in March of 2013; and on M. A. Valentine and A. C. Edmondson, "Team Scaffolds: How Minimal In-Group

Structures Support Fast-Paced Teaming," Harvard Business School Working Paper 12-062.

126 **"Freaky Friday Management Technique":** Ben Horowitz, "The Freaky Friday Management Technique," *Ben's Blog*, January 19, 2012, http://bhorowitz .com/2012/01/19/the-freaky-friday-management-technique/.

127 **"When subordinates request money for a new initiative . . .":** Bernard Smith and John Reed, "General Motors: The Marques Man," *Financial Times*, June 7, 2010, www.ft.com/cms/s/577f45ca-726b-11df-9f82-0144feabdc0, Authorised=false.html?_i_location=http%3A%2F%2Fwww.ft.com% 2Fcms%2Fs%2F0%2F577f45ca-726b-11df-9f82-00144feabdc0.html&_i_ referer=http%3A%2F%2Fjournalisted.com%2Farticle%2F1gva9.

128 **He rejected the "myth" that "it's good to mix it up":** The conclusion about group stability and much of the research that supports it is in J. Richard Hackman, *Leading Teams: Setting the Stage for Great Performances* (Boston: Harvard Business Review Press, 2002). Also see Ali E. Akgün and Gary S. Lynn, "Antecedents and Consequences of Team Stability on New Product Development Performance," *Journal of Engineering and Technology Management* 19, no. 3 (2002): 263–86; Tonya Boone, Ram Ganeshan, and Robert L. Hicks, "Learning and Knowledge Depreciation in Professional Services," *Management Science* 54, no. 7 (2008): 1231–36; Robert S. Huckman and Gary P. Pisano, "The Firm Specificity of Individual Performance: Evidence from Cardiac Surgery," *Management Science* 52, no. 4 (April 2006): 473–88.

128 **bring in at least two or three people who have worked together effectively before:** Kathleen M. Eisenhardt and Claudia Bird Schoonhoven, "Organizational Growth: Linking Founding Team, Strategy, Environment, and Growth Among U.S. Semiconductor Ventures, 1978–1988," *Administrative Science Quarterly* 35, no. 3 (1990): 504–29; Boris Groysberg, Andrew N. McLean, and Nitin Nohria, "Are Leaders Portable?," *Harvard Business Review* 84, no. 5 (2006): 92.

129 **"One plus one with Charlie and me certainly adds up to more than two":** Diana McLain Smith, "For Better, Warren Buffett and Charlie Munger," n.d., http://dianamclainsmith.com/relationships/for-better-or-worse/warren-buffett-and-charlie-munger/, accessed June 13, 2013.

129 **groups with more women performed better on "collective intelligence" tests:** Anita Williams Woolley et al., "Evidence for a Collective Intelligence Factor in the Performance of Human Groups," *Science*, September 30, 2010, doi: 10.1126/ science.1193147, summarized as "Collective Intelligence: Number of Women in Group Linked to Effectiveness in Solving Difficult Problems," *Science Daily*, October 2, 2010, www.sciencedaily.com/releases/2010/09/100930143339.htm.

131 **A fifteen- to sixty-minute nap bolsters alertness:** J. Cardieri, "Churchill Understood Afternoon Naps," *New York Times*, October 2, 1989, www.nytimes .com/1989/10/02/opinion/l-churchill-understood-afternoon-naps-838589. html; Y. Harrison and J. A. Horne, "The Impact of Sleep Deprivation on Decision Making: A Review," *Journal of Experimental Psychology, Applied* 6 (2000): 236–49; S. R. Daiss, A. D. Bertelson, and T. T. Benjamin Jr., "Resting vs. Napping: Effects on Mood and Performance," *Psychophysiology* 23 (1986): 82–88;

Mark R. Rosekind et al., "Alertness Management: Strategic Naps in Operational Settings," *Journal of Sleep Research* 4, no. s2 (1995): 62–66. Quotes from Rosekind were downloaded from Mark R. Rosekind, "Expert Interview," n.d., International Aviation Safety Association, www.iasa.com.au/folders/Safety_Issues/RiskManagement/sleepanddreams.html, accessed February 13, 2013.

131   **the percentage of prisoners pardoned dropped to nearly zero:** Shai Danziger, Jonathan Levav, and Liora Avnaim-Pesso, "Extraneous Factors in Judicial Decisions," *Proceedings of the National Academy of Sciences* 108, no. 17 (2011): 6889–92.

132   **the sportswear giant was plagued with shortages:** Marc L. Songi, "Nike Blames Financial Snag on Supply Chain Project," *Computerworld,* February 27, 2001, www.computerworld.com/s/article/58124/Nike_blames_financial_snag_on_supply_chain_project.

133   **Egon Zehnder's Lindsay Trout told us:** Based on a presentation by Trout to Rao's "Human Resource Management" class at Stanford on May 1, 2012, and was confirmed and refined based on a series of e-mail exchanges between Trout and Rao in November 2012.

133   **"An offensive lineman's job . . .":** Ben Horowitz, "Taking the Mystery Out of Scaling a Company," August 2, 2010, http://bhorowitz.com/2010/08/02/taking-the-mystery-out-of-scaling-a-company.

5. THE PEOPLE WHO PROPEL SCALING

137   **a storm of media interest and individual outrage against United:** Bob Sutton, "United Airlines Lost My Friends' 10-Year-Old Daughter and Didn't Care," *Work Matters,* August 13, 2012, http://bobsutton.typepad.com/my_weblog/2012/08/united-airlines-lost-my-friends-10-year-old-daughter-and-didnt-care.html; Jad Mouawad, "For United, Big Problems at Biggest Airline," *New York Times,* November 28, 2012, www.nytimes.com/2012/11/29/business/united-is-struggling-two-years-after-its-merger-with-continental.html?pagewanted=all; Genevieve Shaw Brown, "Cover Model's Dog Dies on United Flight," ABC News.com, September 21, 2012, http://abcnews.go.com/Travel/united-airlines-killed-golden-retriever-model/story?id=17287486.

138   **the system has beaten them down:** Robert Sutton, "Felt Accountability: Some Emerging Thoughts," *Work Matters,* August 22, 2012, http://bobsutton.typepad.com/my_weblog/2012/08/felt-accountability-some-emerging-thoughts.html.

139   **Purcell emphasized that hiring the most talented people isn't enough:** telephone interview of Paul Purcell, conducted by Sutton on September 10, 2012.

139   **"We believe work is a team sport . . .":** Telephone interview of Leslie Dixon, conducted by Rao and Sutton on June 18, 2012.

140   **"talent density":** Reed Hastings, CEO, Netflix, "Reference Guide on Our Freedom and Responsibility Culture," 2009.

141   **"lack of personal characteristics":** Robert Sutton had multiple conversations with this Netflix manager in the fall of 2011 and fact-checked this story in August of 2012 via a series of e-mails; he prefers to remain anonymous.

142   **Tamago-Ya was decidedly low-tech:** Jin Whang et al., "Tamago-Ya of Japan: Delivering Lunch Boxes to Your Work," Stanford Graduate School of Business, Case No. GS60, 2007 (revised in 2010); this is supplemented by our conversations with Jin Whang about the case.

144   **"like you own the place":** David Novak, *Taking People with You* (New York: Penguin, 2012), 57.

145   **"I own the place and the place owns me":** James R. Barker, "Tightening the Iron Cage: Concertive Control in Self-Managing Teams," *Administrative Science Quarterly* 38, no. 3 (1993): 408–37.

146   **"We found that top performers . . .":** Boris Groysberg, Ahshish Nanda, and Nitin Nohria, "The Risky Business of Hiring Stars," *Harvard Business Review* 82, no. 5 (2004): 92–101; also see Boris Groysberg, *Chasing Stars: The Myth of Talent and the Portability of Performance* (Princeton: Princeton University Press, 2010).

147   **Outsiders were paid about 20 percent more than insiders:** Matthew Bidwell, "Paying More to Get Less: The Effects of External Hiring Versus Internal Mobility," *Administrative Science Quarterly* 56, no. 3 (2011): 369–407.

148   **This trend has grown stronger over the last thirty years:** Peter Cappelli, *Why Good People Can't Get Jobs: The Skill Gap and What Companies Can Do About It* (Philadelphia: Wharton Digital Press, 2012).

149   **"at the expense of younger partners":** Julie Triedman, Sara Randazzo, and Brian Baxter, "House of Cards," *American Lawyer,* July 1, 2012, www .americanlawyer.com/PubArticleTAL.jsp?id=1202560700480&House_of_ Cards&slreturn=20130318125104.

150–51   **"perverse incentives":** Mancur Olson Jr., *The Logic of Collective Action: Public Goods and the Theory of Groups,* 2nd ed. (Cambridge, MA: Harvard University Press, 1971).

151   **"a rational individual should abstain from voting":** Stephen J. Dubner and Steven D. Levitt, "Why Vote?" *New York Times,* November 6, 2005, www .nytimes.com/2005/11/06/magazine/06freak.html?pagewanted=all&_r=0; from an interview Rao and Sutton did with Michael Dearing on May 7, 2012, in Palo Alto, CA.

152   **"Managers who fail to share ideas simply do not get promoted":** Patricia Sellers, "P&G: Teaching an Old Dog New Tricks," *Fortune,* May 15, 2004, http:// money.cnn.com/magazines/fortune/fortune_archive/2004/05/31/370714/ index.htm. The information about partnership decisions at McKinsey and IDEO comes from conversations with senior leaders on both firms; the information about General Electric is from a telephone interview that Sutton did with Susan Peters on June 20, 2013.

155   **"If I discover that you are an asshole, I am going to fire you":** Robert I. Sutton, *Good Boss, Bad Boss: How to Be the Best . . . and Learn from the Worst* (New York: Business Plus, 2010), 99–100.

157   **"Sir, we are withdrawing." :** Thomas E. Ricks. *The Generals: American Military Command from World War II to Today* (New York: Penguin, 2012), 184.

158   **"Before going on the offensive . . .":** Matthew B. Ridgway, *The Korean War* (New York: Doubleday, 1967), 97; Matthew B. Ridgway and Walter R. Winton, "Troop Leadership at the Operational Level: The Eighth Army in Korea," *Military Review,* April 1990, 68.

159   **"the hard decisions are not the ones you make in the heat of battle . . . .":** Matthew B. Ridgway (author), Harold H. Martin (collaborator), *Soldier: The Memoirs of Matthew B. Ridgway* (New York: Harper, 1956), 82–83.

160   **"Guilt proneness predicted emerging leadership . . .":** Rebecca L. Schaumberg and Francis J. Flynn, "Uneasy Lies the Head That Wears the Crown: The Link Between Guilt Proneness and Leadership," *Journal of Personality and Social Psychology* 103, no. 2 (August 2012): 327–42.

160   **Veteran Pixar employee Craig Good told a story to Sutton:** Robert I. Sutton, "Pixar Lore: The Day Our Bosses Saved Our Jobs," hbr.org, January 10, 2011, http://blogs.hbr.org/sutton/2011/01/pixar_lore_the_day_our_bosses.html.

162   **"Guilt prone managers were more likely to support layoffs":** this quote and the next are from Marina Krakovsky, "Why Feelings of Guilt May Signal Leadership Potential," Graduate School of Business, Stanford University, news release, April 13, 2012, www.gsb.stanford.edu/news/research/leadership-guilt-flynn.html.

162   **"honesty box":** M. Bateson, D. Nettle, and G. Roberts, "Cues of Being Watched Enhance Cooperation in a Real-World Setting," *Biology Letters* 2, no. 3 (2006): 412–14; M. Ernest-Jones, D. Nettle, and M. Bateson, "Effects of Eye Images on Everyday Cooperative Behavior: A Field Experiment," *Evolution and Human Behavior* 32, no. 3 (2011): 172–78.

163   **The *India Times* describes another visual image:** Karthikeyan Hemalatha, "Pee Problems? Gods to the Rescue," *Times of India,* November 10, 2012, http://articles.timesofindia.indiatimes.com/2012-11-10/chennai/35033679_1_autorickshaw-driver-compound-wall-station-wall.

164   **"the people make the place":** Vinod Khosla, "Gene Pool Engineering for Entrepreneurs," March 2012, www.khoslaimpact.com/wp-content/uploads/2012/03/Gene_Pool_Engineering_1_31_2012.pdf; Teresa Nelson, "The Persistence of Founder Influence: Management, Ownership, and Performance Effects at Initial Public Offering," *Strategic Management Journal* 24, no. 8 (2003): 707–24; Benjamin Schneider, "The People Make the Place," *Personnel Psychology* 40, no. 3 (1987): 437–53.

164   **"X is shit, Y is genius":** Michael Dearing, "The Five Cognitive Distortions of People Who Get Stuff Done," paper presented at Stanford University, January 31, 2013.

165   **A Neiman employee:** Robert D. Dewar, "Customer Focus at Neiman Marcus: 'We Report to the Client,'" Kellogg School of Management, January 2006, http://cb.hbsp.harvard.edu/cb/web/product_detail.seam?E=68954&R=KEL145-PDF-ENG&conversationId=1553565.

166   **"Perhaps the next CEO will emerge . . .":** Shishir Prasad, Mitu Jayashankar, and N. S. Ramnath, "How Chandra Runs TCS," *Forbes,* July 17, 2011, www.forbes.com/2011/07/18/forbes-india-how-chandra-runs-tcs.html. This de-

scription was updated and revised slightly on the basis of an e-mail exchange between Rao and TCS vice president Pradipta Bagchi on July 5, 2013.

167 **"health concierges":** Bruce Japsen, "Out from Behind the Counter," *New York Times,* October 21, 2011, www.nytimes.com/2011/10/22/business/at-walgreens-pharmacists-urged-to-mix-with-public.html?pagewanted=all&_r=0.

167 **"45 percent of the 6,100 pilots at Southwest Airlines are veterans or reservists":** David Larter, "Commercial Pilot Market Ready for a Boom," *Air Force Times,* July 22, 2011, www.airforcetimes.com/news/2011/07/air-force-commercial-pilot-market-boom-072211w/.

167 **Hundreds of students take "CS 106" each year.:** Sutton has talked to John Lilly at least a dozen times over the years about CS 106 coordinators. Lilly says it is one his favorite topics. The quotes here are from an e-mail that Lilly sent Sutton on April 23, 2013.

168 **Some U.S. charter school chains use a related recruiting strategy:** Caitlin Farrell et al., "Scaling Up Charter Management Organizations: 8 Keys for Success," National Center for Charter School Finance and Governance, 2009, www.uscrossier.org/ceg/wp-content/uploads/2012/02/CMO_guidebook.pdf. Facts about KIPP are from www.kipp.org/, accessed June 18, 2013; facts about YES Prep are from http://yesprep.org/, accessed June 18, 2013; and facts about Rocketship Education are from www.rsed.org/, accessed June 18, 2013.

169 **About 75 percent of Rocketship Education's teachers are in TFA or are TFA alums:** Lyndsey Layton, "Is a Charter School Chain Called Rocketship Ready to Soar Across America?" *Washington Post,* July 29, 2012, http://articles.washingtonpost.com/2012-07-29/local/35486951_1_charter-school-achievement-gap-public-schools/2.

170 **some apparent weaknesses of autistic people:** Gareth Cook, "The Autism Advantage," *New York Times,* November 29, 2012, www.nytimes.com/2012/12/02/magazine/the-autism-advantage.html?pagewanted=all&_r=0.

172 **"I had the gall to apologize":** Robert Sutton, "Felt Accountability: Some Emerging Thoughts," *Work Matters,* August 22, 2012, http://bobsutton.typepad.com/my_weblog/2012/08/felt-accountability-some-emerging-thoughts.html. The original comment said "shares delay" rather than "delay"; we've edited for clarity.

173 **"moments of truth":** Rohit Deshpandé, "Terror at the Taj: Customer-Centric Leadership. Multi-Media Case," Harvard Business School case, 2010; also see Rohit Deshpandé and Anjali Raina, "The Ordinary Heroes of the Taj," *Harvard Business Review* 89, no. 12 (2011): 119–23.

6. CONNECT PEOPLE AND CASCADE EXCELLENCE

174 **"an IED defeat handbook, it was sitting on some guy's desk":** The story of how CALL improved its transmission of information is from Jonathan Koester, "CALL: From Lessons Learned to Educating the Force," *NCO Journal,* July 2011, https://usasma.bliss.army.mil/NCOJournal/Archives/2011/July/PDFs/CALL.pdf.

176   **"ground war":** Hayagreeva Rao and David Hoyt, "Institute for Healthcare Improvement: The Campaign to Save 100,000 Lives," Graduate School of Business, Stanford University, Case No. L-13. In addition, Sutton interviewed Joe McCannon on May 24, 2013, to get more details about the team that he led during the campaign, and they exchanged a series of e-mails in the following two weeks to clarify facts and details.

181   *"To spread excellence, you need to have some excellence to spread.":* Larry Cooley and Richard Kohl, *Scaling Up—From Vision to Large-Scale Change: A Management Framework for Practitioners* (Washington, DC: Management Systems International, 2006).

181   **it is useless for assessing employee traits and potential:** In 1998, Michigan State's Frank Schmidt and John Hunter published a "meta-analysis" of the pattern of relationships observed in peer-reviewed journals during the prior *eighty-five years* to identify which employee selection methods were best and worst as predictors of job performance. Of the nineteen methods, graphology finished second to last, and the authors reported there was no credible evidence that it was a sound employee selection method. See F. L. Schmidt and J. E. Hunter, "The Validity and Utility of Selection Methods in Personnel Psychology: Practical and Theoretical Implications of 85 Years of Research Findings," *Psychological Bulletin* 124 (1998): 262–74; also see Barry L. Beyerstein and Dale F. Beyerstein, *The Write Stuff: Evaluations of Graphology, the Study of Handwriting Analysis* (Amherst, NY: Prometheus Books, 1992).

181   **"I've heard our strategy described . . .":** Brad Garlinghouse, "Yahoo Memo: 'The Peanut Butter Manifesto,'" *Wall Street Journal,* November 18, 2006, http://online.wsj.com/public/article/SB116379821933826657-0mbjXoHnQwDMFH_PVeb_jqe3Chk_20061125.html.

183   **they focused on developing and transferring real excellence:** The information about SPaM is based on Sutton's recollections; on e-mail exchanges with Corey Billington on December 16, 2008, and June 6, 2013; and on descriptions in Andrew Hargadon and Robert I. Sutton, "Building an Innovation Factory," *Harvard Business Review* 78, no. 3 (2000): 157.

184   **the new mindset would have cascaded to far fewer people and places:** Damon Centola and Michael Macy, "Complex Contagions and the Weakness of Long Ties," *American Journal of Sociology* 113 (2007): 7202–34.

184   **most of us are drawn to people who are just like our favorite person:** The standard text here is Robert B. Cialdini, *Influence: Science and Practice* (Boston: Allyn and Bacon, 2001); Sutton heard Khurana tell this evidence-based joke at a research seminar he gave at the Stanford Business School in 2002 or 2003.

185   **Charles Darwin's "four musketeers" are a classic example of this strategy:** Janet Browne, *Charles Darwin: A Biography,* vol. 2, *The Power of Place* (New York: Knopf, 2011).

186   **You need master multipliers:** Based on Hanson's appearances in Rao and Sutton's "Scaling Up Excellence" class on March 1, 2012, and January 17, 2013, and an interview with Rao and Sutton on March 25, 2011.

186   **"bell cows":** Jared Diamond, "Iowa, the Harvard of Coaching," *Wall Street Journal,* December 21, 2011, http://online.wsj.com/article/SB10001424052970 2048790045771107314609895536.html.

187   **"direct, severe, and gentlemanly":** Gerald Imber, *Genius on the Edge: The Bizarre Double Life of Dr. William Stewart Halsted* (New York: Kaplan, 2010).

189   **an "energizer" or a "de-energizer":** See R. L. Cross and A. Parker, *The Hidden Power of Social Networks* (Boston: Harvard Business School Press, 2004); Rob Cross, Wayne Baker, and Andrew Parker, "What Creates Energy in Organizations," *Sloan Management Review* 44, no. 4 (2003): 51–56.

190   **Cox was still giving the welcoming talk:** Chris Cox confirmed this via e-mail on May 25, 2013.

191   **"in the eyes of all, particularly his juniors, the beating heart of the institution":** Imber, *Genius on the Edge,* 226.

191   **Over 80 percent of women who own businesses in the United States were Girl Scouts:** These statistics are from the Girl Scouts of Northern California, *2012 Annual Report,* www.girlscoutsnorcal.org/documents/2013-annual report-paged-web.pdf, with a few updates from CEO Marina Park.

194   **"cackling" in the hallways:** Libby Sartain with Martha I. Finney, *HR from the Heart* (New York: AMACOM, 2003); Byron Reeves and J. Leighton Read, *Total Engagement: Using Games and Virtual Worlds to Change the Way People Work and Businesses Compete* (Boston: Harvard Business Press, 2009).

195   **"gamified application":** Gartner Research, "Gartner Says by 2015, More Than 50 Percent of Organizations That Manage Innovation Processes Will Gamify Those Processes," April 12, 2011, www.gartner.com/newsroom/id/ 1629214.

195   **"putting the lipstick of gamification on the pig of work":** Toby Beresford, "Will Enterprise Software of the Future Be Fun?" *Gamification of Work,* July 15, 2011, http://gamificationofwork.com/2011/07/will-enterprise-software-of-the-future-be-fun/.

195   **"At Rite-Solutions, you start to get the message . . .":** Polly LaBarre, "Provoking the Future," hbr.org, July 20, 2011, http://blogs.hbr.org/cs/2011/07/provoking_the_future.html.

196   **an online game called Mutual Fun:** Hayagreeva Rao and David Hoyt, "Rite-Solutions: Mavericks Unleashing the Quiet Genius of Employees," case study, Graduate School of Business, Stanford University; LaBarre, "Provoking the Future."

197   **"cultivated an almost unshakable loyalty among their people":** LaBarre, "Provoking the Future."

198   **"Supercitizen":** Maria Christina Cabellaro, "An Academic Turns a City into a Social Experiment," *Harvard Gazette,* March 11, 2004.

200   **"If our own employees weren't convinced . . .":** Denny F. Strigl and Frank Swiatek, *Managers, Can You Hear Me Now? Hard Hitting Lessons on How to Get Real Results* (New York: McGraw-Hill, 2011), 106.

201   **the most detailed and bluntest blogs we've ever read:** You can visit *Lizard Wrangling—Mitchell on Mozilla & More* at https://blog.lizardwrangler.com/.

202   **Sutton interviewed Captain Nick Gottuso:** the interview was conducted in Hillsborough, CA, on January 15, 2009.

202   **"grow your own replacement":** Based on a lecture given by Colleen Mc-Creary, Zynga's chief people officer, to Rao's "Human Resource Management" class on April 12, 2011.

204   **"fence-sitters":** Julie Battilana and Tiziana Casciaro, "Overcoming Resistance to Organizational Change: Strong Ties and Affective Cooptation," *Management Science* 59, no. 4 (April 2013): 819–36.

206   **Burt calls these "structural holes":** Ronald S. Burt, *Brokerage and Closure: An Introduction to Social Capital* (Oxford: Oxford University Press, 2005).

207   **the most effective broker whom we know well:** This section is based on the regular interactions that Sutton has had with Kelley since 1994. Sutton met Kelley when he and Andrew Hargadon (now a professor at the University of California at Davis) did an eighteen-month ethnography at IDEO in the mid-1990s—and has since hung around as an IDEO Fellow. In 2002, Sutton joined Kelley's efforts to launch and grow what became the d.school, officially the Hasso Plattner Institute of Design at Stanford. He has had hundreds of conversations with him and has been to at least one hundred meetings with him of all sizes and kinds, ranging from staff meetings at IDEO and the d.school to celebrations of Kelley's wedding and fiftieth and sixtieth birthdays.

207   **the more than fifty classes that the d.school offered:** See "Take a d.school Class," http://dschool.stanford.edu/classes/, accessed June 20, 2013.

209   *He has strong opinions, weakly held:* Sutton first heard the phrase "strong opinions, weakly held" from Bob Johansen at the Institute for the Future, who credited it to former colleague Paul Saffo. The exact origin is unclear, as with many sayings. See this discussion on Sutton's blog for details: "Strong Opinions, Weakly Held," *Work Matters,* July 17, 2006, http://bobsutton.typepad.com/my_weblog/2006/07/strong_opinions.html.

210   **a meeting of the Vermont Oxford Network:** NICQ Quality Improvement Collaborative, Vermont Oxford Network, San Francisco, on September 10, 2008.

211   **StartX:** For information about StartX, see "About StartX," n.d., http://startx.stanford.edu/#about, accessed June 20, 2013; also Colleen Taylor, "StartX, the Stanford-Affiliated Startup Accelerator, Kicks Off Spring 2013 Demo Day with 10 Company Debuts," Techcrunch.com, May 30, 2013, http://techcrunch.com/2013/05/30/startx-the-stanford-affiliated-startup-accelerator-kicks-off-spring-2013-demo-day-with-10-company-debuts/.

212   **when people share rhythms with others they develop stronger emotional bonds:** Xun (Irene) Huang et al., "Going My Way? The Benefits of Travelling in the Same Direction," *Journal of Experimental Social Psychology* 48, no. 4 (2012): 978–81; Scott S. Wiltermuth and Chip Heath, "Synchrony and Cooperation," *Psychological Science* 20, no. 1 (2009): 1–5.

213   "The rhythm that frequency generates . . .": Mr. Darragh told Sutton about his stand-up meetings during a conversation in Northern California on September 24, 2008. I followed up via e-mail with Mr. Darragh to get more details and clarify facts on December 6 and 11, 2008. A different variation of this account appears in Robert I. Sutton, *Good Boss, Bad Boss: How to Be the Best . . . and Learn from the Worst* (New York: Business Plus, 2010), 161–62.

214   "agile" software development methods: See, for example, Dean Leffingwell, *Scaling Software Agility: Best Practices for Large Enterprises* (Upper Saddle River, NJ: Addison-Wesley Professional, 2007).

214   "iteration rhythms" in a "time-boxed environment": The information about Salesforce.com in this chapter is based on an interview that Sutton and Rao did with Chris Fry and Steve Greene on December 6, 2012, at Stanford, CA, about scaling, and a presentation by Chris Fry in our "Scaling Up Excellence" class on March 7, 2013. In addition, Fry's quotes about the job fair come from an e-mail he sent Sutton on June 7, 2013, and Greene's quotes come from an e-mail exchange with Sutton on June 11, 2013.

216   they routinely had in-depth, and often tough, conversations: Michael S. Malone, *Bill and Dave: How Hewlett and Packard Built the World's Greatest Company* (New York: Portfolio, 2007).

218   their tunnel vision condemned them to waste time: Jarrett Spiro et al., "Confirmation Bias in Distributed Sensemaking: Virus Categorization in the West Nile and Sin Nombre Diagnostic Networks," under review, January 2013.

7. BAD IS STRONGER THAN GOOD

219   "dissonant details": From a telephone interview that Rao and Sutton conducted with Karin Kricorian on October 12, 2012; a presentation that Kricorian gave to our Stanford "Scaling Up Excellence" class on February 19, 2013; and Carmine Gallo, "Customer Service the Disney Way," *Forbes*, April 14, 2011, www.forbes.com/sites/carminegallo/2011/04/14/customer-service-the-disney-way. Also, for a detailed description of how the Disney cast creates happiness—and could do an even better job of it—see Lauren Newell, "Happiness at the House of Mouse: How Disney Negotiates to Create the 'Happiest Place on Earth,'" *Pepperdine Dispute Resolution Law Journal* 12 (2012): 415.

221   "Bad is stronger than good": R. F. Baumeister et al., "Bad Is Stronger Than Good," *Review of General Psychology* 5 (2001): 323–70.

221   A variation of the five-to-one rule: Andrew Miner, Theresa Glomb, and Charles Hulin, "Experience Sampling Mood and Its Correlates at Work," *Journal of Occupational and Organizational Psychology* 78, no. 2 (2005): 171–93.

222   how "bad apples" shape work group effectiveness: W. Felps, T. R. Mitchell, and E. Byington, "How, When, and Why Bad Apples Spoil the Barrel: Negative Group Members and Dysfunctional Groups," *Research in Organizational Behavior* 27 (2006): 175–222. Also see "Ruining It for the Rest of Us," episode 370 of *This American Life*, aired December 19, 2008, www.thisamericanlife.org/radio_episode.aspx?sched=1275.

222　**Research on cheating college students:** Rick Grannis, "The Contagion of Cheating and Network Ethics," speech delivered at a seminar at the Graduate School of Business, Stanford University, 2012; Rick Grannis, "The Contagion of Cheating," unpublished book manuscript, 2010. Also see Thao Ta, "The Spread of Academic Cheating," *New University,* January 15, 2013, www .newuniversity.org/2013/01/news/the-spread-of-academic-cheating/.

223　**"convulsed for more than a half hour and then became still":** Laura Batchelor, "NYC Hospital Settles with Family in Waiting Room Death," CNN .com, May 28, 2009, http://edition.cnn.com/2009/US/05/28/ny.hospital .death/index.html; see also AP, "Esmin Green, Who Died on Brooklyn Hospital Floor, Perished from Sitting," *New York Daily News,* July 11, 2008, www .nydailynews.com/new-york/brooklyn/esmin-green-died-brooklyn-hospital-floor-perished-sitting-article-1.347467.

223　**The memo that President Alan Aviles sent to the staff:** Judith Graham, "Esmin Green's Death: The Hospital Chief Responds," *Triage,* July 2, 2008, http://newsblogs.chicagotribune.com/triage/2008/07/esmin-greens-de.html.

224　**one of their first experiments:** Bibb Latané and John M. Darley, "Group Inhibition of Bystander Intervention in Emergencies," *Journal of Personality and Social Psychology* 10, no. 3 (1968): 215–21.

224　**more than 105 studies explored why bystanders often don't take corrective action:** Peter Fischer et al., "The Bystander-Effect: A Meta-analytic Review on Bystander Intervention in Dangerous and Non-dangerous Emergencies," *Psychological Bulletin* 137, no. 4 (2011): 517–37.

225　**"The great majority of the 38 so-called witnesses . . .":** Jim Ramsberger, "Kitty, 40 Years Later," *New York Times,* February 4, 2004, www.nytimes.com/ 2004/02/08/nyregion/kitty-40-years-later.html?pagewanted=all&src=pm.

225　**"diffusion of responsibility":** Latané and Darley, "Bystander-Effect."

225　**Research on schoolyard bullies:** C. Salmivalli, A. Huttunen, and K. Lagerspetz, "Peer Networks and Bullying in Schools," *Scandinavian Journal of Psychology* 38 (1997): 305–12.

227　**"Principals were told . . .":** Michael Winerip, "A New Leader Helps Heal Atlanta Schools, Scarred by Scandal," *New York Times,* February 19, 2012, www .nytimes.com/2012/02/20/education/scarred-by-cheating-scandal-atlanta-schools-are-on-the-mend.html?pagewanted=1&_r=1&ref=us.

227　**"Dr. Hall permitted principals . . .":** Ibid.

227　**"often outperformed wealthier suburban districts on state tests":** Michael Winerip, "Ex-Schools Chief in Atlanta Is Indicted in Testing Scandal," *New York Times,* March 30, 2013, www.nytimes.com/2013/03/30/us/former-school-chief-in-atlanta-indicted-in-cheating-scandal.html?pagewanted= all&_r=0.

227　**uncovered extraordinary swings in test scores at nineteen Atlanta schools:** Heather Vogell and John Perry, "Are Drastic Swings in CRCT Scores Valid?" *Atlanta Journal-Constitution,* October 19, 2009, www.ajc.com/news/news/ local/are-drastic-swings-in-crct-scores-valid/nQYQm/.

227   **"the chosen ones"**: this quote and the following ones in the paragraph are from Winerip, "Ex-Schools Chief."

229   **"In Fresno, PG&E found 41 leaks in 2006 . . ."**: Jaxon Van Derbeken, "PG&E Incentive System Blamed for Leak Oversights," *San Francisco Chronicle,* December 25, 2011, www.sfgate.com/news/article/PG-E-incentive-system-blamed-for-leak-oversights-2424430.php#page-2.

230   **"the sense of mutual regard . . ."**: James Q. Wilson and George L. Kelling, "Broken Windows: The Police and Neighborhood Safety," *Atlantic,* March 1, 1982.

231   **nip bad behavior in the bud:** Robert B. Cialdini, Raymond R. Reno, and Carl A. Kallgren, "A Focus Theory of Normative Conduct: Recycling the Concept of Norms to Reduce Littering in Public Places," *Journal of Personality and Social Psychology* 58, no. 6 (1990): 1015–26.

231   **how these supervisors handled salespeople with problematic behaviors:** Charles A. O'Reilly III and Barton A. Weitz, "Managing Marginal Employees: The Use of Warnings and Dismissals," *Administrative Science Quarterly* 25 (September 1980): 467–84.

232   **"there is a difference between what you do and how you do it":** Cathy Van Dyck et al., "Organizational Error Management Culture and Its Impact on Performance: A Two-Study Replication," *Journal of Applied Psychology* 90, no. 6 (2005): 1228.

234   **"pacific culture":** Robert M. Sapolsky and Lisa J. Share, "A Pacific Culture among Wild Baboons: Its Emergence and Transmission," *PLoS Biology* 2, no. 4 (2004): e106; Natalie Angier, "No Time for Bullies: Baboons Retool Their Culture," *New York Times,* April 13, 2004, www.nytimes.com/2004/04/13/science/no-time-for-bullies-baboons-retool-their-culture.html?pagewanted=all&src=pm; note that this is a heavily edited and revised version of a description of this study that appeared in Robert I. Sutton, *The No Asshole Rule: Building a Civilized Workplace and Surviving One That Isn't* (New York: Business Plus, 2007).

234   **various solutions were tried in these schools:** Marisa de la Torre et al., "Turning Around Low-Performing Schools in Chicago: Summary Report," Consortium on Chicago School Research, February 2012.

238   **So they focused just on fixing the plumbing:** Russ Mitchell, "The Medical Wonder: Meet the CEO Who Rebuilt a Crumbling California Hospital," *Fast Company,* May 2011, www.fastcompany.com/1747629/medical-wonder-meet-ceo-who-rebuilt-crumbling-california-hospital, downloaded 6/24/2013; http://www.healthleadersmedia.com/page-1/LED-274153/HL20-Wright-L-Lassiter-IIImdashGetting-Better-All-the-Time.

240   **making things easy is especially crucial for maintaining customer loyalty:** Matthew Dixon, Karen Freeman, and Nicholas Toman, "Stop Trying to Delight Your Customers," *Harvard Business Review* 88, nos. 7/8 (2010): 116–22.

241   **an intervention designed to reduce bullying in a Connecticut high school:** Elizabeth Levy Paluck and Hana Shepherd, "The Salience of Social Referents: A Field Experiment on Collective Norms and Harassment Behavior in a

School Social Network," *Journal of Personality and Social Psychology* 103, no. 6 (2012): 899–915.

246   **Latham's experience is chock full of lessons:** Gary P. Latham, "The Importance of Understanding and Changing Employee Outcome Expectancies for Gaining Commitment to an Organizational Goal," *Personnel Psychology* 54, no. 3 (2001): 707–16; note that this is a heavily edited and revised version of a description of this study that appeared on Sutton's blog: "An Astounding Intervention That Stopped Employee Theft," *Work Matters,* May 14, 2009, http:// bobsutton.typepad.com/my_weblog/2009/05/an-astounding-intervention-that-stopped-employee-theft.html.

247   **they are more prone to lie and behave unethically:** Hal E. Hershfield, Taya R. Cohen, and Leigh Thompson, "Short Horizons and Tempting Situations: Lack of Continuity to Our Future Selves Leads to Unethical Decision Making and Behavior," *Organizational Behavior and Human Decision Processes* 117, no. 2 (2012): 298–310; H. E. Hershfield et al., "Increasing Saving Behavior Through Age-Progressed Renderings of the Future Self," *Journal of Marketing Research* 48 (2011): S23–S27.

248   **Those employees exposed to the photograph raised substantially more funds:** Amanda Shantz and Gary Latham, "The Effect of Primed Goals on Human Performance: Implications for Human Resource Management," *Human Resource Management* 50 (2011): 288–99.

248   **"We outlined the things we hoped to accomplish . . .":** Lisa Vollmer, "Mulcahy Took a No-Nonsense Approach to Turn Xerox Around," Graduate School of Business, Stanford University, News, December 1, 2004, www.gsb .stanford.edu/news/headlines/vftt_mulcahy.shtml.

249   **the peak—the worst part—and the end:** Daniel Kahneman et al., "When More Pain Is Preferred to Less: Adding a Better End," *Psychological Science* 4, no. 6 (1993): 401–05.

251   **be there to say goodbye to people:** Horowitz gave this advice to our "Scaling Up Excellence" class during the talk that he gave on February 28, 2012. In addition, he made similar points in a September 21, 2010, post on *Ben's Blog* called "The Right Way to Lay People Off," http://bhorowitz.com/2010/09/21/ the-right-way-to-lay-people-off.

252   **"psychological safety":** Amy C. Edmondson, "Learning from Mistakes Is Easier Said Than Done: Group and Organizational Influences on the Detection and Correction of Human Error," *Journal of Applied Behavioral Science* 32, no. 1 (1996): 5–28; Anita L. Tucker and Amy C. Edmondson, "Why Hospitals Don't Learn from Failures," *California Management Review* 45, no. 2 (2003): 55–72.

252   **"error management cultures":** Cathy Van Dyck et al., "Organizational Error Management Culture and Its Impact on Performance: A Two-Study Replication," *Journal of Applied Psychology* 90, no. 6 (2005): 1228.

255   **those in the darker room cheated more:** Chen-Bo Zhong, Vanessa K. Bohns, and Francesca Gino, "Good Lamps Are the Best Police: Darkness Increases Dishonesty and Self-Interested Behavior." *Psychological Science* 21, no. 3

(2010): 311–14; in addition, quote from Association for Psychological Science, "Darkness Increases Dishonest Behavior," news release, March 1, 2010, www .psychologicalscience.org/media/releases/2010/zhong.cfm.

255   **bright lights and other tactics to make employees and customers feel less anonymous:** This is based on an interview Rao and Sutton did with Michael Dearing on May 7, 2012, in Palo Alto, CA, and on an e-mail exchange between Sutton and Dearing on June 30, 2013.

256   **when patients were anonymous, radiologists were far less attentive:** Srini Tridandapani et al., "Increasing Rate of Detection of Wrong-Patient Radiographs: Use of Photographs Obtained at Time of Radiography," *American Journal of Roentgenology* 200, no. 4 (2013): W345–W352; Y. Turner and I. Hadas-Halpern, "The Effects of Including a Patient's Photograph to the Radiographic Examination," paper presented at the ninety-fourth meeting of the Radiological Society of North America, 2008.

256   **The fourth warning sign is *feelings of injustice*:** Tony Simons and Quinetta Roberson, "Why Managers Should Care About Fairness: The Effects of Aggregate Justice Perceptions on Organizational Outcomes," *Journal of Applied Psychology* 88, no. 3 (2003): 432; Jerald Greenberg and Jason A. Colquitt, eds., *Handbook of Organizational Justice* (New York: Psychology Press, 2013).

257   **they will do nothing but sulk and suffer:** Martin E. P. Seligman, *Helplessness: On Depression, Development, and Death* (San Francisco: W. H. Freeman, 1975).

259   **"You're crazy as a bedbug to take that job at your age":** Michael Winerip, "A New Leader Helps Heal Atlanta Schools, Scarred by Scandal," *New York Times*, February 19, 2012, www.nytimes.com/2012/02/20/education/scarred-by-cheating-scandal-atlanta-schools-are-on-the-mend.html?pagewanted=1&_r=1&ref=us.

8. DID THIS, NOT THAT

264   **the premortem technique:** Gary Klein, "Performing a Project Premortem," *Harvard Business Review* 85, no. 9 (2007): 18–19; Karol G. Ross et al., "The Recognition-Primed Decision Model," *Military Review* 84, no. 4 (2004): 6–10; Daniel Kahneman and Gary Klein, "Strategic Decisions: When Can You Trust Your Gut?" interview by Olivier Saboney, *McKinsey Quarterly,* March 2010, www.mckinsey.com/insights/strategy/strategic_decisions_when_can_you_trust_your_gut; "Nobel Prize Winner Daniel Kahneman Describes the "Pre-mortem" to Eliminate Thinking Biases," Vimeo, n.d., http://vimeo .com/67596631, accessed August 21, 2013.

264–65   **Have the other pretend it was a roaring success:** Gary Klein and Daniel Kahneman both describe the premortem as a method for imagining—and preventing—future failure. But Karl Weick demonstrates that the "looking back from the future" method is also useful for imagining the path to success, so we recommend splitting the team into two, with half imagining failure and the other half imagining success. There are two reasons that splitting the group may result in a richer analysis than if you consider only failure or only success. First, factors that propel failure are often different from factors that propel success—so this twist on the premortem may help people develop a more complete picture of the steps required to achieve their goals. Second, influential research by Kahneman and the late Amos Tversky on prospect theory shows that people take different actions when they face losses versus gains. When team members imagine only failure, and possible losses loom large, prospect theory suggests they are prone to take excessive risks to avoid losses, such as desperate steps to avert the cost and embarrassment. The classic prospect theory paper is Daniel Kahneman and Amos Tversky, "Prospect Theory: An Analysis of Decision under Risk," *Econometrica* 47 (1979): 263–91.

266   **Weick uses studies of a professor's itinerary:** Karl E. Weick, *The Social Psychology of Organizing* (Reading, MA: Addison-Wesley, 1979).

266   **experiments by Wharton Business School's Deborah Mitchell:** Deborah J. Mitchell, J. Edward Russo, and Nancy Pennington, "Back to the Future: Temporal Perspective in the Explanation of Events," *Journal of Behavioral Decision Making* 2, no. 1 (1989): 25–38. Quote from Klein, "Performing a Project Premortem," 18.

267   **people are less prone to irrational optimism when they predict the fate of others' projects:** Max H. Bazerman, *Judgment in Managerial Decision Making* (New York: Wiley, 2006), 198.

269   **"the Startup Genome Project":** Garazi Ibarrolaza, "Startup Genome Report on Premature Scaling," *Punchlime,* March 7, 2013, www.punchlime.com/blog/startup/startup-genome-premature-scaling; Bjoern Herrmann and Max Marmer, *Startup Genome,* YouTube video, May 16, 2012, http://www.youtube.com/watch?v=SNOzBZY41jU; Max Marmer, "Startup Genome Report Extra: Premature Scaling," August 29, 2011, http://blog.startupcompass.co/pages/startup-genome-report-extra-on-premature-scal.

269   **"Getting venture money . . .":** Jackson is quoted in Ibarrolaza, "Startup Genome Report."

270   **"we are in it for the long haul":** "Pixar Keeps Its Crises Small, Says Founder Catmull," Graduate School of Business, Stanford University, news release, January 1, 2007, www.gsb.stanford.edu/news/headlines/2007entepreneurship conf.shtml.

271   **"The thrill of the start-up . . .":** Robert X. Cringely, *Accidental Empires* (New York: HarperBusiness, 1992), 157.

271   **Lotus had become a place where its founders were misfits:** this story is in Robert I. Sutton, *Weird Ideas That Work: How to Build a Creative Company* (New York: Free Press, 2007); also see Mitchell Kapor, interview by Andy Goldstein, May 20, 1993, Interview #157, Engineers as Executives Oral History Project, Center for the History of Electrical Engineering, Institute of Electrical and Electronics Engineers, sec. 4.4.4, "Management on a Large Scale," www.ieeeghn.org/wiki/index.php/Oral-History:Mitchell_Kapor#Management_on_a_large_scale.

273   **let's call her Emma:** We are unable to name the company where this manager works. Rao and Sutton heard this story on November 1, 2012, during the

"Customer-Focused Innovation" executive program at Stanford University. We confirmed it and added a few twists based on several e-mail exchanges with Claudia Kotchka and Jeremy Utley in July of 2013.

275   **the U.S. Transportation Security Administration (TSA) developed compelling metaphors:** This story is from an interview that Robert Sutton conducted with Stephanie Rowe at Stanford University on August 29, 2011, as well as several e-mails that Rowe and Sutton exchanged in August of 2012 so that she could review the text, check facts, and clarify several points.

277   **"In both cases, these 23 men and four women . . .":** Karl E. Weick, "Drop Your Tools: An Allegory for Organizational Studies," *Administrative Science Quarterly* (1996): 301.

278   **"still clutching his balance pole . . .":** Ibid.

278   **Michelangelo's famous statue of David:** Michael Hirst, "Michelangelo in Florence: David in 1503 and Hercules in 1506," *Burlington Magazine,* August 2000, 487–92, www.gwu.edu/~art/Temporary_SL/129:255/Readings/david .pdf.

279   **"design depends largely on constraints":** Diego Rodriguez, "Constraints," *Metacool,* March 13, 2006, http://metacool.typepad.com/metacool/2006/03/ last_week_i_pos.html.

279   **a study of college students who played a computer game:** Patricia D. Stokes, "Variability, Constraints, and Creativity: Shedding Light on Claude Monet," *American Psychologist* 56, no. 4 (2001): 355.

280   **the firm's leaders had discovered they needed "guardrails":** Sutton talked with Scott Wyatt at the World Economic Forum in Palo Alto, CA, on June 28 and 29, 2013, and followed up with a telephone interview with him on July 18, 2013.

282   **a rollicking discussion about "creating awesome products":** Sutton attended the "Creating Awesome Products" conversation between Brad Smith and Bill Campbell at Intuit in Mountain View, CA. Additional information was gleaned from phone conversations and e-mail exchanges with Intuit's Cassie Devine and Karen Weiss in late July of 2013.

284   **"There is a strong tendency to hire people like you . . .":** Linda Abraham's remarks here are drawn from a telephone interview (followed by several e-mail exchanges) that Sutton did with her on July 16, 2013.

285   **a story we heard from Ivan Ernest:** Robert I. Sutton, *Good Boss, Bad Boss: How to Be the Best . . . and Learn from the Worst* (New York: Business Plus, 2010), 139. Sutton interviewed Ernest at Google headquarters in Mountain View, CA, on December 15, 2010.

286   **Aaria's story:** John Thomas told this story to Rao on July 25, 2013, and it was fact checked and revised on the basis of an e-mail exchange between Rao and Thomas on July 28, 2013.

288   **Organ Donation Breakthrough Collaborative:** Teresa J. Shafer et al., "Organ Donation Breakthrough Collaborative Increasing Organ Donation Through System Redesign," *Critical Care Nurse* 26, no. 2 (2006): 33–48.

289   **We don't mean false, conceited, arrogant, or selfish pride:** This distinction between "hubristic pride" and "authentic pride" emerged from research by psychologist Jessica Tracy and her colleagues. See, for example, Jessica L. Tracy and Richard W. Robins, "Emerging Insights into the Nature and Function of Pride," *Current Directions in Psychological Science* 16, no. 3 (2007): 147–50.

INDEX

Page numbers in *italics* refer to illustrations. Page numbers beginning with 307 refer to end notes.